HOW COMMUNIST STATES
CHANGE THEIR RULERS

HOW COMMUNIST STATES CHANGE THEIR RULERS

MYRON RUSH

Cornell University Press

ITHACA AND LONDON

ᴸ C

International Standard Book Number 0-8014-0883-0
Library of Congress Catalog Card Number 74-10412

Printed in the United States of America by Vail-Ballou Press, Inc.

Contents

TO MY SISTERS,
MINNIE, BELLE, AND MILDRED

Preface

Succession to supreme office is a good starting point for a study of the politics of Communist states, since the turbulence that accompanies succession tends to raise partially the heavy curtain of secrecy that normally obscures Communist politics. Until now, treatment of the successions that have occurred in Communist regimes has been limited for the most part to the Soviet Union. Despite its half-century history, the Soviet Union has experienced only three instances of succession (in 1923, 1953, and 1964). A consideration of cases of succession in other Communist countries can extend our knowledge of succession in Communist regimes. Moreover, an examination of an important but limited political process that must occur in all Communist regimes may be a useful way of advancing the emergent discipline of comparative Communism. Furthermore, an analysis of how Communist states change their rulers, quite apart from the light it sheds on Communist politics, has some practical importance. Future successions in these countries may significantly affect world politics as well as the fate of Communism.

The present study of Communist succession focuses on Eastern Europe, and particularly on the countries of the Soviet bloc, because these regimes resemble each other much more than they do the Communist governments of Asia and because they have a common susceptibility to Soviet influence; the impending changes in Yugoslavia and China also are treated at length.[1] The six bloc

[1] The two Communist states of Europe which lie outside the Soviet bloc,

states—Bulgaria, Czechoslovakia, East Germany, Hungary, Poland, and Romania—provide abundant materials, since they have experienced succession at the top thirteen times. Yugoslavia and China are important for two reasons: first, because they order their institutions differently from other Communist states, they reveal additional ways in which the transfer of personal power may be effected in Communist regimes; second, because they are outside the Soviet orbit, they indicate the significance of bloc membership to succession.[2]

In analyzing the various instances of Communist succession, I try to maintain a balance between the recounting of history and the application of general ideas. Historians of a certain bent may question whether, in view of the historical differences among the countries studied, it is possible to arrive at significant generalizations about succession in various Communist regimes. On the other hand, political scientists of a behavioral persuasion may question whether historical treatment is even necessary, whether it would not be better simply to identify the key variables involved and analyze the necessary relations among them. My procedure consists in identifying key elements in Communist succession and fashioning from them a framework (Part I) which I apply to an "analytical history" of particular instances of succession (Part II), and in considering major impending successions (Part III). I develop judgments about the politics of the top leadership by viewing them from the special perspective of political succession; while searching for significant similarities, I am sensitive to differences among the various Communist regimes.

Yugoslavia and Albania, have not yet experienced a succession. The same is true of North Korea and the Chinese People's Republic, two of the three Communist states of Asia. Succession was initiated in North Vietnam on September 3, 1969, when Ho Chi Minh died.

   [2] I have written at length on succession in the Soviet Union, and therefore have not treated it extensively in the present work, using the Soviet experience here chiefly for enlightening comparisons. My *Political Succession in the USSR* (rev. ed.; New York: Columbia University Press, 1968) analyzes that succession in depth.

Thus, I attempt to treat each instance of Communist succession with an understanding informed by a study of the others. At the same time, I seek to arrive at valid, if modest, generalizations about this crucial problem of Communist politics. (They are presented throughout the study, but are set forth more systematically in Part IV.)

Because the problem of succession, broadly considered, may embrace all elements of politics, I have found it necessary to narrow the scope of this study, to focus on politics at the top, treating the various forces that make themselves felt at this level and how they influence the replacement of the supreme leader. I have not been drawn, in the present work, into extensive analysis of these forces, striving, rather, to describe them. Since the subject of succession does not lend itself to precise judgments about the future, I seek instead to delimit the range of possibilities, to indicate what may happen in future crises of succession in Communist states, basing my opinions on what happened in the past when these states changed their rulers.

I wish to thank Arnold Horelick, A. Ross Johnson, and Richard Burks for their comments at the outset of my research. I am indebted to Werner Dannhauser, who in difficult circumstances set time aside to read the whole manuscript and give me the benefit of his sharp eye for style and sense. David Mozingo commented helpfully on the chapter dealing with Mao's succession arrangements. I remain responsible, of course, for the book's accuracy, argument, and conclusions. My wife, Terry, generously helped with the index.

I want also to acknowledge the financial support and encouragement I have received from the Committee on Soviet Studies of Cornell University's Center for International Studies, from the Rand Corporation, and from the Earhart Foundation.

MYRON RUSH

Ithaca, New York

PART I

THE PROBLEM

I

Anatomy of
Communist Succession

The Communist states of Eastern Europe and Asia were initially patterned on the Soviet regime. As a result, the problem of succession to supreme office in these states has had the same importance and problematic character as in the USSR. Succession is *important* in Communist regimes because power is highly concentrated and uncontrolled at the top and because their politics are highly variable. The ruler is not independent of his circumstances, but great means are available to him for modifying his circumstances. Moreover, although the policies of a Communist state can change radically without a change in the ruler, their consequences for the country may very much depend on who carries them out; not infrequently a radical change in policy has required a change in leadership. Succession is thus a crucial matter determining the character of politics, and even the general policies, of these states.

Succession is *problematic* in Communist regimes for two reasons: there is no established center for making decisions whose authority is recognized at all times; no reliable means for the transfer of power has yet been devised. While the regimes themselves have acquired a measure of legitimacy because of their performance and durability, the ordering of their institutions and offices remains a problem. The Party organs generally have been superior in authority to those of the government, but this has not

13

always been true, for the relative power of the Party and the government has been a key disputed issue of Communist politics in Eastern Europe. Similarly, there is no rule that establishes whether the leading Party official or the leading government official is supreme. Within the Party, the central committee, which is elected by the Party's congress, formally is the ruling body between congresses. In practice, however, its two executive bodies, the policy-making political bureau (sometimes called the presidium) and the secretariat (the organ for day-to-day administration of party affairs), share power in proportions that are not fixed but vary greatly. Moreover, while personal rule has been customary, there is no constitutional or ideological justification for it, hence no principle by which personal rule can be made legitimate. In the absence of such a principle, the authority of a personal ruler in a Communist state cannot be transferred to another person by a regulated succession. The personal ruler's demise, whether through natural causes (death or physical disability) or as a consequence of political action against him, leads to a distribution of his powers. Even if a successor is chosen without difficulty for the office previously held by the personal ruler, he will still lack the crucial powers of decision that are needed to control the Party's executive organs. Without such control there is no personal rule.

Succession in Communist states thus involves an initial shift from personal rule to oligarchy ("collective leadership"), which has been unstable, tending to shift back to limited personal rule. Since these two phases, or modes of rule, are characteristic of Communist succession, it is useful to specify what is meant by limited personal rule and by oligarchy in the context of Communist politics.

Limited Personal Rule

The decisive feature of the phase of limited personal rule is that major policies cannot be adopted against the will of the leader. He largely determines the composition of the chief organ of rule, the politburo, by appointing and removing its members. The consolidation of his power may be traced in the changes he makes in that body. Until the present time in history, the ruler has had to achieve mastery over the secretariat before he could win decisive authority in the politburo. In the central arena of political struggle during periods of limited personal rule, the ruler is dominant but not absolute. He may have to consult with the politburo, particularly when proposing major policy innovations. He may be opposed on particular questions by individuals or *ad hoc* factions, and this opposition may bring about substantial modification of his proposals before their final adoption or even, on occasion, outright rejection. Such opposition is permitted and is not in itself considered a challenge to his position as ruler. An individual who goes too far in opposition can, however, be removed from the politburo by the leader, though at the possible cost of antagonizing other politburo members, who may feel the security of their own positions jeopardized by such action. Since he cannot employ terror, the limited ruler frequently shifts his subordinates from position to position in order to preserve their sense of dependence on him and to prevent them from forming "family circles" which might become foci of resistance to his will. This practice results in a substantial rate of turnover in the leading bodies, the politburo and the central committee. But in using such means to maintain his authority, the limited ruler must be concerned with how they affect the morale of his lieutenants and their loyalty to him.

Personal rule and its obverse, oligarchy are here defined in terms relevant to Communist states, not to parliamentary or presidential democracies. This point requires elaboration. Of course, a strong British prime minister may dominate his cabinet sufficiently to prevent the enactment of measures of which he disapproves. But even if the prime minister could simply command the cabinet (which he generally cannot), the exercise of such command would confer on him only a fraction of state power, while command over the politburo gives a Communist ruler *formal* control over the entire state system and *effective* control over most of it. Within the politburo, the Communist ruler has far greater control over each member than a prime minister has over individual cabinet ministers. Disaffected cabinet members have countless ways of bringing pressure to bear upon their chief, even to the point of replacing him by means of open political struggle; [1] moreover, should their oppositional activity lead to their expulsion from the cabinet, numerous and varied means would remain available to them for attempts to recover power.

On the other hand, a politburo member who wishes to oppose the ruling figure operates in far more difficult circumstances. He must oppose either as an individual, on selected issues only, or in concert with other oppositionists, which is forbidden by the party statute and may be dangerous. If his object is to oust the ruler, he probably will be compelled to resort to conspiracy. The conspiracy may succeed; however, if it fails, the penalty is severe—at a minimum, expulsion from the central leadership. Once expelled, the purged member may have no further means of opposing the ruler. When politburo oppositionists are faced with such stark and forbidding alternatives, they generally try not to displease the man who is currently master of their fate. Consequently, a Soviet leader who is able to appoint and remove politburo members is able to dominate the politburo, which in turn effectively controls the working of the regime. He has incomparably more political power than a British prime minister, and may be fairly characterized as a personal ruler.

The aims of politics among the second-echelon leaders under a Communist limited ruler are to influence the limited ruler, directly or indirectly, on key questions of policy and personnel; to

---

[1] Even in wartime, Lord Asquith and Neville Chamberlain were replaced as heads of government by parliamentary maneuvers involving their own cabinet officers. A similar fate befell Winston Churchill after winning the war against Adolf Hitler: members of his wartime cabinet belonging to the opposing party contested the 1945 election, won the majority in Parliament, and thus compelled Churchill to resign as prime minister.

strengthen the factions of which they are members and their own positions in them; to limit the power of the personal ruler at its margins, so that it does not grow. The group of subordinates seeks to ensure that the forms of consultation on major policy questions are observed; it attempts to discourage the frequent use of political sanctions against dissident subordinate leaders and especially to keep the ruler from resorting to nonpolitical sanctions (police harassment, threats of prosecution, imprisonment, and so forth).[2] To the extent that the lieutenants are able to place constraints on the ruler's power, they limit the means available to him to protect his position. As a result, he may be deprived of it secretly, by conspiracy, or, if the basis of his personal rule has been severely eroded, even by open political attack.

Oligarchy

The decisive feature of oligarchy is the incapacity of any individual to prevent the adoption of policies to which he may be opposed. Most Communist oligarchs first entered the politburo under the patronage of a personal ruler or were imposed by Moscow and then confirmed by mutual agreement when the politburo constituted itself the sovereign body during the crisis of succession. In the oligarchical phase, membership in the politburo is normally stable, although changing alignments in the politburo, as well as in the larger political arena outside, tend to make oligarchical politics relatively fluid.

Politics among Communists, like all politics, involves struggle. Its focus is the politburo, although there is a tendency for the struggle to expand to wider arenas, particularly to the central committee. When such expansion occurs, interests that are represented in the central committee but not in the politburo may become highly activated politically. These groups include not only institutional entities like the army, the political police, the cultural and the scientific establishments, but also sectional group-

---

[2] Among the lieutenants, however, there may be some who, in the hope that they will benefit, encourage the ruler to extend his authority.

ings like the Party apparatus at the regional level and the economic bureaucracy at the ministerial. The support of these groups is sought by leading oligarchs and they may exert a strong influence on decisions pertaining to their sphere of responsibility. It should be borne in mind, however, that even during the succession there are countervailing agencies at work, most notably the central Party apparatus, which tend to restrict the size of the political arena.

The aims of oligarchs engaged in political struggle are to influence Party and state decisions on policy and personnel; to strengthen their own faction and to prevent the rise to primacy of any other faction; and to strengthen their own position within a faction and to keep any other individual from becoming dominant in it.

To date, oligarchy has been the operative mode of rule in Communist states only intermittently: in periods of *succession,* after the death or political demise of a personal ruler, or of *quasi succession,* when a personal ruler's authority has been severely degraded.[3] Moreover, Communist oligarchies have been short-lived, lasting no more than a few years. The single exception is the oligarchy headed by Leonid Brezhnev, which was established after Nikita Khrushchev's ouster and has lasted a decade. Whether this is an anomaly[4] or portends a change in the character of Communist politics remains to be seen.

Although in key respects succession in the other Communist states of the Soviet bloc[5] is like succession in the USSR, there

[3] This occurred in Hungary between 1953 and 1955, when Matyas Rakosi's authority was undermined by Moscow. In China, Mao Tse-tung's power of decision was sharply reduced in the interval between the Great Leap Forward (1958) and the initiation of the Cultural Revolution (1966).

[4] While the post-Khrushchev oligarchy still rules, its stability has been increasingly threatened by Brezhnev's accumulation of strong powers. Of its current sixteen members, seven have been brought into the politburo since 1971.

[5] Communist states that are not members of the Soviet bloc pose distinctive problems of succession. These include Yugoslavia and Albania, in Eastern Europe, and the Chinese People's Republic (CPR), North Korea, and North Vietnam, in Asia.

are important differences. The Communist governments of Bulgaria, Czechoslovakia, East Germany, Hungary, Poland, and Romania are alien, inasmuch as they were imposed from outside in the aftermath of war, in most cases with the help of Soviet armies of occupation. In the three decades since this happened, these governments have been significantly domesticated; even so, they are far less deeply rooted than the Soviet system of rule, which originated in an indigenous revolution, which defeated a national enemy in a terrible war, and which has lasted more than a half-century. In the USSR succession crises may give rise to radical change in the regime's character, but in the Communist countries of Eastern Europe, if they were left to themselves, such crises could lead to the overthrow of the Communist state. Actually, succession crises in these states of the Soviet bloc are not allowed to run their course. Their potentially disruptive effects are in some measure mitigated by an external factor: the capacity of the Soviet Union to intervene to resolve the succession or prevent its worst consequences. While Soviet influence in the various states of the Soviet bloc has varied greatly during the past two decades, as have the means employed to accomplish Soviet aims in the area, it remains significant and, in the last analysis, is probably still decisive.

While no two successions are precisely alike, it is possible to identify elements which recur in all successions in one form or another. The range of variation in these elements is, of course, smaller within a particular kind of regime than it is in the aggregate of all the regimes. The determining factors are the mode of initiation, the contest for the succession, agencies determining its course and outcome, the policy issues involved, the resolution of the succession, and the depth of the succession crisis.

Mode of Initiation

Succession is initiated by natural or political causes. Voluntary resignation uninfluenced by political circumstance theoretically is a possible third mode, but it is hard to concieve of its happening in Communist states. Natural succession results from a leader's death or physical incapacity that is not caused by political enemies. The first instances of succession in the USSR were natural, or at least appear so, although the activity of political agencies in the illness of Lenin and the death of Stalin cannot wholly be ruled out. In Eastern Europe, the first three instances of succession seem to have been natural, although a shadow of doubt is present in all three: Georgi Dimitrov, the ruler of Bulgaria, died in 1949 after previously receiving extended treatment for illness in the Soviet Union; Klement Gottwald of Czechoslovakia died after catching pneumonia at Stalin's funeral in 1953; Boleslaw Bierut of Poland died after becoming ill on a visit to Moscow for the Twentieth Party Congress in 1956. In each case the demise of the ruler was convenient for Moscow. The only other instances of succession brought on by death—to Gheorghe Gheorghiu-Dej of Romania in 1965 and to Ho Chi Minh of North Vietnam in 1969 —are not similiarly suspect.

All other instances of succession have been politically caused: i.e., the ruler has been forced from power by the political pressures of opponents. Five were removed for one reason or another in 1956, in the aftermath of Nikita Khrushchev's secret speech to the Twentieth Party Congress: Vulko Chervenkov of Bulgaria; Matyas Rakosi, Erno Gero, and Imre Nagy of Hungary; and Edward Ochab of Poland. Five more politically caused successions have occurred since October 1964, starting with the ouster of Khrushchev himself. Antonin Novotny of Czechoslovakia was forced out in January 1968, and his successor, Alexander Dubcek, was deprived of effective power by the Soviet invasion of August; Wladyslaw Gomulka was ousted in Poland in 1970; and Walter Ulbricht resigned under pressure in East Germany in 1971.

Politically induced succession, since it involves dissatisfaction with the ruler's performance, tends to be more disruptive than succession due to natural causes, although the latter also has produced crisis. Political succession since 1956 (the year of successions in Eastern Europe) has no longer been the result of political campaigns initiated in Moscow but has originated primarily in indigenous developments and in Moscow's reaction to them.

Contest for Succession

A contest is necessary to determine the successor. It generally involves several candidates, each of whom commands some of the forces that may contribute to victory in the struggle. In most cases these candidates—who constitute what may be termed the circle of succession—are currently in the higher ranks of leadership, but they need not be, even to succeed. In Eastern Europe the circle of possible successors has been far less restricted than in the USSR. Nagy of Hungary and Gomulka of Poland were mere Party members, and Janos Kadar of Hungary had recently held a minor post when they were propelled into positions of pre-eminence. All three men had previously been disgraced politically, but this did not disqualify them for the leadership. In the USSR, on the other hand, no one who has been expelled from the leading bodies has ever again become a serious candidate for the succession. In Eastern Europe men who were responsible for the political police, such as Imre Nagy and Janos Kadar, on occasion subsequently became pre-eminent, but this has not yet occurred in the USSR. Moreover, former rulers (for example, Chervenkov, Ochab, and Ulbricht) have played an important role in some countries of Eastern Europe, but not as yet in the USSR.

Three kinds of succession contests are distinguishable according to their intensity and consequences: a limited contest of succession involving a relatively orderly transfer of power; an extended contest for the succession, in which a dominant leader, after overcoming social disorder or defeating powerful challengers, finally establishes stable personal rule; and an indecisive contest, in which a dominant leader, after winning substantial power, fails to consolidate his position, causing a new crisis or the continuation of an existing one.

Agencies Determining the Succession

Succession generally has resulted from the interaction of four chief agencies: the Soviet leadership; the leadership of a nation (broadly speaking, the politburo); subelites; and the nation at large.

The Soviet Leadership

The influence of Soviet leaders has been predominant. In his day, Stalin designated all the top leaders in the Eastern European states. At times, particularly in 1956 and again in 1968, it appeared that Moscow might be losing its decisive voice in Eastern European succession, but the appearance proved deceptive. Moscow has generally been able to influence succession even without directly intervening, since a national leadership's understanding of what would be acceptable to the Soviet leaders has significantly affected the outcome.

The National Leadership

In some states, the Party's politburo has played a key role in a succession, even on occasion in opposition to Moscow. In 1956, the politburo in Poland chose Gomulka, despite Moscow's reservations about him. In Romania, in 1965, the oligarchy accepted Gheorghiu-Dej's choice of Nicolae Ceausescu to be his successor as first secretary of the central committee; [6] Moscow had no say in the matter. The Soviet leaders also probably had no active part in the Czechoslovak leadership's choice of Dubcek to succeed Novotny as first secretary in 1968, although they may have possessed veto power which they failed to exercise.

---

[6] In Communist editorial practice the first letter of this title is usually capitalized: "First secretary of the central committee." On the other hand, the initial letter in the titles of first secretaries of *provincial* Party committees is not capitalized.

Subelites

One result of a contest for succession is that the great concentration of power at the center is reduced and, consequently, so is the domination of the state over the society. As the candidates for the succession reach out to particular institutions and functional groups for support, the bargaining power of these bodies is enhanced. They become better able to defend thier autonomy against encroachments from the center and may acquire a growing influence on the deliberations, and even the decisions, of the top leadership. In all Communist states the political influence of government administrators, army generals, and provincial leaders, and of the institutions with which they are associated, tends to be enhanced during the succession. Furthermore, in developed states (East Germany, Czechoslovakia, and Poland, as well as Hungary and Yugoslavia) the political potential of economic managers and of writers may in significant measure be realized. In periods of succession, writers have been especially adept at loosening the shackles of censorship and greatly extending their influence on events. These effects of succession in the USSR are similar to those in Eastern Europe. In Eastern Europe, however, they may be reinforced by nationalism, a very powerful sentiment that is normally held in check among functionaries but that may acquire a new and explosive force, which is directed against the USSR during crises of succession. This happened in 1956 in Poland and Hungary, and to a lower degree in Czechoslovakia, both before and after the ouster of Novotny. Moreover, if an Eastern European state has strong Western traditions, and especially if the country's intellectuals still have significant ties with the West, the effects of a reduction in central Party control may be progressive. Restoring central control and resolving the crisis of succession will be more difficult, as was the case in Czechoslovakia in 1968, when the Soviet army was required.

The Nation

The influence of public opinion and national sentiment has generally been diffuse, although they have played a critical, perhaps decisive, role on four occasions: (1) Popular dislike of Gero in Hungary led to massive demonstrations against his authority in October 1956. In attempting to suppress them, Gero provoked the revolution which swept him from power. At this juncture popular feeling brought Nagy to the fore. (2) In Poland, a few months after Bierut's death, Ochab realized that he lacked the popular support needed to consolidate his position within the top leadership. Consequently, at the time of "the Polish October" of 1956, Ochab felt obliged to resign in favor of Gomulka, who then had great popular prestige because he had suffered for his resistance to Stalin's policies in the late 1940's. (3) Novotny's ouster from personal rule in January 1968 was due not only to growing opposition in the ruling oligarchy, but also to popular opposition, which made it difficult for him to carry out necessary economic reforms. (4) The violent workers' demonstrations in Gdansk, Gdynia, and Szczecin in December 1970 enabled Gomulka's rivals in the Polish leadership to remove him from power. The popular will has several times been disregarded by Moscow and the local oligarchy, as in the Soviet overthrow of Nagy in 1956, and of Dubcek in 1969.

The large social groups that have produced important changes in the leadership and have influenced succession are the *youth*, particularly students, who played a key role in Hungary and Poland in October 1956, and in Czechoslovakia in the late sixties; the *working class*, which played a crucial role in East Germany in 1953, in Hungary in 1956, and in Poland on several occasions (at Poznan in May 1956, at Warsaw in October 1956, and in the Baltic port cities in December 1970); the *intellectuals*, particularly writers and academic figures, who actively influenced developments in Hungary and Poland in 1956 and in Czechoslovakia in 1968, and whose inaction at times has also significantly influenced developments (for example, in East Germany in 1953); and, though to a lesser extent, the *peasantry,* who played an important role in Hungary in June 1953 and a less significant one in October 1956, and whose support helped Gomulka consolidate his position after coming to power in Poland in October 1956.

Policy Issues in Successions

The key policy issues in the Eastern European states of the Soviet bloc have generally paralleled those in the USSR, although relations with Moscow have been a distinctive and, at times, an overriding issue. Sharp changes of policy initiated by Moscow, particularly in connection with Soviet succession, have tended to create instability in the politics of the Eastern European states, sometimes actually inducing crises of succession, but in any event provoking controversies over policy. These controversies have involved such fundamental issues as liberalization, including increased automony for particular institutions and functional groups; the role of the Party apparatus in economic management and the proper balance of central direction and local initiative; economic policy, particularly the allocation of resources among consumer goods, arms, and investment; measures to win popular acceptance and support, as supplements and alternatives to reliance on brute force and Soviet intervention to maintain Communist rule; and the rehabilitation of victims of previous rulers.

A key question related to policy issues is how the successor shall treat the preceding ruler. By attacking him, the successor may lessen or destroy his prestige, thus facilitating broad changes in the predecessor's policies and perhaps making him the scapegoat for current failures. The archetype is the attack on Stalin at the twentieth congress of the Communist Party of the Soviet Union (CPSU) by Khrushchev, who in turn was sharply criticized by the men who ousted him. This precedent has been generally followed by the Eastern European members of the Soviet bloc.[7] An

[7] Todor Zhivkov of Bulgaria criticized Chervenkov. Ochab and Gomulka spoke of Bierut's deficiencies, and Gomulka, in turn, was harshly criticized

indication that criticizing the predecessor is advantageous is the
fact that even Ceausescu in Romania and Erich Honecker in East
Germany, though each benefited from his predecessor's patronage,
found it expedient to criticize him. Of all the men who formerly
ruled in Communist states only Lenin, Dimitrov, and Ho Chi
Minh, to my knowledge, have so far escaped public criticism by
their successors.

Resolution of the Succession Crisis

Even if a candidate for the succession quickly establishes his
primacy in the leadership, personal rule may still elude him. For
one thing, his pre-eminence makes him the principal target of
other candidates. To stabilize his position in the succession, a
leader must win control of the decisive levers of power and
undermine the position of rival candidates and potential opponents. Unless he purges his opponents from the politburo and
replaces them with his own supporters, it is doubtful that he can
maintain political stability.[8] At a minimum, a personal ruler must
have unimpaired control over the Party secretariat. Moreover,
"election" by the central committee to the post of first secretary
need not imply that the central committee will support the incumbent's bid for personal rule. While he may not find it necessary to
purge the central committee extensively, he must make sure that
his partisans are strongly represented and that potential rivals
within the central committee cannot organize to oppose him.

A distinction must be made between the power a leader needs
to resolve the succession by establishing personal rule and the
power he needs after attaining rule to make it secure, that is, to

---

after he was ousted. Gero, Nagy, and Kadar all condemned Rakosi. Novotny,
though he did so reluctantly, finally found it necessary to criticize Gottwald;
Novotny in turn was attacked by Dubcek, who had helped force Novotny
from power; finally, Dubcek was blamed by Gustav Husak for the disorder that led to the Soviet invasion of Czechoslovakia.

[8] Whether a crisis of succession can be effectively resolved without the
establishment of personal rule—i.e., under oligarchy—is moot. The question
is discussed in Chapter 1 and in Part IV, below.

protect himself against an open challenge by his lieutenants or against a conspiratorial coup d'état. In Stalin's view, what was necessary to secure his rule was the capacity to destroy or terrorize defeated rivals and potential opponents. His requirements may have been excessive; yet if Stalin could learn what has happened, in the two decades since he departed the political scene, to rulers who were deprived of this ultimate authority, he no doubt would be confirmed in his belief that terror is needed to make personal rule secure.

Depth of the Succession Crisis

Disturbances accompanying succession may affect the entire nation or only the leadership. Factional conflict is almost invariably intensified within the leadership, usually leading to the extensive turnover of officials (e.g., in Bulgaria, 1956–1962). Among the people, succession produces uncertainty about the direction of events, which in extreme cases may lead to riots, as in Czechoslovakia in 1953, or even to revolution, as in Hungary in October 1956.

There are two critical points in Communist succession: when the senior secretary is replaced and when the new leadership consolidates its rule. The difficulties encountered in coping with these critical periods may vary markedly. In a particular succession, the replacement of the senior secretary might be accomplished without difficulty yet the attempt at consolidation produce deep disturbances. This happened, for example, in Poland in 1956, when Bierut was readily replaced but the new leadership's efforts to consolidate rule met with great obstacles and finally failed. On the other hand, Gomulka's replacement by Edward Gierek in 1970 in Poland was attended by violent popular disturbances and by a virtual *coup d'état*, yet the new leadership consolidated its rule with compartive ease.

The depth of the crisis of succession may be measured not only by the disturbances that accompany it but, more important, by its effects on political development. While changes in policy and in the composition of the leading bodies are virtually certain to occur during a succession, only a crisis of some depth will produce major changes in the ordering of institutions and in the character of the regime. Such changes did occur in the Soviet bloc following Stalin's death, which brought an end to rule by personal despotism. In the USSR, the Party apparatus, headed by Khrushchev, and the government bureaucracy, headed by Georgi Malenkov, struggled for supremacy. There was a parallel struggle in Hungary from 1953 to 1955 between Nagy and Rakosi, whose bases were, respectively, the government bureaucracy and the Party apparatus. The two struggles ended almost simultaneously, in early 1955, as the victory of the Party apparatus in Moscow produced a similar victory in Budapest. In Hungary, however, the government achieved ascendancy in the last days of October 1956, and the revolution actually destroyed the Party apparatus as an effective instrument of rule. As a result, when Kadar assumed power with the support of Soviet bayonets, he found it necessary to construct a new Party apparatus and to make it the basis of his rule. Although the Party apparatus was subsequently able to achieve sovereignty throughout the Soviet bloc, the issue is not finally resolved and tends to re-emerge in periods of succession.

Both the extent of the disturbances in a succession and its effects on the future course of political development have been highly variable. There was only a minor crisis in Bulgaria when Dimitrov died in 1949, since both he and his successor, Chervenkov, were Stalin's creatures.[9] On the other hand, the Hungarian crises of succession in 1956—when first Rakosi and then Gero proved unable to rule—led to a popular revolt that was violently suppressed by the Soviet army and had lasting consequences.

Although the severity of Communist succession crises in Eastern

[9] That Dimitrov tried to act independently of Stalin in fostering a Balkan union did not alter their relationship, as can be seen from the outcome: Dimitrov acquiesced in Stalin's veto and in addition suffered a weakening of his position of leadership.

Europe has depended on several factors, it has tended to be least in the following circumstances: when succession has been due to natural rather than political causes (e.g., in Romania in 1965); when Moscow has been able to control the succession (e.g., in East Germany in 1971); when there have been no strong alternative candidates (e.g., in Poland in 1970); and when external pressures have constrained the leaders to limit their mutual struggle (in North Vietnam in 1969; in Romania in 1965).

PART II

ANALYTICAL HISTORY OF SUCCESSION IN THE SOVIET BLOC

2

Stalin Designates Rulers
(1945–1953)

The thirteen instances of succession (and the several of quasi succession) in the Communist states of Eastern Europe cannot be discussed without reference to developments in the USSR, which have invariably affected succession in Eastern Europe and have often determined the outcome.[1] Four periods can be usefully distinguished.

1. Designation and succession under Stalin (1945–1953). While Stalin lived, he chose the rulers of most of the Communist states of Eastern Europe almost as he chose provincial chiefs of the

[1] Parts II and III use the following sources: Soviet newspapers and periodicals; *Peking Review;* the daily *Eastern Europe* publications of the Foreign Broadcast Information Service; and documentary and other materials in background reports of Radio Free Europe Research (RFE) in Munich. I have also used documents collected in the following books: Alexander Dallin, ed., *Diversity in International Communism: A Documentary Record, 1961–1963* (New York: Columbia University Press, 1963); William Griffith, ed., *Albania and the Sino-Soviet Rift* (Cambridge, Mass.: M.I.T. Press, 1963); William Griffith, ed., *Sino-Soviet Relations, 1964–1965* (Cambridge, Mass.: M.I.T. Press, 1967); Branko Lazitch, *Biographical Dictionary of the Comintern* (Stanford, Calif.: Hoover Institution, 1973); Robin Remington, ed., *Winter in Prague* (Cambridge, Mass.: M.I.T. Press, 1969); and Paul Zinner, *National Communism and Popular Revolt in Eastern Europe: A Selection of Documents on Events in Poland and Hungary, February–November, 1956* (New York: Columbia University Press, 1956). The principal secondary works used are separately listed in a footnote at the beginning of various sections.

33

USSR.[2] Consequently, succession was no great problem. The single instance of succession under Stalin was occasioned by the illness and death of Dimitrov, who was readily replaced by Chervenkov; both were long-time agents of the Communist International (Comintern).

2. Post-Stalin collective leadership (1953–1955). Stalin's death in 1953 led to the institution of a "collective leadership" to replace his autocratic rule in the USSR, and a similar arrangement was prescribed for the Eastern European states. As a result, two states, Hungary and East Germany, experienced quasi-succession crises: the authority of the ruler was undermined, initiating a sharp struggle for power. In Czechoslovakia, where Gottwald died within a few days of Stalin, there was a full-scale crisis of succession. These crises in the leadership exacerbated factional controversy over the scope and timing of "the new course" domestic policy, which also emanated from Moscow.

3. The Khrushchev de-Stalinization campaign (1956–1964). Khrushchev's secret speech in 1956 attacking Stalin raised a more fundamental question about the legitimacy of the rulers of Eastern Europe. Stalin had not only chosen them, but he had also helped them to eliminate their chief rivals by the same brutal methods whose use in the USSR was exposed by Khrushchev. Furthermore, by rehabilitating many of those whom Stalin had purged in the USSR, Khrushchev posed the parallel question of rehabilitating the purged leaders of Eastern Europe. This became a disruptive issue and led to full-scale succession crises in Poland, Bulgaria, and Hungary. Six of the thirteen instances of Eastern European succession (including the death of Bierut) occurred in the nine-month period following Khrushchev's secret speech.

4. Post-Khrushchev succession. In the post-Khrushchev period

2 There are some exceptions. Stalin chose Tito to lead the Yugoslav Communist Party in 1938, but later could not remove him. Gheorghiu-Dej, in Romania, probably was not freely chosen by Stalin initially, although later he accepted him. Gomulka was chosen by local leaders of the Polish Party during the war and later was purged by Stalin. In China, Mao established his supremacy in opposition to Moscow's favorites.

succession in the Soviet bloc of Eastern Europe has originated in indigenous developments and in Moscow's reaction to them, not in Soviet-initiated political campaigns. Moreover, it appeared for a time that Soviet influence on the whole process of Eastern European succession was declining. The USSR apparently had no voice in Nicolae Ceausescu's succession to Gheorghe Gheorghiu-Dej, or in Alexander Dubcek's to Antonin Novotny. Even when the Soviet army invaded Czechoslovakia, it at first appeared that no important Communist would accept the leadership from Soviet hands. With the passage of time, however, Moscow succeeded in ousting Dubcek as Party first secretary and replacing him with an acceptable candidate, Gustav Husak. Subsequently, Moscow apparently was consulted by the Polish leadership when Edward Gierek suddenly replaced Wladyslaw Gomulka in December 1970 and played an active role in the replacement of Walter Ulbricht by Erich Honecker in May 1971.

Long before Communists took power in the states of Eastern Europe, Stalin exercised a decisive influence in selecting the heads of the local Communist parties and in eliminating leaders of whom he disapproved.[3] While this influence was felt in all the parties

[3] This chapter, in addition to primary sources, draws upon the following: Franz Borkenau, *European Communism* (London: Faber and Faber, 1953); J. F. Brown, *Bulgaria under Communist Rule* (New York: Praeger, 1970), chap. i; Zbigniew Brzezinski, *The Soviet Bloc* (New York: Praeger, 1967), chaps. i–vii; Richard Burks, *Dynamics of Communism in Eastern Europe* (Princeton, N.J.: Princeton University Press, 1961); Peter Calvocoressi, *Survey of International Affairs, 1947–1952* (New York: Oxford University Press, 1952–1955); Milovan Djilas, *Conversations with Stalin* (London: Penguin, 1963); M. K. Dziewanowski, *The Communist Party of Poland* (Cambridge, Mass.: Harvard University Press, 1959); Stephen Fischer-Galati, *The New Rumania* (Cambridge, Mass.: M.I.T. Press, 1967), chaps. i–iii; Hansjakob Stehle, "Polish Communism," and François Fejto, "Hungarian Communism," in William Griffith, ed., *Communism in Europe* (Cambridge, Mass.: M.I.T. Press, 1964–1966), Vol. I; Ghita Ionescu, *Communism in Rumania* (New York: Oxford University Press, 1964), chaps. i–ix; Josef Korbel, *Communist Subversion of Czechoslovakia* (Princeton, N.J.: Princeton University Press, 1959); Hugh Seton-Watson, *East European*

of the Communist International after 1928, when Stalin seized
control of it, it was especially strong in Eastern Europe.[4] Most of
the governments in power there were repressive, and many Communists had to go underground or into exile, frequently to the
neighboring Soviet Union. Partly as a result, Stalin became
deeply and personally involved in the appointment and removal
of the region's Party leaders. During the great purge of the late
thirties, the leadership of the Polish, Yugoslav, and Hungarian
parties was almost wiped out, and the Bulgarian and Romanian
parties suffered large losses. When the purge was over, only two
Party heads (Klement Gottwald in Czechoslovakia and Georgi
Dimitrov in Bulgaria) retained their positions.

Stalin was personally involved in choosing the replacements for
the Party heads he had purged. Josip Tito, with the support of
Georgi Dimitrov of the Comintern, was chosen in 1938 to rebuild
the Yugoslav Party. Dimitrov told Milovan Djilas, a top Yugoslav
leader who was later purged, "You know, when the question arose
of appointing [sic] a Secretary of the Yugoslav party, there was
some wavering, but I was for Walter [Tito's Party name]."[5] The
other replacements as Party heads were chosen in the following
years—in some instances, ironically, with the cooperation of the
Nazis. During the period when the Nazi-Soviet Pact was in effect,
Stalin chose to have Matyas Rakosi released from a Hungarian
prison in an exchange agreement, but left another high Hungarian

---

Revolution (New York: Praegar, 1956), chaps. ii, viii, xi; Carola Stern,
Ulbricht (New York: Praeger, 1965), chap. iv; Adam Ulam, *Titoism and
the Cominform* (Cambridge, Mass.: Harvard University Press, 1952); Paul
Zinner, *Communist Strategy and Tactics in Czechoslovakia* (New York:
Praeger, 1963); and *News from behind the Iron Curtain* (monthly, New
York), issues of 1952 and January–April 1953).

[4] In Asia, Stalin's influence was less, although even in China it was not
until 1935 that Mao established his supremacy in the Party.

[5] Djilas, *Conversation with Stalin*, p. 30. Wilhelm Pieck, a leading German Communist, was also a partisan of Tito in 1938, according to Vladimir
Dedijer, *The Battle Stalin Lost* (New York: Viking, 1970), p. 127. As a
consequence of Dimitrov's early support for Tito and his continuing political
friendship with him, he came under a shadow in 1948, when Stalin decided
to expel Tito from the Soviet bloc.

Communist, Laszlo Rajk, to languish in prison. Similarly, Stalin chose to have Ana Pauker and Vasile Luca, both leading Communists, released from prison and brought to the USSR in an exchange, while the future leader, Gheorghe Gheorghiu-Dej, remained behind in a Romanian prison. (Later, Gheorghiu-Dej was the last Communist leader in Eastern Europe, except for Ulbricht, to receive Moscow's permission to establish a personal dictatorship.)

The new Party head in German-occupied Poland, Wladyslaw Gomulka, was not designated by Moscow at this time, but apparently was chosen initially by the Communist underground during a temporary break in communications with Moscow. Stalin's subsequent choice to rule in Poland, however, was not Gomulka but Boleslaw Bierut, who returned to Poland in 1944 with the Red army. Bierut first headed the new Polish state, but he later replaced Gomulka as the Party's general secretary when the latter was purged in 1949. Walter Ulbricht, Stalin's choice to head the Party in East Germany, was also delivered to his fief by the Red army.

By the time the war was over, then, Stalin had chosen the Party heads who later led the Communists to power in Eastern Europe: Georgi Dimitrov, Klement Gottwald, Josip Tito, Matyas Rakosi, Boleslaw Bierut, and Walter Ulbricht. They all had proved their loyalty to Stalin while serving as Comintern agents on various assignments in Europe and during extended stays of varying duration in the USSR.

Romania was an exception. Ana Pauker and Vasile Luca, themselves experienced Comintern agents, returned with the Red army, only to find that Gheorghe Gheorghiu-Dej had ousted the Party leader, Stefan Foris, a Jew, and taken the position for himself.[6] This occurred in 1944, at a time when communications

---

[6] After Gheorghiu-Dej died, a party panel rehabilitated Foris, who had been executed as a traitor in 1946. The panel asserted that he had been accused falsely and sentenced without trial. Although Gheorghiu-Dej had gone to considerable lengths to argue that Ana Pauker had all along been his enemy, not his ally, the panel charged the crime against Foris to Gheorghiu-Dej as well as to Pauker.

with Moscow were poor, although an emissary from Moscow, Emil Bodnaras, had recently come to Romania. Like Gomulka in similar circumstances, Gheorghiu-Dej subsequently was confirmed in his post (October 1945). Nevertheless, while Stalin accepted the situation that had developed, he was slow to give either Gheorghiu-Dej or Gomulka even the measure of confidence that he bestowed on such surviving Comintern figures as Bierut and, at least for a time, Pauker.

The problems posed for Stalin by the presence of strong nativist leaders in Romania and Poland were also encountered in other states of Eastern Europe, particularly Yugoslavia. By early 1948, Tito had disappointed Stalin's expectations by his unwillingness to submit to Soviet controls that other satraps docilely accepted. Stalin responded by trying to subvert Tito's leadership with the help of dissident figures like Andrija Hebrang and by finally expelling Yugoslavia from the bloc in 1948. In the months that followed, Stalin gradually increased Soviet economic pressure on Yugoslavia and brought to bear sharp military pressure from the satellite states, all to no avail. Tito, by using repressive measures himself, invoking strong nationalist feelings, and accepting huge subsidies from the "imperialists," succeeded in retaining power and courageously preserved Yugoslav independence.

Soon after Tito's defection, Stalin turned his attention to the other Communist states of Eastern Europe, initiating purges of nativist leaders who he feared were potential Titoists. These were men who had remained in their native countries during the war, in the anti-German underground or in prison. The very fact that they had survived these dangers gave rise to Stalin's unjustified doubts of their devotion to Communism. In any case, they had not been trained in the Stalin school of leadership during an extended residence in the USSR, nor had they been fully subject to Stalin's methods of selecting leaders. In the purge of nativists, Gomulka was removed as Party general secretary in Poland and placed under house arrest. Laszlo Rajk of Hungary and Traicho Kostov of Bulgaria were tried for treason and executed. These executions not only enabled Stalin to inoculate the satellites against the Titoite heresy, but they also helped the established rulers to get rid of potential alternatives to themselves. If Rajk and Kostov had survived, even in disgrace like Gomulka, after Khrushchev's attack on Stalin in 1956 they might have challenged their persecutors, Rakosi and Chervenkov, and perhaps replaced them in power. As it was, they could only be rehabilitated posthumously.

The purge spread outward in these states, encompassing less powerful nativist leaders. In Poland, Gomulka's personal associates, Marian Spychalski, Zenon Kliszko, and Waclaw Komar, were imprisoned and forced to testify against him. In Hungary, Janos Kadar, minister of the interior, after being used to entrap Rajk, was himself imprisoned and tortured. The minister of the interior in Bulgaria, Anton Yugov, was also purged from his post, for alleged failure to protect the ruler against the conspiracies of his enemies.

The purge of nativists in Poland, Hungary, and Bulgaria (and the futile attempt to oust them in Yugoslavia) was only the first round. Subsequently, having checked the danger of Titoism, Stalin initiated a second round of purges in 1951 with a different category of victims. It was directed at Czechoslovakia and Romania, which previously had been struck lightly. This time the beneficiaries were nativists like Gheorghiu-Dej in Romania and Antonin Novotny (along with Klement Gottwald) in Czechoslovakia. The purged leaders were Jews (Rudolf Slansky, Bedrich Geminder, and other members of the Slansky group in Czechoslovakia; Ana Pauker and Teohari Georgescu in Romania) and minority nationals (the Hungarian Vasile Luca in Romania; the Slovaks Vladimir Clementis and Gustav Husak in Czechoslovakia). The trial of the Slansky faction, in particular, gave a strong impetus to the anti-Semitic campaign that was about to be mounted in the USSR itself.[7] One result of the second round

---

[7] The purges in Czechoslovakia and Romania probably were linked to the impending purge of Lavrentii Beria in the USSR.

of purges, and presumably one of its key objectives, was to turn national feeling in the two countries against minority groups and thus win some measure of popular support for the Communist rulers. Another result (as in the first round of purges) was to strengthen the autocratic tendency in the states of Eastern Europe.

Autocratic rule in the Eastern European satellites did not appear full-blown but developed over time, especially after the purge of Tito. By 1949 blood purges in Hungary, Bulgaria, and Albania had removed the rivals of Rakosi, Chervenkov,[8] and Enver Hoxha, enabling them to establish personal rule—subject of course to Moscow's will. In Poland, Gomulka's arrest set the stage for Bierut to rule, though he seemed to prefer to share substantial power with Jakub Berman and Hilary Minc, men of ability who, because they were Jews, never received public authority commensurate with their power. In East Germany, Ulbricht succeeded in purging a number of his opponents in 1953, especially after the June uprising, although he was to face strong opposition on several occasions in the next few years. In Romania and Czechoslovakia a rough balance was maintained between the nativist and Muscovite factions in the leadership until relatively late.

In Romania, Gheorghiu-Dej had been chosen general secretary by an indigenous leadership during the war, as had Gomulka in Poland. For this reason, Stalin held in reserve for both countries alternative leaders who could replace them if necessary. Gomulka, indeed, was purged and his power handed over to Bierut.[9] Gheorghiu-Dej was not, although his power was limited in the

---

[8] Georgi Dimitrov was unable to exercise strong personal rule on his return to Bulgaria after the war, because of illness. Subsequently Stalin's suspicion of him after the abortive attempt to form a "Balkan federation" further undermined his power.

[9] Such a replacement of nativists by Muscovites also took place in Bulgaria. Kostov became general secretary of the central committee in 1940, but Dimitrov and Chervenkov, at that time in Moscow working for the Comintern, subsequently returned to Bulgaria and took over the leadership.

early years of the regime, particularly during the purge of Titoists (1948–1951). He was unable to control policy, he later asserted, even though he occupied the post of general secretary:

Ana Pauker, [Vasile] Luca, and Teohari Georgescu, continuing to act as a separately constituted group, outside the elected bodies, ignored the Central Committee; the Secretariat replaced, in point of fact, the Political Bureau, which acted almost as a commission of the former— the most important problems of the party and state leadership being solved by the Secretariat, where they had a majority and where the General Secretary, on many of the most important problems, was isolated and put in a minority.[10]

This state of affairs continued, according to Gheorghiu-Dej, until May 1952. Since this was the period of Stalinist excesses for which Gheorghiu-Dej was trying to deny personal responsibility, he had reason to exaggerate the extent of his impotence, but it it is clear that he was not in control.

In early 1952 the struggle in Romania between Muscovites and nativists, headed by Gheorghiu-Dej and including Gheorghe Apostol, Chivu Stoica, and Nicolae Ceausescu, reached a climax with the victory of Gheorghiu-Dej. After purging the opposing faction, Gheorghiu-Dej made himself head of the government. (Since 1944 he had been general secretary in the Party.) There is no reason to suppose that this outcome was contrary to Moscow's wishes, since the Romanian Party was then highly dependent on Moscow. Rather, *this was a time when Stalin favored nativist leaders against those whose ethnic background was a handicap in the effort to win a measure of domestic support.* (Pauker was a Jew, Luca a Hungarian; oddly, they were accused of being rightists, perhaps because they sought to compensate for their handicap by offering material concessions to the people.) Stalin retained powerful figures within the leadership circle in Romania who still looked to Moscow, notably Iosif Chisinevschi, the sole remaining highly placed Jew, and Emil Bodnaras, a former Soviet

[10] Report of Gheorghiu-Dej to the central committee, *Scinteia* (Bucharest), December 7, 1961; trans. in Dallin, p. 372.

citizen. Though strengthened, Gheorghiu-Dej remained vulnerable.

In Czechoslovakia, as in Romania, the nominal leader, Klement Gottwald, for several years did not exercise personal rule. Although he headed the Party (as chairman of the central committee) as well as the state, Gottwald did not actually control the Party machinery. Until July 1951, it was largely in the hands of the general secretary of the central committee, Rudolf Slansky.[11] While the Slansky faction dominated the Party apparatus, Gottwald concentrated on the leadership of the economy and the state bureaucracy.[12] Slansky testified at his own trial: "I bypassed Party authorities; I solved many important political and organizational matters on my own, without presenting them to the Party Chairman (Gottwald) and the Party Presidium. In this way I isolated the Chairman and the Presidium from the rest of the Party." [13] Just as Gheorghiu-Dej exaggerated his own helplessness under Stalin in order to escape responsibility for Stalinist policies, so Slansky was compelled at his trial to exaggerate his own power in relation to Gottwald's in order to serve as a scapegoat for the regime's failures and to document his alleged attempt to usurp power. Yet it remains true that the nominal leader's authority in Czechoslovakia and Romania was for several years circumvented by the party secretariat, probably acting as Stalin's executive organ in the two satellite states.

The purge of the Slansky faction in 1951 and 1952 removed this limitation on Gottwald's power and established the conditions for

[11] While both leaders had spent the war in Moscow, a number of the men later associated with Gottwald had been in the underground or in concentration camps; on the other hand, the Slansky faction included numerous Jews who had survived the war only because they had been out of the Nazis's reach, in the USSR or in the West. Slansky himself, however, had returned to Czechoslovakia in 1944 to take part in the Slovak uprising against the Nazis.

[12] Eugen Loebel, *Stalinism in Prague* (New York: Grove, 1969), p. 54.

[13] *Ibid.*, p. 126.

the exercise of personal rule. Though it might be assumed that a purely egoistic struggle for power is waged in Communist states, Gottwald did not himself initiate the moves against Slansky, nor did he desire Slansky's removal from power so that he could enlarge his own. On the contrary, Gottwald evidently relied on Slansky to lessen his own labors. According to Novotny, "after his election to the presidency, Comrade Gottwald transferred all his work to the Prague Castle. The *de facto* leader in the Party was Slansky, who, owing to Comrade Gottwald's passivity, became the middleman between the Party and Comrade Gottwald." [14] The campaign to make Slansky the Czechoslovak Rajk—that is, to expose him as the leader of a vast "conspiracy" against the Party—developed outside the sphere of Gottwald's control.

Gottwald's misgivings about the purge of Slansky are documented in two key articles on Czechoslovakia's political trials that were published in 1968, when censorship was relaxed during the Prague Spring.[15] The author, a Czechoslovak historian named Karel Kaplan who had access to the Party's archives, noted that, following the break with Tito and the start of the trials of alleged Titoites in Eastern Europe, Gottwald came under pressure to "request" the services of Soviet security advisers, who were sent to Prague in October 1949. From this point on, the Czechoslovak political leadership lost effective control over its own security agencies. Since they were engaged in gathering information on

---

[14] Antonin Novotny, Report to the central committee of the Czechoslovak Communist Party, November 15, 1961, *Rude Pravo* (Prague), November 21, 1961; trans. in Dallin, ed., *Diversity in International Communism*, pp. 305–306.

[15] Karel Kaplan, "Thoughts about the Political Trials," *Nova Mysl* (Prague), Nos. 6, 7 (June 5, July 10, 1968); trans. in *Studies in Comparative Communism*, April 1969, pp. 97–116. Kaplan subsequently was expelled from the Communist Party. See also *The Czechoslovak Political Trials, 1950–1954*, ed. Jiri Pelikan (Stanford, Calif.: Stanford University Press, 1971), the report, still secret in Czechoslovakia, of a commission set up by the Czechoslovak central committee in April 1968 to inquire into the political trials of the 1950's and the subsequent cover-up by Novotny.

an alleged conspiracy within the leadership, this meant that decisive control over the Party's higher politics had passed into the hands of Soviet security advisers acting on behalf of the political authorities in Moscow. The search for the leader of the "conspiracy" reached higher and higher; finally, on the prompting of the police interrogators, some of the fifty high officials already arrested began to implicate Slansky.

At this point Stalin wrote to Gottwald (July 20, 1951) that he had "received incriminating documents concerning Comrades Slansky and [Bedrich] Geminder," but considered the evidence insufficient for prosecution.[16] A cat-and-mouse game now developed between Stalin and Gottwald. After Gottwald expressed agreement with this assessment of the evidence, Stalin invited him to Moscow to discuss the matter. Pleading illness, Gottwald sent Alexis Cepicka, his son-in-law, who conferred with Stalin and the Soviet politburo. As a result of this conference, Stalin sent Gottwald a letter in which he reaffirmed his skepticism regarding the evidence incriminating Slansky but said, "I think he should be moved into another position" from the post of general secretary, on the grounds that some of Slansky's appointees had proved to be subversive. Stalin thus accepted some of the results of the investigation into the conspiracy but left open the question of Slansky's involvement. In his original draft of a reply to this letter, Gottwald expressed trust in Slansky and opposed his removal: "I must admit that I myself never considered this eventuality. . . . My concept is based, first, on my trust in the political and personal honesty . . . of Comrade Slansky; and secondly, on the fact that even now I fail to see how I could replace Comrade Slansky in his key position." [17] This draft, however, was not sent. Instead, Gottwald wrote Stalin a letter accepting his suggestion that Slansky be transferred to another, less sensitive, position. This was done on September 6, 1951. Two months later, Stalin sent a top aide, Anastas Mikoyan, to Prague, "allegedly" with a request that

16 Kaplan, in *Studies in Comparative Communism*, April 1969, p. 109.
17 *Ibid.*, p. 110.

Gottwald arrest Slansky "on the grounds of an incipient attempt to escape abroad." [18] Again Gottwald resisted at first but finally, on the basis of Stalin's request and documents purporting to show that Western intelligence agencies were planning to help Slansky escape, Gottwald ordered Slansky's arrest (November 24).

The stage was set for the establishment of personal rule in Czechoslovakia, just as earlier it had been set in Hungary and Bulgaria. The chief barrier to Gottwald's personal power, the Slansky machine, was destroyed. Slansky was not only out of the office of general secretary, but the central committee declared that the post was not to be filled and that instead its duties were to be assumed by Gottwald as Party chairman (September 6, 1951). Slansky, like Rajk and Kostov, was charged with trying to usurp the position of the country's supreme leader. Kaplan says that, as the atmosphere of terror deepened, "any trust or confidence that party members could cling to centered now solely on the person of Gottwald, since the leading cadres could not be sure whose turn would come next." [19] In their efforts to avoid personal political danger, Party members were provided a single fixed point of reference, the cult of Gottwald. These circumstances would have made it easy for Gottwald, subject to Moscow's control, to seize absolute power in Czechoslovakia.

Yet this was not the outcome, nor was it Gottwald's aim. Having tried to protect Slansky, having written that he did not see how he could "replace Comrade Slansky in his key position" of general secretary, Gottwald lacked the heart and the vitality to grasp the power that had been wrenched from Slansky. Gottwald's death eighteen months later (March 1953) ended a period of personal decline resulting from illness, mental depression, and heavy drinking. Several years later, Novotny recalled Gottwald's weakened condition in the period after Slansky's arrest.

---

[18] *Ibid.*, p. 112. The commission report says flatly that "Stalin now insisted on Slansky's immediate arrest" (Pelikan, ed., *The Czechoslovak Political Trials*, p. 106).

[19] Kaplan, in *Studies in Comparative Communism*, April 1969, p. 113.

On the strength of my own experience in 1952, when I came into contact with Comrade Gottwald, I can confirm that the unmasking of Slansky, in whom Gottwald had placed great trust, affected him very strongly and brought on a certain depression. Comrade Gottwald admitted to himself his own guilt for having let things go so far in the Party. He felt personally responsible to the Party, and this situation was a very heavy burden on his mind. Understandably, this did not improve his health. On the contrary, his condition grew rapidly worse.[20]

It would be charitable to suppose that Gottwald's depression was due at least in part to his awareness that the charges he was compelled to make against Slansky were false. Fear for his own life doubtless also contributed to the "very heavy burden on his mind" during Stalin's last years.

Even earlier, according to Novotny, following the Communist seizure of power in February 1948, Gottwald's poor health was incapacitating and contributed to Slansky's ascendancy:

After 1943, when he had suffered his first stroke in the USSR, his health was not good, and his condition continued to deteriorate. I think that the Central Committee should know that Comrade Gottwald was aware of the grave state of his health. His state of health was very effectively exploited by many people, including Slansky, who also exerted pressure on him.

These people, in particular Slansky, exploited this situation to the full, telling party officials that they could not disturb Comrade Gottwald, that he needed rest, and so forth. Thus a halo of inaccessibility and superiority was created around Comrade Gottwald. His views were made known to us in the Party through Slansky or Gottwald's secretary.[21]

In his last years, according to Karel Kaplan, "Gottwald participated only very sporadically in meetings of the Political Secretariat." [22] In view of Gottwald's evident physical deterioration, it seems strange that Stalin allowed the burdens of rule in Czechoslovakia to weigh still more heavily on Gottwald's shoulders. The

[20] Report to the central committee of the Czechoslovak Communist Party, *Rude Pravo*, November 21, 1961; trans. in Dallin, p. 306.

[21] *Ibid.*   [22] Kaplan, in *Studies in Comparative Communism*, p. 109.

reason may be that Stalin intended Slansky's former power to be exercised by Novotny, who in fact replaced him in the Party presidium. As it turned out, Novotny was the chief beneficiary of the Slansky purge. His power grew appreciably from November 1951 until February 1953, when he was suddenly dropped from the secretariat. If Gottwald instigated this check to Novotny's fortunes, he did so too late. A month later Gottwald was dead and Novotny had returned to the secretariat.

The development of autocracy clearly made good progress in the Soviet bloc in the last years of Stalin's life, as in several states the dominant leader eliminated factional opponents of his rule, but the pace of progress differed. The difference was due in part to Stalin's evaluation of the political character of the top men in these states, but it was due also to significant differences in the intensity of these leaders' drive toward power. Gottwald, like Bierut in Poland, did not thirst for absolute power but seemed to prefer an arrangement which allowed his colleagues to exercise considerable authority independent of his own. Gottwald and Bierut, however, were exceptions. In other states, the struggle for power was more in accordance with the customary assumptions of Western observers: Rakosi, Chervenkov, and Gheorghiu-Dej proved they needed little encouragement from Stalin to kill their rivals if this was required to strengthen their own position, and Ulbricht, while he stopped short of executing his opponents, was just as ruthless in divesting them of power.

Besides strengthening autocratic tendencies in the Soviet bloc, the purges had more lasting consequences. In Bulgaria, Hungary, and Poland, especially where eligible candidates were executed or disgraced, the purges reduced the size of the circle of succession. Initially this tended to stabilize politics, but the subsequent outcome was a deepening of the crises of succession which overtook the three states in 1956.

Personal rule, once attained, was symbolized by formal changes in the offices held by the leader. In the first years after the war,

the dominant figure of a nation generally headed the Party and
exercised a measure of control over state bodies in his capacity
as a deputy to the nominal head of government, who was not
usually a long-standing Communist and did not exercise the full
authority of his office. As the nominal heads of government were
retired, in the early fifties, the Party leaders assumed their offices,
creating within a state a single center of authority.[23]

That Stalin encouraged this autocratic trend is puzzling, especially since it gained strength after Tito's defection had pointed
up the danger that a strong leader enjoying the personal allegiance of his Party and army and the patriotic support of the
entire nation might succeed in taking a Communist state out of
the Soviet bloc. Tito, of course, was unique; he had created the
guerrillla force that won power, had inspired Yugoslav Communism to become a mass movement, and had founded the
Communist state. Only in Yugoslavia was Stalin prevented from
placing his agents in key posts. Elsewhere the Communist states
were largely a creation of the Soviet army; their leaders had
questionable legitimacy and were in varying degrees dependent
on the Soviet Union. To maintain control over these states Stalin
evidently did not believe it necessary to foster a wide dispersal
of power in their leading bodies or factional conflict in them so
that he could play the arbiter. These were the methods he used
to dominate the top Party and state organs in Moscow, though in
the Soviet provinces, as in the Eastern European states of the
Soviet bloc, he generally ruled through autocratic bosses working
under the close surveillance of his local agents.

While Stalin had grounds for expecting his carefully selected
satraps in Eastern Europe to be loyal, far more important for a
man as suspicious as Stalin were the powerful means of control
that he commanded. Soviet occupation forces were present in
some of the satellites (in Hungary, Poland, East Germany, and

[23] This happened in all the Communist states of Eastern Europe except
Czechoslovakia, where Gottwald exercised great authority under the constitution as president of the republic after the 1948 coup, and East Germany, where the head of the Party, Walter Ulbricht, remained for several
years a deputy of Otto Grotewohl, the head of government.

Romania, but not in Albania, Bulgaria, and Czechoslovakia). After the purge of Tito, when autocratic tendencies in Eastern Europe were accentuated, the Soviet security police penetrated much more deeply into the ruling institutions of these states. Furthermore, the leading bodies in the satellites included some men with a special feeling of loyalty to Moscow, or of dependence on it.

Because Stalin commanded these instruments of control, autocratic rulers in the satellites, though they could wield great power, could do little to make that power secure. Consequently, to be a satellite dictator was to be a dictator in a special, restricted sense. By working through them, Stalin could reduce his personal involvement in everyday affairs of the seven dependent states, while keeping a rein on their policies.

The Dimitrov Succession

The single instance of Eastern European succession while Stalin lived was in Bulgaria in 1949, after Georgi Dimitrov died. Dimitrov's political position had been weakened early in 1948 after his discussions with Tito about a Balkan federation were condemned by Stalin. Moreover, he had been chronically ill for several years, and for this reason had returned belatedly to Bulgaria after its liberation by the Red army. For several months in late 1948, Dimitrov was hospitalized in Moscow. As Dimitrov became weaker, physically and politically, some of his power passed into the hands of his protégé, Vulko Chervenkov.[24]

Chervenkov was married to Dimitrov's sister, a fact that may have had a bearing on his succession. Marriage has played a not insignificant role in the political alliances of Communist leaders, including their arrangements for the succession. Stalin's daughter, Svetlana Alliluyeva, married the son of Andrei Zhdanov, who before his death in 1948 was Stalin's heir presumptive. Alexei Adzhubei received significant promotions after he married Nikita Khrushchev's daughter, Rada; while it is doubtful that Adzhubei

---

[24] During the great purge, Dimitrov had saved Chervenkov from arrest. See Djilas, p. 31.

had a central place in Khrushchev's plans for the succession, he did rely on his son-in-law to perform important confidential assignments. In Czechoslovakia, Alexis Cepicka advanced rapidly after marrying the daughter of Klement Gottwald, and when Gottwald died was a contender for the succession. In the thirties, Ana Pauker achieved a position of leadership in the Romanian Communist Party while married to its head, Marcel Pauker. His execution in the great purge did not damage her prospects; rather, it enhanced them. When important Communist leaders who had remained in Romania were purged toward the end of the war, Ana Pauker became perhaps the most prominent figure in the party.

It should be noted that blood ties, as well as marriage, play a significant role in Communist succession arrangements. This is particularly true in two developing states, North Korea and Cuba. Kim Il-sung appears to favor his younger brother, Kim Yong-chu, as his heir. Fidel Castro has gone so far as to make his younger brother, Raoul, second secretary of the Party, first deputy chairman of the council of ministers, and head of the Cuban armed forces.

Whatever the significance of the marital connection between Chervenkov and Dimitrov, the heir clearly had Stalin's backing. Chervenkov was permitted to execute his chief rival, Traicho Kostov, to demote another serious rival, the minister of interior, Anton Yugov, and to become the first satellite leader to take the top posts in the Party and government.

From the establishment of Communist power in Eastern Europe until Stalin's death in 1953, the sole instance of succession was occasioned by death, not political causes—a testimony of Stalin's sagacity in the choice of rulers for the satellites, as well as of the effectiveness of his system of controls. Stalin's single failure, his designation of Tito in 1938 to head the Yugoslav Party, of course, had grave consequences. Even here, however, it is to Stalin's credit that at an early stage he truly discerned Tito's political talents, if not the use he was to make of them.

3

The Campaign for Collective Leadership (1953–1955)

The succession crisis initiated in Moscow by Stalin's death in 1953 governed political developments in Eastern Europe for several years. While it lasted, Moscow lacked a single voice to arbitrate controversies in the other states of the Soviet bloc. The crisis did not end until July 1957, when Khrushchev resolved the succession by purging his rivals and establishing limited personal rule. The interval of four years was marked by an event in Moscow that had severe repercussions in Eastern Europe: Khrushchev's secret speech initiating the anti-Stalin campaign. The Stalin succession crisis thus falls into two periods: the early post-Stalin period, when Moscow inaugurated a campaign for "collective leadership" (1953–1955);[1] and the Khrushchev de-Stalinization campaign (1956).

[1] This chapter, in addition to primary sources, draws upon the following: Victor Baras, "East Germany in Soviet Foreign Policy: The Objectives of the New Course and the Impact of the Uprising of June 17, 1953," an important Ph.D. dissertation, Cornell University, 1972; Arnuif Baring, *Uprising in East Germany* (Ithaca: Cornell University Press, 1972); Heinz Brandt, *Search for a Third Way* (Garden City, N.J.: Doubleday, 1962), chaps. vii–ix; Brown, *Bulgaria under Communist Rule*, chap. ii; Brzezinski, *The Soviet Bloc*, chaps. viii–xi; Ionescu, *Communism in Rumania*, chap. x; Flora Lewis, *A Case History of Hope* (Garden City, N.J.: Doubleday, 1958); Tibor Meray, *That Day in Budapest* (New York: Funk & Wagnalls, 1969); Imre Nagy, *On Communism* (New York: Praeger, 1957), *passim*, especially Introduction and chaps. xxii–xxiv; Richard Staar, *Poland, 1944–1962* (Baton Rouge: Louisiana University Press, 1962); and Carola Stern, *Ulbricht.*

While Stalin lived, the USSR maintained its hegemony in Eastern Europe through a system of local autocrats. When Stalin died, the USSR experienced a severe crisis of succession which in some instances shook the power of the little Stalins, causing quasi succession crises. The Soviet succession crisis was reflected in Eastern Europe in two ways. First, the virulent factional struggle to which the Stalin succession issue gave rise was projected into Eastern Europe by the search for partisans in other states of the Soviet bloc. Second, after his death Stalin's power was divided among his chief lieutenants in accordance with the resurrected doctrine of "collective leadership," and the little Stalins were called upon to divide their authority similarly. The aim, no doubt, was to preserve doctrinal uniformity as a means of Soviet control. The Soviet leaders may also have believed that, in view of their own divisions, it would be easier to enforce their will on a similarly divided satellite leadership than on an individual dictator.

The rulers of Eastern Europe were not quick to redistribute their own power. Changes did take place, but not in all the states at once, or to the same degree. A key change was the separation of the top posts, head of government (or of the state) and head of the Party (general secretary, or first secretary, of the central committee). The division of posts, which occurred in the USSR on March 14, 1953, was almost immediately effective in Czechoslovakia, where Klement Gottwald had just died; not long afterward it was imposed on Hungary. Perhaps because of the disturbances that followed the division of offices in Czechoslovakia and Hungary, there was an interval of more than six months in which no top leader in another state divided his offices. Then, in the first half of 1954, the process was resumed: in Bulgaria, Poland, Romania, and finally in Albania, more than one year after Stalin's death, the leader gave up one of his chief offices. Thus the combination of the top Party and government posts in the person of the ruler—which in some instances had been effected as late as the last months of Stalin's rule—was reversed. This did not restore the situation that had existed before these offices were combined, however. In several states the change was more formal than substantive. In East Germany and Hungary, on the other hand, real changes in the distribution of power took place, and the crises that resulted had their origins in Moscow and reflected Moscow's factional struggles. Finally, in Czechoslovakia, the death of Klement Gottwald led to a full crisis of succession, which was made more acute by the turbulence of the succession in Moscow.

Quasi Succession in East Germany

The most serious quasi succession crisis, stemming from a weakening of the personal ruler's authority, occurred in East Germany. At the time Stalin died, Ulbricht had attained considerable personal power, although a number of his opponents remained in the politburo and he still lacked some of the attributes of legitimate authority. Moscow had no need to effect a division of the top posts in East Germany, since Ulbricht, alone of all Stalin's satraps, headed only the Party, not the government or the state.[2] Ulbricht, on the other hand, saw the need to consolidate his position, and at a meeting of the central committee in mid-May he took several steps toward this end.

Ulbricht purged Franz Dahlem, a long-standing and powerful rival whose responsibility for organization and cadres gave him a key power base. Ulbricht's ability to remove Dahlem from all his posts and to link him with the Slansky case in Czechoslovakia at a time when Moscow was downgrading the whole idea of political trials suggests that Ulbricht was receiving strong support from a minority faction in Moscow. His move against Dahlem may have been crucial. If Dahlem had remained in the politburo,

---

[2] Ulbricht in 1953 was deputy chairman of the council of ministers, the post held by party heads in the other people's democracies before they became heads of government. He acquired the more elevated title of first deputy chairman in 1955, but not until 1960 was he able to make himself head of state (chairman of the council of state).

Moscow would have had an experienced *apparachik* available as an alternative to Ulbricht after the June 17 riots.

Besides eliminating Dahlem from the leadership at the May session of the central committee, Ulbricht stepped up preparations for a mammoth celebration of his sixtieth birthday on June 30, thus raising to new heights the cult of Ulbricht. Finally, in an effort to deal with economic difficulties stemming from East Germany's year-old program for the "systematic building of socialism," Ulbricht got the central committee to raise work norms by 10 percent. All these measures ran counter to the dominant Soviet policies at this juncture, which were averse to political trials, cults of personality, and the placing of added burdens on the working class.

On June 5 the new Soviet high commissioner of East Germany, Vladimir Semenov, arrived in Berlin. At a meeting of the politburo he criticized the political leadership and presented the new program (termed "a series of measures") just drawn up for East Germany by the Party presidium in Moscow. This program required the abandonment of the drive to achieve socialism which Ulbricht had initiated the previous year. Instead, there was to be a major effort to improve the people's living conditions, including a series of concessions to the urban middle class and private peasants. At the politburo meeting Semenov apparently was persuaded to allow the increase in labor norms to stand, although it ran counter to the ameliorative policies being introduced.[3]

The effect of Moscow's decision to change East German domestic policy radically was to weaken Ulbricht's position in the leadership, since he had been closely identified with the old policy of "building socialism" which was now being criticized and abandoned. Moreover, this happened at a time when Ulbricht, despite his success in purging Dahlem, was under concerted attack inside the politburo. According to available evi-

[3] An attempt was later made to justify the increase in work norms as necessary to provide the increased output for better living conditions.

dence, at least three members of the politburo were opponents of Ulbricht: Wilhelm Zaisser, Rudolf Herrnstadt, and Hans Jendretzky.[4] Thus the introduction of the New Course in East Germany became enmeshed with the efforts of Ulbricht's opponents to weaken his authority and, if possible, to remove him. It is unclear, even two decades after the events, how the Party presidium in Moscow viewed these efforts of Ulbricht's opponents.

While the *effect* of the new policies imposed by Moscow was to weaken Ulbricht's authority, this was not necessarily Moscow's intention. Moscow's intervention against the growing cult of Ulbricht was in accord with general post-Stalin policy and may not have been directed against Ulbricht personally. Imposition of the New Course threatened Ulbricht's leadership only if Moscow did not intend him to implement the program. While it is true that Ulbricht was given little time, before the New Course was introduced, to disassociate himself from the old, now discredited, policy of building socialism, this may have been owing to Moscow's desire to hasten negotiations on Germany with the West.[5] The new policy was not announced by Ulbricht personally, but was issued collectively, in the name of the East German politburo.[6] In Hungary, similarly, the new policy was not announced by Rakosi. The top Soviet leaders did, however, discuss it and the accompanying personnel changes at length with Rakosi and other Hungarian leaders before they were in-

[4] Brandt, *Search for a Third Way.* Brandt's book is a crucial source for any account of these events, particularly for what he saw and heard as a key subordinate of Hans Jendretzky, the party first secretary in East Berlin. However, his inferences about developments in the East German politburo and, even more, about deliberations of the Soviet presidium necessarily are based in part on rumor and conjecture.

[5] Moreover, Ulbricht had previously been advised by Moscow (in April) to ease the pace of East German economic development. (See below.)

[6] On the other hand, the decree increasing work norms begins with a reference to the "criteria established by the General Secretary of the SED, Comrade Walter Ulbricht" (Baring, p. 117).

troduced, while East Germany's New Course program was simply brought to Berlin by Vladimir Semenov.[7] When Moscow inaugurated the New Course in East Germany, it clearly intended to reduce Ulbricht's authority at least to the very substantial degree to which it reduced Rakosi's in Hungary. Moscow's intervention may have provided Ulbricht's opponents in Berlin with an opportunity to try to remove him from the leadership altogether, but there is no firm evidence that the Soviet presidium intended such an outcome or even that Moscow would have permitted it.

According to Heinz Brandt (who based his account on information he had received from his chief, Jendretzky), "Rudolph Herrnstadt was assigned the task of formulating his own proposals for a new Politburo, a new secretariat of the Central Committee, and a whole new Central Committee, and presenting them to the party leadership as the basis for drawing up new resolutions." [8] Brandt does not specify who "assigned" Herrnstadt the task of drawing up proposals on the composition of a new leadership, but it seems very unlikely that he had been designated to do so by a united leadership in Moscow.[9] Particular Soviet leaders—most notably Beria—may, however, have intended Herrnstadt to replace Ulbricht; subsequently, the purge of Beria led to the purge of Herrnstadt and Zaisser, and Ulbricht asserted (but gave no evidence) that the two were linked with the purged leader in Moscow. While it seems exceedingly doubtful that the Soviet presidium authorized Herrnstadt to pro-

---

[7] According to Heinz Brandt, Semenov brought resolutions of the Soviet central committee which were subsequently drawn up in the form of theses and "adopted by the [East German] Politburo word for word. 'Up to now we have been merely translators and have created nothing of our own,'" Brandt was told by Jendretzky (p. 191).

[8] Brandt, p. 186.

[9] Carola Stern treats Herrnstadt's list of proposed changes in the leadership as a factional maneuver. See *Ulbricht,* pp. 142–143. In any case, Brandt's conclusion does not seem warranted that "Ulbricht was now only formally general secretary of the party, the leadership had already been taken away from him" (Brandt, p. 186).

pose changes in the leading bodies, Moscow probably did insist that opponents of Ulbricht be given important tasks in implementing the New Course, as happened in Hungary, where Imre Nagy became the new head of government.

Moscow's attempt to impose radically new policies on a Communist state may give rise to a difficulty bearing on the problem of succession in that state. If the new policies are to be forcefully administered and accepted as authoritative by the people for whom they are intended, it probably will not be possible to retain the old leadership intact. On the other hand, the introduction of new policies, particularly in conjunction with criticism of the ones being abandoned, causes instability, which may be dangerously compounded if at the same time the personal ruler is removed. The best solution, probably, is to retain the top leader in order to promote stability, while bringing new men into responsible posts, preferably earlier advocates of the policies being adopted. There are risks in this procedure also: the new leaders and the old may quarrel along factional lines, thereby jeopardizing both stability and the new course. Nevertheless, this seems to be the solution the USSR has favored. When introducing a radical new policy in a Communist state, it has preferred not to replace the personal ruler but rather to dilute his power with new blood. Personal rulers have been removed by Moscow only when they have become ineffectual (like Rakosi and Gero in 1956) or when they have refused to obey Moscow's commands (like Chervenkov and Nagy in 1956 and Dubcek in 1968 and 1969).[10]

Ulbricht's personal calculations with regard to the 1953 New Course are unclear. Even after Stalin's death, he had adopted onerous measures that imposed new hardships on the population, thereby causing an increase in the flow of refugees to the West and a further weakening of the economy. It seems unlikely that Ulbricht would have resisted an unequivocal policy promulgated by Moscow; presumably he either did not know that the

[10] The forced resignation of Ulbricht in 1971 because of Soviet dissatisfaction with him is discussed below.

dominant Soviet leaders were determined to impose a new course on East Germany, or, if he knew, he relied on hard-liners in the Soviet leadership to obstruct its implementation. Like leaders in the other people's democracies (for example, in Czechoslovakia and Poland), Ulbricht was in no hurry to respond to suggestions emanating from Moscow until he could determine more certainly where, among the contending factions, the real power lay. Once Semenov arrived in Berlin with the new program, however, Ulbricht no longer had grounds for resistance. While unenthusiastic about the New Course, to which he was opposed by conviction and which threatened to lead to a reduction in his power, Ulbricht doubtless was prepared to carry it out. His chief concern probably was to prevent his opponents from using the opportunity to weaken his authority.

The deep divisions in the East Germany leadership, which corresponded to similar cleavages in the Soviet presidium, complicated the problem of relaxing Ulbricht's oppressive regime. Beria supported the Zaisser-Herrnstadt faction and was hostile to Ulbricht, who subsequently boasted, "Beria was indignant when I opposed his policy in regard to the German question in 1953." [11] Ulbricht probably had the support of Vyachaslav Molotov and Lazar Kaganovich, and perhaps of Khrushchev as well.[12] While the entire Soviet leadership favored a new policy in East Germany, the Beria faction apparently saw it as necessary to facilitate serious negotiations with the West to settle the German question, an objective the other Soviet leaders may not have fully shared. Similarly, inside East Germany there was disagreement over the limits of the New Course; the Zaisser-Herrnstadt faction seemingly wanted it to bring fundamental change, including an end to the "systematic building of social-

[11] Report to the central committee of the Socialist Unity Party of Germany (SED), November 23–26, 1961; in Dallin, ed., *Diversity in International Communism*, p. 353.

[12] Khrushchev did not lean toward liberalization in the early post-Stalin period but favored Matyas Rakosi in Hungary and Edward Ochab in Poland.

ism," while Ulbricht and his key followers, Erich Honecker and Hermann Mattern, sought to limit the scope of the New Course.[13]

The disagreement between the two politburo factions was reflected in a public controversy that erupted a few days before the June 17 riots on an issue that was central to the uprising. The status of the increased work norms set by a government decree in the last half of May was brought in question by the politburo's June 11 announcement, without any preparation, of a radical change in policy. (The effect of the decree was to require additional work to receive the old wages.) On June 14 the Party newspaper, *Neues Deutschland*, without mentioning the May decree voiced opposition to setting work norms by administrative means, and thus implied that the decree was wrong; two days later, however, the trade union newspaper, *Die Tribune*, explicitly reaffirmed the validity of the higher work standards under the New Course. The Party newspaper was edited by Rudolf Herrnstadt and reflected the views of his faction, which evidently sought to rescind the decree setting higher norms; on the other side, arguing for the preservation of the higher work standards, were Ulbricht and his followers. This quarrel fed the discontent of the Berlin construction workers, first encouraging them to believe that the decree on higher norms had been withdrawn, then dashing their hopes. The June 16 article provoked the construction workers to go into the streets of East Berlin that morning to demonstrate against the increased work norms.[14]

[13] Ulbricht revealed his real attitude toward the New Course only in 1955, after Malenkov and his policies had been defeated in the USSR: "Some of you may be surprised that I did not use the expression 'New Course.' . . . The most remarkable thing about such a course would not be that it is new but that it is wrong. . . . We never had any intention of taking such a wrong course, and we never will take it" (speech at the Twenty-fourth SED Central Committee Plenum, June 1 and 2, 1955; quoted in English by Carola Stern, "East Germany," in Griffith, ed., *Communism in Europe*, II, 74).

[14] This was flatly and plausibly asserted by a high East German official, Otto Nuschke. See the account of his interview with the West Berlin radio station, RIAS, in Baring, p. 157.

When the demonstrations began, the politburo was having its regular Tuesday weekly meeting. Its discussion of measures to implement the New Course had hardly begun when it was interrupted by news of the construction workers' demonstration and their demands for a withdrawal of the new work norms. After some hours of deliberation, the politburo had the decree on work standards rescinded, and by evening the East German leaders believed the demonstrations had come to an end. However, the next day, Wednesday, June 17, the demonstrations spread from East Berlin to all of East Germany, involving a large proportion of the industrial work force. No longer limited to economic aims, the demonstrations now embraced political objectives, including the removal of Ulbricht. This same issue apparently had come under discussion in the politburo itself, for as its deliberations continued through Monday night, Ulbricht came under open and severe attack. The curtain of secrecy on this meeting of the politburo was lifted for a moment for an official, Heinz Lippmann, who came to consult with his superior, politburo candidate Erich Honecker, Ulbricht's protégé and subsequently his successor. Lippmann reports:

[Honecker] seemed nervous and was apparently not listening to what I said. When I asked if he were ill, he shook his head and said resignedly: "They're all attacking Walter [Ulbricht]. He'll probably be defeated. But the worst thing is that I don't know what I should do myself." He sounded weary and depressed; I had never heard him talk like that before. He was in no hurry to go back into the meeting —almost as if he hoped to avoid having to make a decision.[15]

Honecker did avoid making a decision at this time. Ulbricht "postponed a decision by demanding that the opposition put its views in writing and discuss them with a commission."[16] Members of the politburo dispersed. When the regime's coercive or-

[15] Heinz Lippmann, *Honecker and the New Politics of Europe* (New York: Macmillan, 1972), p. 158. Lippmann, who was Honecker's deputy in the youth movement from 1951 to 1953, subsequently moved to West Germany and became a journalist.
[16] *Ibid.*

gans proved ineffective, the Soviet army intervened and the uprising collapsed.

It is often said that the workers' demonstrations, by placing a premium on stability in the leadership, inadvertently saved Ulbricht from being ousted.[17] So far as is known, however, Ulbricht's rule, though weakened by the advent of the New Course, was not subjected to open attack by his politburo opponents until *after* the demonstrations, when Honecker suddenly discovered on June 17 that Ulbricht's position was in serious jeopardy. The central committee's statement of August 22, 1953, in its explanation of why the opposition was emboldened to try to win control of the leadership, links the advent of the New Course and the June 17 demonstrations and makes them *jointly* responsible: "After the announcement of the New Course and after the fascist putsch attempt of June 17, Zaisser and Herrnstadt considered the time right for them to undertake an attack on the party leadership in order to take it for themselves." It was only then, "in a commission created by the Politburo"—presumably the commission referred to by Heinz Lippmann that Ulbricht proposed on June 17—that Zaisser and Herrnstadt "made the proposal to change the party leadership in such a way that they, Zaisser and Herrnstadt, would have unlimited influence. Comrade Zaisser further proposed that Comrade Herrnstadt be elected First secretary of the Central Committee. Herrnstadt received this proposal with the comment: 'I know that the party apparatus is solidly against me, but the masses are behind me.' " [18]

[17] It should be noted, however, that the Hungarian demonstrators in October 1956 did not save Gero but, on the contrary, were the immediate cause of his removal. See below the discussion of why Ulbricht survived hostile workers' demonstrations while Gero did not.

[18] *Chronologische Materialien zur Geschichte der SED* (West Berlin: Informationsbüro West, 1956), pp. 410 ff. This key statement was never published in East Germany and has been neglected in the literature on the June uprising. It was called to my attention by Victor Baras, who analyzes it at length in his dissertation, "East Germany in Soviet Foreign Policy." The translation used here is by Baras.

The crushing of the revolt, although it ended the masses' active participation in the politics of the leadership, did not immediately resolve the quasi succession crisis in East Germany. The two factions now struggled to blame each other for the uprising, and Herrnstadt actually succeeded in becoming the author of the central committee's public account of what had happened and what needed to be done.[19] The outcome of the struggle, and Ulbricht's fate, depended more than ever on the leaders in Moscow, whose attention and anxieties were now focused on the situation in East Germany.

In an analogous situation in Hungary in October 1956, when Soviet troops were called into Budapest to suppress a popular revolt, Moscow moved immediately to oust Erno Gero and replace him with Janos Kadar—even though a key demand of the demonstrators in Hungary was the ouster of Gero, just as in East Germany they had called for an end to Ulbricht's rule. The situation in East Germany differed, however, in important respects. There the Soviet army intervened only when it clearly was required, and then decisively, ending the revolt and restoring public order. In Budapest, Gero's initial decision to request the use of Soviet troops was obviously premature and worsened the situation, necessitating further urgent measures to end the crisis. Moreover, while Ulbricht was Moscow's original choice to rule in East Germany and had kept its confidence for eight years as the dominant leader, Gero came to power only four months before the Hungarian revolt and quickly proved his incompetence. Finally, acceptable candidates to succeed Gero were available in the very first days of the revolt in Hungary, including both a man in whom the people had confidence (Imre Nagy) and an able and experienced *apparachik* (Janos Kadar); in East Germany, on the other hand, even before the purge of Beria made Zaisser and perhaps Herrnstadt ineligible, there was no Communist who had wide popular support, and the most experienced

[19] Resolution of June 21, 1953; in Baring, pp. 160–173.

apparachik, Franz Dahlem, had just been purged, with Moscow's approval, and thoroughly discredited.[20] If there was serious danger to Ulbricht's position it was from his key opponent in Moscow, Lavrentii Beria, but the East German uprising compromised Beria. Only when he was purged, *nine days after the uprising,* was Ulbricht's continuance as Party leader at long last assured. The question that remained was, To what extent would he be permitted to act against his enemies? Zaisser, as minister of state security, was an early casualty following the purge of Beria. By the end of July, Ulbricht succeeded in also purging four politburo candidates (Rudolf Herrnstadt, Hans Jendretzky, Anton Ackermann, and Elli Schmidt) from the leading bodies. Ulbricht adapted himself to the requirements of the New Course, and once Malenkov was removed (February 1955), his position was reasonably secure. It remained so until 1956, when Khrushchev in some measure unsettled it once more by his secret speech.

Quasi Succession in Hungary

The quasi succession crisis in Hungary was the direct result of Moscow's decision to reduce the power of Matyas Rakosi. Like the other personal rulers in Eastern Europe, he was made to divide his offices in accordance with the newly proclaimed doctrine of collective leadership. Rakosi was, however, compelled to do so long before the others; moreover, unlike them, he was not permitted to choose his successor as head of government. Moscow did the choosing, and instead of selecting one of Rakosi's

---

[20] According to Carola Stern, discussing the situation as it was in 1950, "the men with the best personal ties with the Russian Communist Party, Herrnstadt and Zaisser, . . . showed little ambition at first to Party leadership. Both were considered *éminences grises* operating in the background. . . . [Herrnstadt was] an unlikely candidate. The Party functionaries did not care for his cold and cynical intellectuality" (*Ulbricht,* pp. 118–119. Yet in the maneuvering against Ulbricht in June 1953, it was rumored that Herrnstadt was to replace Ulbricht as first secretary (*ibid.,* pp. 142–143).

close subordinates, they picked Imre Nagy, a sharp critic of Rakosi.

Although it is not entirely clear why Rakosi was singled out for an early reduction in power, a clue may be found in Stalin's policy with respect to the leadership in the Soviet bloc during his last years. It will be recalled that in 1952 a number of Jewish leaders were purged in Romania and Czechoslovakia. It seems plausible that Stalin also harbored plans to purge Rakosi—the only Jew he ever allowed to become head of a ruling party—as well as Rakosi's numerous Jewish lieutenants.[21] Incidentally, it should be noted that Stalin's anti-Semitism was not a blind and uncontrolled prejudice. When it was expedient to place Jews in high positions in the newly installed Communist regimes of Eastern Europe, Stalin apparently imposed few restrictions on their employment. It was only after they had served their purpose and had become a hindrance to efforts at winning popular support that Stalin indulged his hatred and suspicion of Jews. At this point death intervened to put an end to Stalin's incipient anti-Semitic campaign, and in particular to attacks on Jewish leaders as unpatriotic accomplices of the state of Israel. One objective of the campaign was, however, retained by his successors: to reduce the prominence of Jews among Eastern Europe's leaders. (Later, in 1956, Jews were ousted from the top leadership of both Hungary and Poland.) It may be conjectured that Rakosi, saved by Stalin's death from being purged, was instead made a special target of the new leaders' campaign to reduce the personal power of Eastern European dictators.

The way in which Moscow brought about the early division of offices in Hungary and the resistance the division met from Rakosi are described in a major document, titled "Dissertation," authored by Imre Nagy in 1955, after his initial purge from the leadership.

[21] In January 1953 the Jewish head of the political police, Gabor Peter, was arrested. Powerful secondary Jewish leaders in Poland, such as Hilary Minc and Jakub Berman, probably were also on Stalin's list.

The question of the relation of Party and state was also discussed very sharply in the conference held with the Soviet comrades prior to the June, 1953, meeting of the [Hungarian] Central Committee. . . . At this conference Comrade Malenkov pointed out that, in May, 1953, they had discussed with Matyas Rakosi the personal [personnel] questions also that concerned the separation of Party and state leadership. "We asked, 'Whom do you recommend as your deputy [to be the head of government, or "premier"]?' He could name no one. He had objections to everyone whose name was mentioned; he had something against everyone. Everyone was suspected except he alone. This appalled us very much," said Comrade Malenkov. Comrade Malenkov declared that Matyas Rakosi had said that he did want a Premier, "but he wanted a Premier who would have no voice in the making of decisions." Comrade Khrushchev noted, "The matter involved was that the leadership of the Party and the state should not be concentrated in the hands of one man or a few men; this is not desirable." . . . In his speech at the April [1955] meeting of the Central Committee, Matyas Rakosi allegedly said that he felt heavy responsibility for the fact that I had become Premier on July 4, 1953, thereby suggesting that he at least "recommended" me for Premier. For the sake of truth, it must be stated that it was not Matyas Rakosi, but the Soviet comrades—Comrades Malenkov, Molotov and Khrushchev—who recommended what Comrade Rakosi and all members of the Hungarian delegation accepted with approbation. Thus Rakosi is innocent in this question; there is no basis for his remorse, because he bears no responsibility at all for my nomination as Premier.[22]

From this passage it is clear that Moscow chose Nagy and that Rakosi, after temporizing, was obliged to accept the decision. Actually, Nagy's special patron was Malenkov, whose New Course policies Nagy strongly favored; Rakosi, on the other hand, was a partisan of Khrushchev's hard-line policies and subsequently received his support. For twenty months the struggle in Hungary paralleled the struggle in Moscow. Finally, shortly after Malenkov's defeat and removal from the post of head of the Soviet government in early 1955, Nagy fell from power. As a result, Rakosi was virtually restored to his former position as the unrivaled leader, although with diminished authority and with-

[22] Nagy, *On Communism*, pp. 250–252.

out access to the means of repression that Stalin had provided him with to protect his power.

Quasi succession in Hungary led to controversy over the pace and scope of the New Course program enjoined by Moscow, which in turn provoked popular disturbances. The New Course was introduced by Nagy, not Rakosi, in a fervent speech that sharply criticized the methods used in forcing peasants to become members of collective farms.[23] Many peasants misconstrued the speech as an invitation to dissolve them. Their unauthorized dissolution of numerous collectives damaged the economy and complicated the implementation of the New Course. In the following months the struggle between Rakosi and Nagy continued, culminating in Rakosi's victory in early 1955. Having conspicuously espoused the cause of the people's welfare, however, Nagy acquired wide popularity and thus in 1956 became an important factor in the Rakosi succession.

The Gottwald Succession in Czechoslovakia

Klement Gottwald's death, several days after he attended Stalin's funeral in Moscow, resulted in only the second instance of Communist succession in Eastern Europe. Not as orderly as the 1949 succession to Dimitrov in Bulgaria, the succession to Gottwald was complicated, and strongly influenced, by the succession in Moscow. Gottwald's power and his offices were divided: Antonin Zapotocky became president; Antonin Novotny returned to the secretariat (from which he had been removed a month previously) as its senior member; Viliam Siroky replaced Zapotocky as premier. This arrangement gave the appearance of a triumvirate, but of the three only Novotny was a serious candidate to replace Gottwald as ruler. Zapotocky was an experienced and respected figure whose opposition to Novotny posed an obstacle, but he was too old to be an effective rival for personal rule. Siroky was a Slovak; although Slovaks have since

[23] Speech delivered July 4, 1953; trans. in *News from behind the Iron Curtain*, August 1953.

been heads of the party, at that time the office was beyond their reach. Thus Novotny, unlike Khrushchev, did not have to cope with a formidable rival like Malenkov. Novotny received the title of first secretary of the central committee in September 1953, shortly after Khrushchev received the same title in the USSR. Even Khrushchev's secret speech, which shook the power of several well-established rulers in the Soviet bloc, did not prevent Novotny from consolidating his position. His rule was confirmed when he assumed the post of president of the republic in November 1957, a few months before Khrushchev made himself head of government.

Succession to Gottwald was not accomplished without popular disorder. The uncertainty about the succession in Czechoslovakia during the first months after Gottwald's death, added to the uncertainty about the succession in the Soviet leadership, complicated the execution of new policies. In early June, riots in Pilsen, occasioned by a painful currency reform, foreshadowed the urban riots that were about to occur in East Germany and the rural disturbances in Hungary. For several years afterward there was an acute struggle in the leadership. Yet the disorder and disarray were not serious, and on the whole the succession was accomplished at no great cost to the leadership. There were two reasons: first, Khrushchev's victory over domestic rivals was translated into a victory for his protégé, Novotny, in Czechoslovakia; second, Novotny, though a typical *apparachik* and a man of limited capacities, was far superior to his opponents in the power struggle.

Novotny's situation when Gottwald died was complicated but basically favorable. Although he was an *apparachik*, Novotny had not been a member of the Slansky faction during the period when Slansky ran the central Party apparatus as general secretary and staffed most of the Party's provincial posts. As first secretary of the Prague city organization, Novotny had played a key role in the purge of Slansky and his partisans in the fall of 1951. He had also been its chief beneficiary, for he replaced Slansky in the central secretariat and the politburo. Although Novotny was obviously allied with Gottwald, their relationship was apparently one of mutual dependence in executing the purge enjoined by Moscow. As president of the republic and chairman of the Party central committee, Gottwald was pre-eminent, though with the rise of Novotny in Slansky's place he once again had a powerful subordinate and potential rival. Three months after Slansky's trial, however, Novotny was transferred from the Party secretariat, the source of his power, to the government. A few weeks later, after Gottwald became ill with pneumonia and soon afterward died, Novotny was quickly restored to the secretariat "in order to concentrate on work in the Central Committee." The same phrase was used at this time in the USSR with respect to Khrushchev, whose personal strategy now became the model for Novotny.

In view of Novotny's removal from the secretariat shortly before Gottwald's death, he could hardly have been Gottwald's choice as successor. If Gottwald was thinking of an heir, it may have been his son-in-law, Alexej Cepicka, who unsuccessfully opposed Novotny in the following years. The relative orderliness of the Gottwald succession, then, cannot be credited to Gottwald's arrangements for the succession. Since he was apparently struggling to protect his own power and was physically weakened in the months before he died, it is unlikely that Gottwald could devote much effort to arranging the succession. Its relative orderliness was apparently due to Khrushchev's effective support of Novotny, and to Novotny's personal superiority to his rivals in the struggle for power.

Novotny was not well-known in the country when Gottwald died. Since he was a poor speaker, he was not well-equipped to win popularity by placing himself before the public. In the closely confined politics of Czechoslovakia in 1953, however, this proved no great handicap. Good fortune compensated for the lack. The purge of the number-two man, Slansky, by an external agency (Stalin) had earlier removed a formidable barrier to

Novotny's rise. Others, of course, also benefited, including Cepicka. Novotny's second stroke of fortune was the death of Gottwald, which at once removed the number-one man and weakened the prospects of his protégé, Cepicka, and enabled Novotny to return to the secretariat from which he had just been expelled. The way was clear for him to arrogate to himself Gottwald's former powers and thus resolve the succession.

Stable Leadership in Bulgaria, Poland, and Romania

In three states, after Stalin's death, there were neither actual nor quasi succession crises. Boleslaw Bierut's position in the Polish leadership was unchallenged. In Bulgaria, the man chosen to be first secretary, Todor Zhivkov, was evidently a Chervenkov protégé when appointed. Zhivkov, who at age forty-two was young for the post, subsequently was helped by the Russians to supplant Chervenkov as head of the government. Some of Chervenkov's future difficulties were foreshadowed by the fact that men whom he had earlier downgraded, such as Anton Yugov and Boyan Bulgaranov, became more active and prominent in the early post-Stalin period.

Gheorghiu-Dej, in Romania, was more successful than Chervenkov in protecting his position while appearing to accommodate himself to Moscow's policy favoring collective leadership. He remained head of the government and chose a close subordinate, Gheorghe Apostol, to be nominal head of the party secretariat. To ensure that actual control of the secretariat remained in his own hands, Gheorghiu-Dej replaced the veterans in that body (Miron Constantinescu, Chisinevschi, and Alexandru Moghioros) with young protégés, particularly Nicolae Ceausescu and Mihai Dalea. Gheorghiu-Dej also took the precaution at this time, in 1954, of executing a political prisoner, Lucretiu Patrascanu, who otherwise might have become a formidable rival to him when Khrushchev initiated de-Stalinization.[24] This was the only politi-

---

[24] Later in 1954, Vasile Luca, who had been removed from the leadership in 1952, was sentenced to life imprisonment for political crimes.

cal execution in Eastern Europe after Stalin's death, except for
the 1958 execution of the Nagy group, at Soviet insistence, for its
role in the Hungarian uprising. Gheorghiu-Dej's resort to political
execution after it had ceased to be respectable in the Communist
regimes of Eastern Europe was resisted by some of his own
followers—or so at least Nicolae Ceausescu was to claim after
Gheorghiu-Dej had died.[25] The execution of Patrascanu is testimony, not only to Gheorghiu-Dej's ruthlessness in his struggle
for power, but perhaps also to his willingness to take decisive
action without first seeking Moscow's approval.[26]

In all three states—Poland, Bulgaria, and Romania—New
Course policies were adopted in 1953, but they did not bring the
confusion and disorder that accompanied their introduction into
the other Communist states of Eastern Europe. The reason, it is
clear, is that higher politics in the three states remained stable and
orderly during the early post-Stalin period, while upper-level
politics in Czechoslovakia, East Germany, and Hungary were in
disarray, leading to confusion and disruption when the New
Course was introduced. The difference in leadership stability is
not attributable to general features distinguishing the two sets of
states but, rather, to the specific circumstances that led to a
weakening of the leadership in particular states. In Czechoslovakia the succession crisis initiated by Gottwald's death caused
instability in the leadership. The higher politics of Hungary and
East Germany, on the other hand, were disrupted by gross Soviet
intervention, probably inspired by different motives in each instance: the special Soviet aim in Hungary was to weaken the
hold of Jewish leaders on the leadership in an effort to secure
greater popular support for the regime; the special aim in East
Germany was, at the very least, to rekindle hope in the West that

[25] A central committee resolution rehabilitated Patrascanu on April 26,
1968.

[26] In the USSR itself, only leaders associated with the political police,
like Lavrentii Beria and Mir Dzhafar Bagirov, were executed after Stalin
died.

a negotiated settlement might lead to the unification of Germany, thereby raising a serious obstacle to American plans for the rearmament of West Germany.

That circumstances, rather than a predisposition to leadership stability in particular states, account for the differences among them observed in 1953 appears from their subsequent history. The Czechoslovak leadership, unstable in 1953, was relatively untouched by the bloc crises of 1956 and 1961; in the mid-sixties, however, the leadership in Czechoslovakia once again was seriously weakened. On the other hand, the leadership in Bulgaria, stable in 1953, was wracked by deep divisions in 1956 and 1961 that significantly weakened it. Poland, strong in 1953 and 1961, was weakened by conflict among its leaders in 1956 and 1968. East Germany and Hungary, unstable in 1953 and 1956, had strong and unified leaderships in 1961. Circumstances that partly account for the episodic weakening of the leadership of particular bloc states are the occasional situational crises that confront all states, as well as the irregular emergence of outstanding leaders who are able to dominate their colleagues; but more important is the fact that episodic instability characteristically results from the need to change rulers and the consequent weakening of leadership that usually attends such a change in Communist states. Only in Romania and North Vietnam, perhaps, has the leadership been able throughout a quarter-century of rule to avoid the most acute internal crises; there are no grounds for supposing that these countries will always be free of them.

4

De-Stalinization Results in
a Year of Successions (1956)

Events in the immediate post-Stalin period revealed how difficult it was for a divided Soviet leadership to maintain order in
Eastern Europe. A weakening of the satellites' leadership at the
same time, whether through internal causes or Soviet intervention,
had particularly serious consequences. When the Soviet bloc had
almost recovered from the divided leadership in Moscow produced by Stalin's death, a new shock emanated from the Kremlin.
It shook the authority of leaders in Eastern Europe, led to new
Soviet interventions in their politics, and helped to create deep
crises of succession in three states.

The shock originated in Nikita Khrushchev's secret speech
against Stalin in 1956 at the Twentieth Party Congress.[1] In attack-

[1] This chapter, in addition to primary courses, draws upon the following:
Adam Bromke, *Communist States at the Crossroads* (New York: Praeger,
1965); Brown, *Bulgaria*, chaps. iv–viii and Appendixes I and II; Brzezinski,
The Soviet Bloc, chaps. viii–xvi; Fischer-Galati, *The New Rumania*, chaps.
iii–iv; Andrew Gyorgy, "The Internal Political Order," in Stephen Fischer-
Galati, ed., *Eastern Europe in the Sixties* (New York: Praeger, 1963);
Ghita Ionescu, *Break-up of the Soviet Empire in Eastern Europe* (London: Penguin, 1965), chaps. ii–iv; Ionescu, *Communism in Rumania*, chaps.
xi–xvi; Paul Kecskemeti, *The Unexpected Revolution* (Stanford, Calif.:
Stanford University Press, 1961); Melvin Lasky, ed., *The Hungarian Revolution* (New York: Praeger, 1957); Lewis, *A Case History of Hope;* Richard
Lowenthal, *World Communism* (New York: Oxford University Press,
1966), chaps. ii–iii; Meray, *That Day in Budapest;* Stern, *Ulbricht*, chaps.

ing Stalin, Khrushchev raised a general question about the legitimacy of rule by all the leaders whom Stalin had elevated to power and whose authority therefore depended on Stalin's good name. This question was a source of embarrassment to Khrushchev himself, as it was to other Communist leaders—in the USSR, in Eastern Europe, and in Communist parties elsewhere in the world. Moreover, Khrushchev's specific charge that Stalin falsely accused devoted Communists of treason and had them killed struck a particular blow at the little Stalins in Eastern Europe. These men, encouraged or prodded by Stalin, had themselves staged trials of their opponents in order to eliminate them, thereby consolidating their own personal rule. Presumably their victims were as innocent as Stalin's, and equally deserving of rehabilitation. But if they were rehabilitated, the authority of the ruler who had persecuted them would be put in jeopardy. Just as the imposition of Stalinism in Eastern Europe gave rise to an autocratic trend, de-Stalinization tended to weaken personal rule.

Khrushchev was of course aware of this tendency, though he did not realize how difficult it would be to control it. He intended the anti-Stalin campaign to extend into Eastern Europe, though not everywhere with equal force. The campaign was evidently not aimed at leaders currently allied with Khrushchev, such as Rakosi in Hungary and Novotny in Czechoslovakia; Chervenkov, on the other hand, was an early target. But anti-Stalinism could not be manipulated like a surgeon's tool, nor was Khrushchev a surgeon. His questioning of the purge trials was bound to have a particularly strong impact in Hungary and Bulgaria, where the purged leaders, Rajk and Kostov, had been Communists with nationalist tendencies and some popular support. Their rehabilitation threatened the position of the countries' rulers, who in each instance had staged and benefited from the purge. The immediate consequences in the two states, however, were different: Chervenkov soon fell, while Rakosi survived for a time. The difference may

---

vii–viii; and Paul Zinner, *Revolution in Hungary* (New York: Columbia University Press, 1962).

have been partly due to the fact that Rakosi moved with the blow, becoming in late March the sponsor of Rajk's rehabilitation, while Chervenkov resisted the rehabilitation of Kostov. Another reason was that Khrushchev continued to show solicitude for Rakosi, as he had during the latter's controversy with Nagy, but he apparently used the rehabilitation of Kostov to discredit Chervenkov and to replace him.

The Chervenkov Succession in Bulgaria

The rehabilitation of Kostov in April was accompanied by an unexpected development. Chervenkov was criticized for his arbitrary rule and demoted from his post as government head. Since Chervenkov had been the effective ruler in Bulgaria for a half-dozen years without serious challenge, it seems clear that internal opposition alone did not cause him to fall; the hand of Moscow also was at work. Chervenkov had been in Moscow for several weeks in late 1955. It is possible that his talks with Soviet leaders did not go well or that subsequently Chervenkov did not carry out what he had undertaken. Once the decision was made, for whatever reason, to undermine Chervenkov, Moscow could capitalize on a vulnerability: he ruled the country from a post outside the secretariat, as head of the government. In Romania, when Gheorghiu-Dej was required to choose between the supreme office of the Party and of the government, he originally made the same decision as Chervenkov, but subsequently, when he observed the primacy of the first secretary in the USSR, he assumed this post himself, vacating the office of premier. Chervenkov, however, for some reason failed to switch. This may have facilitated Moscow's efforts to subvert Chervenkov's control over the Party apparatus, particularly by encouraging Zhivkov to add real power to his nominal authority as first secretary. However it was accomplished, Moscow achieved its aim. Chervenkov was subjected to public criticism and, like Malenkov a year earlier, was demoted to the post of deputy to the head of the government. Whatever the grounds in 1956 for doubt about

Chervenkov's loyalty to the Soviet cause (or to that of the dominant faction in the Soviet leadership), two years later he provided excellent grounds: after a visit to the Chinese People's Republic in 1958, Chervenkov strongly advocated that Bulgaria also engage in a "great leap forward."

Moscow's intervention against Chervenkov was its first attempt since the 1948 fiasco against Tito to replace an established ruler with someone more satisfactory. It was not to be the last, however, and not all were as successful as this one. Moreover, although the removal of Chervenkov was readily accomplished, Bulgaria was not spared an extended succession crisis. The division of posts, a merely formal action when initially carried out in 1954, now reflected a real division of power. In place of Chervenkov as a single personal ruler there was a small oligarchy, or "collective leadership," centered on the triumvirate of Zhivkov, Yugov, and Chervenkov, each a rival of the other two. Zhivkov, no longer Chervenkov's subordinate, occupied a pre-eminent position as the head of a Soviet-supported faction based in the secretariat. Anton Yugov was Chervenkov's new chief as head of the government. He had been minister of the interior from 1944 until 1949, when Chervenkov demoted him for lack of vigor in the purge of Kostov. Finally, Chervenkov, although publicly discredited, remained a powerful figure because he retained the support and allegiance of numerous functionaries. An unequal struggle among the three leaders continued for a half-dozen years, until decisive Soviet support enabled Zhivkov to remove Chervenkov in 1961 and Yugov the following year, thereby resolving the succession.

Why it took Zhivkov six years to consolidate his power, despite Moscow's strong support, is not altogether clear. Subtle forms of resistance to Soviet pressure may have been employed by Zhivkov's opponents, and it is possible that Soviet pressure was itself moderated in order not to provoke an anti-Soviet reaction. In any case, after the downgrading of Chervenkov in 1956, Zhivkov required two Party congresses (1958 and 1962) to win control of the top bodies. The 1954 politburo, chosen while Chervenkov was still dominant, continued in office without substantial change until 1962, when Zhivkov was finally able to appoint a majority of the politburo.[2] Change, when it came, however, was thoroughgoing: of the 9 members then elected, only 2 (besides Zhivkov) remained from the 1954 politburo. Moreover, of the 11 men chosen for the 1966 politburo, 9 first entered it after Zhivkov became the leading figure in April 1956.

The central committee of 1954, like Chervenkov's politburo, was also stable in the early years of Zhivkov's tenure as first secretary. Only 3 of its members were not re-elected in 1958 and, despite its increased size, 70 percent of the voting members of the 1958 central committee had been first chosen while Chervenkov still ruled. On the other hand, 28 voting members of the 1958 central committee were not re-elected at the next Party congress in 1962. Not until then, apparently, did Zhivkov succeed in purging his opponents from the central committee. Of the 101 full members of the 1962 central committee, almost two-thirds had entered it after Chervenkov's ouster in 1956. At the next Party congress (1966), Zhivkov strengthened his control over the central committee still further by increasing its voting members from 101 to 137—more than twice the size of the 1954 central committee. By then only a conspiracy could unseat Zhivkov. Earlier a conspiracy actually had been attempted, shortly after the one that removed Khrushchev; its failure eased the further consolidation of Zhivkov's rule.

The Bierut Succession in Poland (*March–October 1956*)

The crisis of succession in Poland began shortly after Khrushchev's secret speech, although the two events were not directly connected. The sixty-four-year-old Boleslaw Bierut died on March 12, after an illness that began in Moscow, where he had attended the Twentieth Congress. When the central committee

[2] In 1957, however, Zhivkov took advantage of Khrushchev's purge of "the anti-Party group" to replace an able young rival, Georgi Chankov.

met on March 20 to pick his successor as first secretary, Khrushchev attended and spoke. He warned against having Jews prominent in the leadership, thus voicing privately and in a sterilized version the theme that Stalin had enunciated more ominously at the time of the doctors' plot.[3] Before the year was out, two of the three Jews in the politburo, Jakub Berman and Hilary Minc, had been ousted.

The man chosen to succeed Bierut was Edward Ochab. According to the testimony of Colonel Josef Swiatlo, a former high official of the Polish political police, at the time of his defection in 1953, it was generally understood that Ochab "was assigned to work exclusively in the party sector and for a long time has not occupied any government position. He is being trained and educated to be a future party leader, Bierut's successor. . . . Today he is regarded as Bierut's successor."[4] Swiatlo was well placed to receive such information, and evidence is lacking of a subsequent decline in Ochab's fortunes. If Bierut was grooming Ochab as his heir and this was widely known in leadership circles, it is understandable that the central committee would accept him in the absence of other strong candidates. As the number-two man in the secretariat, Ochab was in any case a logical candidate to succeed Bierut.[5] Furthermore, Ochab was very acceptable to the Moscow leadership, and particularly to Khrushchev. Ochab, in speeches delivered during the factional struggle between Malen-

---

[3] The doctors' plot was an alleged conspiracy manufactured by Stalin in the last months of his life. According to a Soviet announcement in January 1953, a group of doctors, most of them Jewish, had plotted to kill leading Soviet military figures, but after Stalin's death the so-called plot was said to have been a fabrication.

[4] *News from behind the Iron Curtain,* March 1955, p. 10. This was published a year before Ochab was chosen for the post.

[5] Others who have succeeded from that post in various countries are: Novotny in 1953 (although he had been transferred from it a few weeks before Gottwald died); Gero in 1956; Brezhnev in 1964; Ceausecu in 1965; and Honecker in 1971. Malenkov was second in seniority to Stalin, but Khrushchev, who was third, forced Malenkov out of the secretariat when Stalin died and became first secretary of the central committee.

kov and Khrushchev, had strongly supported Khrushchev's views. Like Rakosi, Novotny, and Zhivkov, Ochab at this time apparently was an adherent of Khrushchev's faction.[6]

The selection of Ochab seems to have been made by a narrow circle of leaders without serious controversy, in accordance with Bierut's intention and with the participation of Moscow in the person of Khrushchev. The Polish people, of course, had no say, and the central committee probably very little, but both were yet to be heard from. The elevation of Ochab did not resolve the succession. He still faced the problem of winning the allegiance of the Party apparatus, which he now headed, and of consolidating power in the other institutions of rule. When he failed to accomplish these goals quickly, Poland entered upon an interregnum of several months, during which state authority was weakened and political uncertainty became widespread. Before it was over, large elements of the leadership, numerous intellectuals and writers, and the masses of workers would play their part in Polish politics.

The unsettled situation created by Khrushchev's secret speech complicated Ochab's problem of consolidation. The chief victim of Stalinist practices in Poland who had to be rehabilitated was Wladislaw Gomulka, a man who then held a strong attraction for the Polish people because he had advocated that Poland follow its own national road to socialism, and had suffered for his advocacy with dignity and strength. Gomulka was very much alive; and, though still deprived of his Party card, he had become a potent factor inside the Party. Throughout this period, Gomulka's

---

[6] According to an assertion of Zbigniew Brezezinski, "based on personal sources in Warsaw . . . Khrushchev's first choice was F. Mazur (reputedly an agent of the MVD [Soviet Ministry of Internal Affairs]), and Ochab was a compromise choice" (*The Soviet Bloc*, p. 534). According to the same sources, the politburo's candidate for the post of first secretary was a Jew, Roman Zambrowski (p. 245). Flora Lewis' informants, on the other hand, told her that Khrushchev's candidate was Zenon Nowak (*A Case History of Hope*, p. 102), and that Zambrowski was nominated for "one of the secretaryships," but this "had never been meant seriously" (p. 103).

powerful political personality cast a shadow over Ochab's. Since Gomulka was expected to assume a responsible position, it was necessary to negotiate the terms of his rehabilitation—and the terms he set were hard. These negotiations, which began soon after Ochab's election and lasted until the crisis reached its peak in the "October days," considerably hampered Ochab's efforts to consolidate his power.

Three factions took shape; their lines hardened and their controversy became increasingly open, particularly after the Poznan riots in late June. (1) The center faction, which supported Ochab, recognized the need for changing the old ways but wanted reform to be closely controlled by the leadership and its organs. (2) A liberal faction, the Pulawska group, consisting of some young Party leaders and numerous writers and other intellectuals, sought renewal; it advocated bold criticism, radical reform, greater independence of Moscow, and strong efforts to win popular support. (3) The conservative faction, which included the Natolin group,[7] wanted to keep reform to a minimum and to preserve close censorship over the press; it relied heavily on Moscow for support. Ochab headed the centrist faction, but it was only one of three and did not control the politburo, where the conservative faction initially was strong. Throughout the interregnum Ochab made little progress in winning influence over the other factions or in extending his control over the leading bodies.

In late June workers in Poznan staged a demonstration to protest their living conditions. It turned into an uprising which the army suppressed. Thus once again, as in 1953 in Czechoslovakia, East Germany, and Hungary, divisions in the leadership reflecting crises of succession (or quasi succession) led to popular disturbances. This time, however, instead of helping to unite the leadership against a common enemy, the riot exacerbated divisions in the leadership, which could not agree on its causes or its implications for national policy. The conservatives subscribed

---

[7] The names of the groups derived from the Warsaw suburbs in which they met.

to Moscow's view that counterrevolutionary intrigue abetted by a too liberal press was responsible; liberals spoke of the workers' justified grievances that had to be remedied; the centrists found it increasingly difficult to maintain a coherent middle position between the widening extremes. All of this complicated the efforts of Ochab, the chief centrist, to consolidate his position as Bierut's heir.

With the workers entering the political arena, Gomulka's popularity became a growing asset. On the other hand, the conservatives' condemnation of the Poznan uprising hurt them. Ordinary Party members in factory cells passed resolutions attacking the Natolin faction and calling for Gomulka's election as first secretary.[8] As the crisis deepened and the existing leadership proved unable to act effectively, the conservatives relied increasingly on a hoped-for Soviet intervention or a military coup to reverse the course of developments, while the centrist faction increasingly saw a need to break with the past and to enlist popular support by placing Gomulka at the head of the Party. Ochab himself came to believe that he lacked sufficient support in the leadership and the nation to govern. Although apparently not under strong pressure to do so, he finally resigned in favor of Gomulka.[9] At a meeting of the politburo in October, Gomulka was designated to replace him as first secretary; the decision was to be formally confirmed by the central committee. For the first time, a ruling Party in the Communist bloc was choosing its new leader without consulting Moscow.

The politburo decision on succession apparently was secretly conveyed to the Kremlin by Moscow's partisans in Warsaw. The Soviet leaders were disturbed. Previously their views had never

[8] Lewis, p. 198. The Natolin faction had also negotiated with Gomulka on the terms of his return to a position of leadership, but their views were too far apart for any agreement to be reached.

[9] The extent of popular rejection of Ochab is indicated by the results of the contrived but relatively free state elections held several weeks later, in January 1957, when Ochab did poorly. Gomulka, on the other hand, did very well.

been overridden; this time they had not even been taken into account. At a time when Moscow had accepted the need for some devolution of authority to the capitals of Eastern Europe, the political character of a ruler became even more important than before. If the ruler was not to be designated by Moscow, it was necessary that the USSR retain at least a veto of each Party's choice. Moscow was disturbed also by the particular choice of Gomulka, a man who had stood against Stalin and the previous Polish leadership in 1948 and thereafter, and who had never acknowledged his errors.

As the Polish central committee met to effect the change in its leadership, a Soviet delegation arrived, unannounced, in Warsaw for talks. It included Khrushchev, Mikoyan, Kaganovich, and Molotov. Whether they came determined to prevent the change in leadership is not known; certainly they came unreconciled to it, since they ordered armored units of the Soviet army in Poland to move toward Warsaw. The resulting confrontation of the delegation with Gomulka (as well as with other members of the Polish politburo) was a kind of political examination, a verbal test to determine whether Stalin's judgment against Gomulka should stand. The Soviet leaders evidently were satisfied that Gomulka was not disloyal to the USSR. He could be allowed to assume his post, especially since Moscow retained the means for a new intervention should it prove necessary. The Polish central committee, on the recommendation of its politburo, then proceeded to elect Gomulka first secretary.

Once again, as in 1955 with Tito, Khrushchev had reversed Stalin's judgment as to who could be relied upon to rule a Communist state in accordance with Soviet interests. But Khrushchev had also learned how difficult it was to judge the reliability of a ruler. Ochab had failed to justify Soviet expectations of both his capacity to rule and his unquestioning loyalty to the Soviet cause. In Ochab's report to the plenum on October 20, he is said to have "mentioned in passing that never before in his life did he have so much bitterness to swallow as in recent days and that unjustified, unheard-of accusations were leveled against him by 'our Soviet friends.' " [10]

Ochab's resignation as first secretary of the central committee, which surprised and angered the Soviet leaders, also posed a difficulty for Western observers. It was apparently a personal decision, and had not been forced on him. While little is known of the circumstances in which Ochab decided to resign, his sense of failure is reflected in his remarks to the central committee admitting "his and the Politburo's culpability for using traditionally superficial methods" of analysis, particularly with regard to the Poznan uprising. [11] In any case, Ochab's decision to resign while still in control of important levers of power does not accord with the theory of a pure struggle for power. The range of conduct of Communist leaders is greater than is often supposed.

In the aftermath, Gomulka, unlike Ochab, consolidated his personal rule and thus resolved the succession. He early proved himself a reliable ally of the USSR, which had opposed his coming to power, while he disappointed Polish youth and liberal intellectuals, who had helped force him on a reluctant Party leadership. (Dubcek, when faced, a dozen years later, with a similar choice between the USSR and his own people, chose differently.) By suppressing his supporters Gomulka won the confidence of his former opponents.

In consolidating his position after becoming first secretary in October, Gomulka was aided by several circumstances. His popularity was tremendous, and he had the support of countless people who did not know his true views. Moreover, the example of Hungary, where revolt had just been violently suppressed, was a fresh reminder to all sides of what could happen to Poland if Gomulka failed. Even the Catholic Church in Poland restrained the opposition and for a time gave Gomulka a measure of support. Nevertheless, in view of the obstacles he faced, Gomulka's success

[10] Brzezinski, *The Soviet Bloc*, p. 254.

[11] *Ibid.*, p. 255. While Ochab, by his admission, discredited the old politburo, Gomulka came to power without confessing any past mistakes.

in establishing his personal rule is remarkable. His personal supporters in the top leadership, men like Marian Spychalski, Zenon Kliszko, and Waclaw Komar, constituted a very small group. Others, like members of the Pulawska faction, offered conditional support because they thought Gomulka could do the necessary job of reform. A third group, the Natolin faction, was compelled to accept him because of his wide support.

Gomulka dealt with the problem of a divided leadership cautiously but firmly during the next year. With the help of the reformers, he withstood the last-ditch attacks of Stalinists while conciliating those members of the Natolin faction who accepted an accommodation with him. It was largely by balancing the opposing factions, not by replacing them with his own protégés, that Gomulka broadened the base of his support in the Party and succeeded in stabilizing his personal power.

Gomulka early won control over the Party apparatus by a purge which reduced its size.[12] He won its allegiance by adopting some conservative policies of which it could approve. The Party apparatus became the effective instrument of his rule, although his failure to staff it or the leading organs of Party and government with his own men limited the scope of his power. It could be jeopardized whenever the established equilibrium was seriously upset, as by the rise of Mieczyslaw Moczar's oppositional faction in 1968, or by the 1970 riots, which actually led to Gomulka's removal. He left himself without the means of carrying out a program of radical reform, although he clearly lacked the will quite as much as the power.

Gomulka's rule was a triumph of centrism. He continued the reduction in the power of the political police that had already begun. He reached an accommodation with the Church by moderating religious policy, and one with the peasants by abandoning efforts at collectivization. Both accommodations lasted throughout the period of his rule. Although industry ad-

---

[12] According to Brzezinski, it was reduced from about thirteen thousand to five thousand (p. 347, n. 1).

vanced, the economy was inefficient and the workers were not satisfied that their material condition had improved in the same measure. That Gomulka stayed in power for fourteen years was not so much because of the success of his policies, which was quite limited, as because of his effective use of the means available to a Communist ruler to preserve his power. It is difficult to change even a mediocre ruler in a Communist regime, but it is not impossible, as events in Poland in 1970 were to show once more, and as events in Hungary in October 1956 also demonstrated.

A Period of Successions in Hungary (July–November 1956)

No other people's democracy experienced greater political instability in its first decade than Hungary. In part Hungary's instability was due to the weakness of Communism in Hungary before the Soviet army imposed it on a reluctant nation, but Communism was perhaps no stronger in Romania or Poland, which were relatively stable. Stalin's errors in dealing with the Hungarian leadership were crucial, and they were compounded by the mistakes of his successors. Stalin's basic error was to give the hegemony to Rakosi and then order him to purge and *execute* Rajk; the crucial error of Stalin's successors, particularly Khrushchev, was to confirm Rakosi's hegemony (in 1955) and then order him to *rehabilitate* Rajk. Khrushchev's blunder in having the murderer rehabilite his victim is all the more remarkable since he showed an early awareness that a fundamental contradiction was involved. According to Imre Nagy, in his 1955 memorandum to the Hungarian central committee:

On the occasion of our Moscow talks prior to the Third Congress [May 1954], Comrade Khrushchev likewise said the following: "Rakosi is responsible for the arrests. Therefore he does not want to release these people. He knows that he is guilty and will compromise himself. It is not permissible to denounce men and to throw suspicion on them." Comrade Khrushchev advised that "the rehabilitations should be carried out so as not to destroy Rakosi's authority." But, so that his words would not be misinterpreted, he added, "We will protect

Rakosi's authority only in so far as it is not prejudicial to Party authority. It may happen that on the pretext of protecting Rakosi's authority, the old policy will be reinstated and the freeing of the prisoners will not proceed. Of course, it is difficult for Rakosi to free the prisoners," Comrade Khrushchev said, "because he ordered the arrests. Despite that, what happened must be told." [13]

The rehabilitations of which Khrushchev spoke excluded the key victim, Laszlo Rajk. When, three years later, following Khrushchev's secret speech, Rakosi was compelled to rehabilitate Rajk also, the ingredients had been assembled for a whole series of political explosions.

The Rakosi Succession

By ousting Imre Nagy from the government in the spring of 1955, Matyas Rakosi succeeded in re-establishing his unrivaled leadership. Although he no longer was personally challenged within the top leadership, Rakosi increasingly found himself challenged outside it by disappointed partisans of the New Course and, in particular, by restive intellectuals. For those who were dissatisfied, Nagy represented an alternative to Rakosi's rule. While Communist politics do not sanction an *opposition*, a group that stands just outside the portals of power and actively restrains the government, it cannot always prevent the existence of an *alternative* to the government, a group or prestigious individual that stands ready to replace the government and has a basis of support. Gomulka constituted such an alternative in Poland. If he had been executed earlier, Ochab conceivably might have been able to consolidate his position as leader. Rakosi saw a comparable danger to himself from Imre Nagy and persisted in a campaign to discredit him. He had Nagy formally condemned by the central committee for his political errors and, in September 1955, had him expelled from the Communist Party.

Rakosi's progress in consolidating his position was interrupted by Khrushchev's secret speech to the Twentieth Congress. At a

[13] Nagy, *On Communism*, p. 296.

time when Rakosi was still seeking to rid himself of a living rival, the speech raised grave questions about the means he had used to dispose of one who was dead. Domestic pressures and exhortations from Moscow for the rehabilitation of Rajk gave Rakosi no choice. He announced the move and, aping Khrushchev, blamed the injustice to Rajk on the former head of political security, Gabor Peter, who was Hungary's Beria. The concession only whetted the appetites of his most vocal critics, the writers and journalists, and won Rakosi only a short reprieve.

Nagy increasingly served as the rallying point of opposition to Rakosi, yet in the aftermath of the Twentieth Congress, Rakosi could not get Moscow's approval to arrest or execute him. As a result, the politics of Hungary from March to October 1956, like the politics of Poland, was haunted by the specter of an *alternative* to the leader—in Poland, Gomulka; in Hungary, Nagy. Similarly, Rakosi's threats of repressive measures against his critics proved to be empty, since Moscow did not permit him to carry them out. Nevertheless, while denying Rakosi the means he needed to protect his waning power, Moscow persisted in supporting him against his critics. Tito reported that when he tried, in June 1956, to persuade "the Soviet comrades" to remove Rakosi, they answered that "he was prudent, that he was going to succeed, and that they knew of no one else whom they could rely upon in that country." [14] After the June riots in Poland showed where events might lead, Moscow had to face again the question of who should rule in Hungary. Personal animosity to Rakosi had become so strong and widespread that, unless he could repress his opponents, his presence in the leadership would now be a provocation and a source of weakness. When he proposed to arrest hundreds of dissidents, including Imre Nagy, Moscow refused its approval and decided instead to remove him.

The Soviet leaders doubtless were influenced in their decision

---

[14] Speech at Pula, November 11, 1956, published in the Party newspaper, *Borba,* five days later, November 16; trans. in Zinner, ed., *National Communism and Popular Revolt in Eastern Europe,* p. 524.

by the paralyzing divisions that were developing in the top bodies of the Hungarian Workers Party (the Communist Party in Hungary) and by the related erosion of support for Rakosi. According to Gero:

For various reasons the Politburo did not feel that it could rely on the unanimous support of the Central Committee. They felt that no unanimous views were held within the Central Committee as regards relations to the Politburo or to its individual members [presumably an allusion to disagreements in the central committee regarding Rakosi in particular], and that on the other hand there was no full unanimity among the members of the Central Committee as regards the policy of the Party. In this respect the onus must mainly rest with the Politburo for failing to show enough resolve and courage in eliminating the retarding factors.[15]

Dissident elements in the Hungarian leadership may have solicited Moscow's intervention, but evidence of this is lacking. In any case, Mikoyan arrived unexpectedly in Budapest on July 18 to inform a surprised and angry Rakosi that he had been dismissed from his post. Moscow thus unceremoniously ousted a loyal ruler in a Communist state of Eastern Europe as it has done on four other occasions: in Bulgaria two months previously, when Chervenkov was ousted; in Hungary again, three months afterward, when Gero was removed; thirteen years later, in 1969, when Dubcek was ousted as the nominal head of the Party in Soviet-occupied Czechoslovakia; and in 1971, when Ulbricht was demoted in East Germany.

Publicly, Rakosi was relieved of his post "at his own request," but one of his opponents later wrote that he had been "called upon by the supreme body of the Party [i.e., the central committee] to give up his post."[16] The published letter of resignation spoke of Rakosi's illness (hypertension); unlike Novotny in 1968, however, Rakosi was also compelled to acknowledge his

[15] Erno Gero, report of the politburo to the central committee, *Szabad Nep* (Budapest), July 19, 1956; *ibid.*, p. 345.

[16] Zoltan Horvath, in *Nepszava* (Budapest), October 14, 1956; *ibid.*, p. 338, n. 4.

"mistakes," since Moscow's purpose in removing him was to divest the Hungarian leadership of the burden of Rakosi's evil reputation.[17]

The matter of Rakosi's replacement posed a difficulty. Nagy was at this time unacceptable to either Moscow or the Hungarian leadership, which not many months before had expelled him from the Party. The men who had been closest to Rakosi could provide continuity of leadership, but most of them were Jews, and Khrushchev had just warned the Poles that keeping Jews in prominent positions was an unnecessary affront to national sentiment. Nevertheless, a Jew was chosen, in the person of Gero. According to Tito, the Soviet leaders even "made it a condition that Rakosi would go only if Gero remained." [18] The reason seems clear: Gero's Soviet backers hoped that he, as Rakosi's closest associate, would be able to maintain continuity in policy and to hold the Party together without having to bear the full onus of Rakosi's reputation for repression and injustice. Possibly, Moscow viewed Gero as a transitional leader, as Khrushchev later hinted in a letter dated November 9, 1956, addressed to Tito: "You were fully satisfied with the fact that the Central Committee of the CPSU, since the summer of this year, in connection with the removal of Rakosi, has tried to have Comrade Kadar made First Secretary of the Central Committee of the Hungarian Workers Party." [19] If this really was the Soviet intention when Gero was appointed in July 1956, however, it is difficult to understand why

[17] After noting his "mistakes" with respect to the cult of personality and the violation of socialist legality, Rakosi hinted at Moscow's role in his removal: "After the 20th Congress of the CPSU and Comrade Khrushchev's speech it became clear to me that the weight and effect of these mistakes were greater than I had thought." For the subsequent failure to carry out reforms Rakosi acknowledged his personal responsibility as first secretary (*Szabad Nep,* July 19, 1956; *ibid.,* pp. 341–342).

[18] Tito, Pula speech, November 11, 1956; *ibid.,* p. 524.

[19] The existence of the letter and part of its contents were revealed by Enver Hoxha of Albania in a speech, November 7, 1961, on the October revolution anniversary; in *Zeri i Popullit* (Tirana), November 8, 1961; trans. in Dallin, p. 115.

Moscow went to such lengths in the following months to try to stabilize Gero's position. It seems more likely that Kadar—who was elevated to the top three Party bodies (the central committee, the politburo, and the secretariat) in July when Rakosi was ousted—was not intended to replace Gero unless Gero failed to stabilize Hungarian politics.

The decision to have Gero succeed Rakosi doubtless was made in consultation with Rakosi's lieutenants, and perhaps with Rakosi himself. Rakosi apparently had mixed feelings about Gero. According to some accounts, Gero was ambitious and coveted the supreme position. Rakosi, in turn, had expressed doubts about Gero. "The mutual jealousy between these two men had gone on for decades." [20] Georgi Malenkov is quoted as saying that in May 1953, Rakosi voiced "objections to everyone whose name was mentioned" for the post of head of the Hungarian government. "He could name no one. He had . . . something against everyone. Everyone was suspect except he [sic] alone." [21] No doubt those suspect included Gero. Yet when Rakosi was being expelled from the leadership in July 1956, he probably had good reason to prefer Gero as the successor most likely to preserve what he had created. In any case, such friction between a Communist ruler and his most powerful subordinate is not uncommon. In Czechoslovakia, it led to the split that emerged in 1967 between Antonin Novotny and Jiri Hendrych, his secretary for cadres, while in East Germany, Ulbricht twice found it necessary to purge the number-two man: Franz Dahlem in 1953, and Karl Schirdewan in 1958.

Once Moscow decided that Rakosi's successor as first secretary was to be Gero, there was no difficulty in having him named to the post. Dissident opinion could be disregarded. But questions remained: Could possession of the office be translated into effective power? Could the new Party head establish his personal authority? Gero had several counts against him. Although he now

[20] Meray, *That Day in Budapest,* p. 49.
[21] Quoted by Nagy, *On Communism,* p. 250.

made it a point to criticize Rakosi's failings publicly, in the eyes of dissidents the new leadership could not disassociate itself from the old. Furthermore, Tito, whose rapproachement with Moscow had won him a certain influence in Eastern European affairs, was against the appointment and continued to oppose Gero for two months. Gero was also pressed to take further measures to rehabilitate Rajk, whom Stalin had had executed. The pressure led to a massive funeral procession and Rajk's reinterment, which kept alive the memory of Gero's involvement in the affair. At the same time, Gero had to negotiate with Nagy for Nagy's return to the Party (which occurred early in October) and to the leadership.

Gero failed to understand that the crisis he faced did not involve simply a transfer of personal power, but also a potentially explosive social revolt. He spent several weeks taking control of the levers of power and consolidating his position in the Party, but then departed from Hungary on September 8, 1956, for the USSR, to meet with Khrushchev and Tito; later he met with Mikoyan and Mikhail Suslov, the two Soviet leaders who then were charged with implementing policy toward Hungary. Gero was away from Hungary during five of the six weeks preceding the revolution, acting as though the key to a solution of Hungary's crisis lay, not in Hungary, but in the USSR and Yugoslavia.[22] Kadar, now the second-rank secretary in the Hungarian Party, was also out of the country during most of this period, perhaps encouraged to travel by Gero, who doubtless was reluctant to have a potential rival active in Budapest while he himself was away. The result was to remove the two chief figures of the leadership from the capital. When, a week before the outbreak of revolution, he departed for Yugoslavia to receive Tito's public acceptance of him as Hungary's ruler, Gero obviously did not suspect what lay ahead.

Gero received Tito's blessing in Belgrade almost at the moment the Hungarian people intervened to express their own views on

[22] Zinner, *Revolution in Hungary*, p. 223.

who should be the ruler. When Gero returned to Budapest on October 23, he was confronted by a huge demonstration of students and young workers.[23] Emboldened by developments in Poland, where Gomulka had returned to power, the demonstrators demanded a change of policy and the return of Imre Nagy to high councils of the government. Gero responded with a provocative speech on the radio, and the demonstration turned into a riot in which the police fired upon the crowd. The politburo, in emergency session on the evening of October 23, now dropped its demand that Nagy acknowledge his past mistakes as a condition of his return to the leadership.[24] Under the pressure of developments in the streets of Budapest, the politburo summoned a midnight meeting of the central committee at Party headquarters, which Nagy was allowed to attend. He and some of his closest followers were elevated to the central committee and the politburo. Moreover, Nagy once again became head of the government, the position he had held from Stalin's death, when the New Course was instituted, until March 1955, when Rakosi ousted him. This was clearly a concession that the people of Budapest had forced from Gero, who still clung to power.

The circumstances of Nagy's return to the leadership in the early hours of Wednesday, October 24, indicate that the decision was made by Gero himself, not by Moscow. Gero apparently hoped to use Nagy's personal authority as the Communist most acceptable to the Hungarian people in order to mollify the demonstrators and re-establish public order, an aim Nagy shared. The terms on which Nagy and his closest followers entered the leadership—presumably the result of bargaining between the

[23] The revolution began as a blow struck by youth. The activity of writers and intellectuals, which was crucial in preparing the uprising, continued during the revolution but was no longer so prominent or efficacious. In fact, Hungarian writers have been fairly quiescent since the fall of 1956, having even failed to react strongly to the Soviet invasion of Czechoslovakia.

[24] In Poland, Gomulka's return to the leadership was the outcome of negotiations with the Party that had been completed, but there too the Party was unable to impose its terms.

two men—suggest that Gero remained in charge. The central committee "confirmed" him in the post of first secretary and made his henchman, Andras Hegedus, till then head of the government, first deputy to Nagy.[25] Moreover, Gero evidently was employing a two-pronged strategy, for at about the same time that he elevated Nagy he called for the dispatch of Soviet army units to Budapest to help maintain Communist control in the city.

The Gero Succession

Moscow was troubled by Gero's failure to restore order and by his hasty judgment that units of the Soviet army stationed in Hungary were needed in Budapest for use against the demonstrators. It will be recalled that the Soviet authorities withheld the use of force when the demonstrations in East Berlin first began on June 16, 1953, and did not commit units of the Soviet army until the afternoon of the second day. When the rapid commitment of Soviet forces against the demonstrators in Budapest failed to restore order but instead provoked violent and desperate resistance, Moscow once again dispatched Mikoyan to effect a change in the Party leadership in Hungary. This time he was accompanied by Suslov, perhaps as a representative of a leadership faction opposed to Khrushchev. The two men arrived in the early afternoon of October 24 at the central committee building, from which the government, as well as the Party, was then operating. The next morning, Gero's ouster was announced.[26] Since Gero had been confirmed as first secretary only

[25] Central committee announcement over Radio Kossuth on October 24, 1956; trans. in Lasky, ed., *The Hungarian Revolution*, p. 59.

[26] *Ibid.*, p. 74. Oddly, although, according to the announcement, Gero was relieved of his post at a meeting of the central committee, Kadar's appointment to replace him was decided at a meeting of the politburo. It seems questionable, in the confused circumstances, whether quorums of either body could be assembled. Three days later, the powers of the central committee and the politburo were assumed by a new body, the presidium.

hours before Mikoyan and Suslov arrived, his removal from the post doubtless was a Soviet decision.

Gero's replacement by Janos Kadar was apparently also decided by Moscow. Kadar enjoyed a measure of prestige as a man whom Rakosi had kept in prison until 1954. When Rakosi was ousted in July 1956, Kadar was taken into the secretariat and the politburo, thus becoming virtually the number-two man to Gero. Whether or not he had been favored by the Soviet leaders to become first secretary following Rakosi's removal in July (as Khrushchev said in his November 9 letter to Tito), Kadar evidently was being groomed to succeed Gero if the latter failed. When he did fail, the Gero-Nagy duumvirate that Gero had engineered in a desperate effort to remain in power was replaced by a new duumvirate. It consisted of Kadar, who apparently had the confidence of the Soviet leaders, and Nagy, who, because of his performance as head of the government in 1953 and 1954, evidently did not. Nagy was accepted by the Soviet leaders, as he had been by Gero, as a necessary means of mollifying the demonstrators and restoring order. It is very doubtful that he figured in Moscow's long-term plans for Hungary's leadership.

Not much is known about relations between Nagy and Kadar or about their relative authority in the circumstances in which they now found themselves. At first they worked in close proximity in the central committee building, under the eyes of the two Soviet representatives. Even so, their speeches seemed to reflect different orientations; Nagy was concerned equally with the need to restore order and the need to proceed with reform, while Kadar placed primary stress on the need to suppress "fascist counterrevolution." After October 26, the problem of coordinating their actions became more complicated, as Mikoyan and Suslov departed for the USSR (taking with them Gero and Hegedus), and Nagy moved from the central committee's offices to nearby quarters in the parliament building where he had worked during his previous tenure as head of the government.

It is always hard in a duumvirate to maintain a balance between the two top figures, especially, as in the present instance,
when the duumvirate is not so much the product of political
contrivance as the resultant of contending forces. With the collapse of the regime, only two effective political agents remained:
the Hungarian people surging in the streets and, subsequently,
in the countryside, who had raised Nagy to power; and the Soviet Union and its occupation forces, which had elevated Kadar.
As late as October 28, partisans of the USSR attempted to balance Nagy's pre-eminence in the government by subordinating
him to Kadar in the Party. A presidium was created to exercise
"the Central Committee's mandate to lead the Party," of which
Kadar was the chairman and Nagy merely one of five members,
none of them his supporters. If the aim was to subject Nagy to
Party discipline in a body dominated by his opponents, the attempt failed. As the Party *apparat* collapsed and Soviet military
forces withdrew from Budapest in the last days of October,
power shifted from the Party to the government, which was seen
as representing the popular will. The government now made the
major decisions and referred only in passing to the concurrence
of the Party presidium. Premier Nagy announced on October 30
that "the cabinet abolishes the one-party system"—a measure
which in effect deprived the Hungarian Workers Party of sovereignty.[27] Kadar, speaking after Nagy on the radio, could only
sound an echo: "Every member of the Presidium of the Hungarian Workers Party agrees with today's decisions by the Presidium of the Council of Ministers." [28] The presidium and the
Party that it was "mandated" to lead both passed out of existence
on November 1, just four days after the Party presidium was established. Kadar announced the formation of a new Party which
would "break away from the crimes of the past once and for all." [29]
How far power had shifted from Kadar to Nagy, even in Party
affairs, was revealed by the composition of the preparatory com-

[27] *Ibid.*, p. 139.   [28] *Ibid.*,p. 140.
[29] Radio address by Kadar, November 1, 1956, *ibid.*, p. 179.

mittee that was to form the new Party: whereas Nagy had been isolated in the presidium, Kadar was isolated in the new committee, which Nagy and five of his partisans dominated. Moreover, whereas Kadar was chairman of the presidium, in the preparatory committe he had no special title.

Nagy's ascendancy over Kadar within the duumvirate clearly was not the result of his skill at political maneuvering or his passion for power, both of which were quite limited. Such personal characteristics doubtless are needed in ordinary times when the chief aim of a candidate for succession is to take possession of the established levers of power, but in the Gero succession the institutions controlled by these levers were already crumbling. To consolidate his position as head of the government in the revolutionary situation that had developed, Nagy had to achieve three objectives: to identify himself with the revolution; to control its movement so that it did not turn against the Communists; and to win Soviet acquiescence in the measures necessary for these purposes.

Once the insurrection had achieved the scale of a revolution, it was hypostatized: association with the revolution became a touchstone by which leaders were judged. Nagy initially was favored, in his efforts to associate himself with the revolution, by his reputation as an opponent of the Rakosi-Gero regime against which the revolution was directed. His efforts were soon complicated, however, by the deception in which Gero and Hegedus had engaged in the early hours of the revolution, when they made it appear that Nagy was responsible for calling Soviet troops into Budapest to suppress the disturbances. This time, in contrast to what happened June 17, 1953, in East Germany, the revolution did not collapse when it encountered the Soviet army but, rather, turned its fury against it. Rage at the Soviet army's intervention became a central feature of the developing Hungarian revolution. In time Nagy denied responsibility for the decision to bring Soviet troops into Budapest, but earlier, probably under Soviet pressure, he said in a radio speech that their "intervention in the fighting was necessitated by the vital interests of our socialist order." [30] The continuing linkage of Nagy with the Soviet intervention led to a questioning of his commitment to the revolution that put him on the defensive. When revolutionary delegations from Budapest and the provinces visited his offices in the parliament building to demand that he rid Budapest and all Hungary of Soviet troops, Nagy made their demands his own. He even denied (contrary to fact) that he had said Soviet troops were "necessary for the reestablishment of peace and order." [31]

The Soviet leaders, already doubting Nagy's reliability, were further antagonized by the denial. Yet, since Nagy's power was based on the people—on factory workers and students in Budapest and the provincial cities, on peasants and members of the professions in the countryside—as a revolutionary wave swept popular opinion, it carried him along. Responding to the demands of the revolutionary delegations as well as to the crossing of new units of the Soviet army into Hungary, Nagy called on October 31 for Hungary's withdrawal from the Warsaw Pact, which was being used to justify the intervention. The following day Kadar, after proclaiming the formation of the new Party with its organizing committee dominated by the Nagy faction, secretly left Budapest and defected to the Russians. Caught in a crossfire, Nagy ended by helping to provoke a new armed Soviet intervention against his government without winning the revolutionaries' wholehearted support. The stage was set for the suppression of the revolution by the Soviet army and the renewed dominance of the USSR in Hungarian politics.

The Nagy Succession

The Soviet invasion did not immediately end the political contest between Nagy and Kadar, just as it did not end the contest between the Hungarian people and the Soviet state. The people

[30] Radio speech, October 25, 1956, *ibid.*, p. 75.
[31] Interview with foreign journalists October 31, 1956, broadcast by Austrian radio, *ibid.*, p. 156.

remained an active political force for a time, as they did in Czechoslovakia after August 1968, although not for as long. The working class, in particular, organized in workers' councils in the factories, continued to resist by a general strike. Lacking an articulate political program of their own, the workers called for the return to leadership of Imre Nagy. However, on November 22, Nagy was betrayed into leaving his sanctuary in the Yugoslav embassy and was made captive by the Russians. Not long afterward the workers' organized resistance was itself broken. From then on, for all practical purposes Nagy ceased to be a significant factor in Hungarian politics.

A final scene had still to be played out. When Nagy was tried and executed in 1958, he assuredly was not a dangerous alternative to Kadar's rule. He was victimized, in all probability, chiefly to deter other Communist leaders who someday might be tempted to betray Moscow's confidence.[32] Nagy, to this day, is the only ruler in the Soviet bloc since the time of Stalin who has been brought to execution. The fate of the other former rulers in Hungary was different. Rakosi and Gero, as well as their closest associates, having served the Communist cause in Hungary in accordance with Soviet precepts and to the best of their ability, were merely cursed for their political sins and retired to private life.[33] From them neither Moscow nor Kadar had anything to fear.

Soviet intervention in Hungary was politically far more successful in the short run than the 1968 intervention in Czechoslovakia. The chief reason was the availability of Kadar and important members of the former leadership. It is not clear at what point Kadar and his partisans decided to break with Nagy and the

[32] Dubcek has also been punished, though it was expedient for a time to allow him to remain as first secretary. Then, in a series of steps, he was expelled from the leadership and from the Party so that his example would serve as a deterrent to others. Ochab, while he proved unreliable for Moscow's purposes during the "October days" in Poland, did not endanger Communist rule; hence he was allowed to remain in the leadership.

[33] Fejto, "Hungarian Communism," in Griffith, ed., *Communism in Europe,* I, 267–268.

revolution. They had grounds for deep concern, after October 28, at the rapid decline of their faction in the leadership. Even more important, they had reason to fear that, following the dissolution of the Hungarian Workers Party, the immediate withdrawal of the Soviet army from Hungary, which Nagy was demanding, would mean the end of Communist rule. On the other hand, at some point they probably were led to understand that the USSR in no event would permit the withdrawal of Hungary from the Warsaw Pact. Whatever their reasoning or motivation, they fell from sight at the end of the day on Thursday, November 1, only to reappear three days later proclaiming a new "revolutionary worker-peasant government." Thus the Soviet army succeeded in establishing a satellite government made up of experienced and well-known Hungarian leaders, at least some of whom, like Kadar, did not bear the stigma of the former Rakosi-Gero clique.[34]

This government at first had little substance. The situation has been described by Paul Zinner:

The government existed in name only. It did not control the executive machinery of the state, nor did it have the personnel to staff that machinery. . . . For a period of several weeks, Hungary lived under a veritable interregnum, with the Soviet military wielding effective power, the Hungarian government in the throes of painful reconstruction, the object of derision and ridicule, and the workers' councils, spontaneous bodies of the people's will, exercising *de facto* political power to the point of being consulted by the Soviet military as well as Hungarian government organs.[35]

The problem that Kadar faced in consolidating his succession resembled the one Nagy had faced in October: not to transfer the powers of an existing office into his own hands, but to create

[34] Even after he defected from the Nagy leadership to set up a new government, Kadar continued to speak positively of the October revolution until early 1957, when he began to characterize the uprising as simply a counter-revolution.

[35] *Revolution in Hungary*, pp. 338–339.

a new basis of rule. In a sense, then, Kadar was not Gero's successor but the founder of a new regime; more precisely, he had to rebuild a regime whose functionaries deeply distrusted him and whose subjects looked upon him as a traitor.

Kadar had certain advantages, however.[36] Not only did Tito approve of him, but, unlike Rakosi and Gero, Kadar could now rely on brute force as well as large Soviet subsidies to induce the nation to accept his personal rule. To enhance his authority, he assumed the post of head of government in addition to that of head of the Party (which he had to rebuild), and undertook to conciliate the nation. With the passage of time he was basically successful in winning popular acceptance of his rule, in sharp contrast to Gomulka, who ultimately failed, in more favorable circumstances, to do so in Poland.

Developments in Hungary from March 1953 to November 1956 are here treated as though they comprised three political successions (as well as one quasi succession). This is warranted, since on three occasions it was necessary to replace the supreme official, and to try to stabilize the leadership on a new basis. At the same time, it could be said that throughout this period, Hungary experienced a single crisis of succession, since at no time did it have an unchallenged leader, or leading body, whose authority was acknowledged widely enough for stable rule. (At no point, incidentally, was Moscow unable to determine the succession, except when street demonstrations—and perhaps Gero's preemptive decision—forced it to accept Nagy as head of the government.) What might be regarded as a single crisis of succession was finally resolved by the Soviet army when it suppressed the nation's revolt and installed Kadar as the ruler in a newly established Communist regime.

[36] It is interesting to speculate about what might have happened if, in July 1956, Kadar rather than Gero had succeeded Rakosi. He probably would have had the immediate support of Tito and, himself a victim of Rakosi, might conceivably have won a measure of popular support. Whatever the merit of this speculation, it illustrates the problem the Soviet leaders face when the leaders in Eastern Europe are chosen.

Reverberations

Khrushchev's de-Stalinization campaign encouraged criticism of rulers everywhere, even where a ruler's position appeared strong. In the weeks following the Twentieth Congress (February 1956), personal rulers in several Communist states of Eastern Europe were openly criticized by dissident Party leaders at major Party meetings—not only in Bulgaria, where Chervenkov was actually unseated, but also in Romania, Albania, and East Germany.[37] That Khrushchev instigated these attacks on the dominant leaders cannot be demonstrated, but the author of the secret speech against Stalin clearly was responsible for the widespread phenomenon. Moreover, while Khrushchev may not have meant Gheorghiu-Dej, Ulbricht, and Hoxha to suffer Chervenkov's fate, he apparently did not mind if they became apprehensive that such was his intention.

In Romania the chief victims of the purges in Stalin's day had been Jews and members of other ethnic minorities; they were not Communists of the dominant nationality, like the victims in Bulgaria and Hungary. It was therefore easier for Gheorghiu-Dej to avoid rehabilitating the victims. Although the leaders purged in 1952 had not been executed and were still alive, Gheorghiu-Dej did not rehabilitate them but, despite their unpopularity, treated them as a potential threat to his power.[38] A more serious threat, however, was posed by the men still in high office who favored a wider-reaching policy of de-Stalinization and liberalization, notably Miron Constantinescu, an ethnic Romanian, and Iosif Chisinevschi, a Jew who remained responsive to Moscow's wishes. Emboldened by Khrushchev's secret speech, they attacked Gheorghiu-Dej at a meeting of the central committee in

[37] The extensive criticism of Rakosi in Hungary following the Twentieth Congress, on the other hand, did not come from powerful Party leaders, but chiefly from the intelligentsia.

[38] In the case of Lucretiu Patrascanu, a politically important ethnic Romanian who was executed in 1954, Gheorghiu-Dej succeeded in delaying rehabilitation until after his own death in 1965.

March 1956, accusing him of responsibility for the Party's use of Stalinist methods.[39] Gheorghiu-Dej was the victor in this confrontation, but his antagonists remained in the leadership, perhaps protected by Khrushchev.

While Gheorghiu-Dej was able within a few months to limit the consequences for himself and for Romania of Khrushchev's secret speech, in Albania and East Germany the potential dangers were greater and took longer to deal with. In Albania the chief victim of Stalinist repression had been Koci Xoxe. Until his execution in 1949, Xoxe was sponsored by Tito, while his rival, Enver Hoxha, was at that time aligned with Moscow. The question of rehabilitating Xoxe, which was closely linked with the question of improved Soviet relations with Yugoslavia, thus posed a double threat to Hoxha's personal power.

Khrushchev's secret speech stimulated Albanian dissidents to speak out for more extensive de-Stalinization measures. At a conference of Party organizations in the capital city, Tirana, in April 1956, they criticized the leadership's failure to implement collective leadership, to improve relations with Yugoslavia, and to rehabilitate Koci Xoxe.[40] Later, after Albania's split with Moscow, the chief Albanian newspaper claimed that this attack on the leadership was "encouraged" by developments at the Twentieth Congress of the CPSU and had as its aim "to overthrow" the Albanian leadership.[41] Whatever its source or its aim, Hoxha quickly suppressed it and severely disciplined those who had spoken out. He did not become reconciled with Tito, and he has never rehabilitated Xoxe.

Presumably, Moscow was determined only to pressure Hoxha into carrying out the policies it favored, and did not at this time

[39] Ionescu, *Communism in Rumania*, pp. 260–261. Gheorghiu-Dej's version of this confrontation is in speeches published July 9, 1957, and December 7, 1961, in the Party newspaper, *Scinteia*. Later, after Gheorghiu-Dej died, his chosen successor, Ceausescu, renewed these charges.

[40] Speech by Hoxha, November 7, 1961; trans. in Dallin, ed., *Diversity in International Communism*, p. 121.

[41] Editorial in *Zeri i Popullit*, January 9, 1962; trans. in Dallin, p. 176.

seek to replace him. The danger to Hoxha's position was, however, made clear to him. The contents of a letter sent by Khrushchev to Tito on November 9, 1956, were immediately conveyed to Hoxha, who learned that the CPSU central committee had been trying since the preceding summer, in connection with the removal of Rakosi, to have Comrade Kadar made first secretary of the central committee of the Hungarian Workers Party.[42] Hoxha later remarked somewhat disingenuously that this demonstrated Khrushchev's willingness "to interfere even in a question that is so important . . . as the choice of a particular person for the post of first secretary of a fraternal party." [43] Actually, if Hoxha ever had doubts about Khrushchev's interference in such matters, they should have been dispelled six months earlier, when Chervenkov was replaced. In the aftermath of the Hungarian revolt, however, Moscow's pressure for de-Stalinization relaxed. The danger to Hoxha's position abated, only to become serious once more in 1960, when the Sino-Soviet dispute emerged as a disruptive factor in bloc relations.

In East Germany, Ulbricht's position, which had not yet been fully repaired following the events of June 1953, was newly shaken by Khrushchev's revelations about Stalin and by the resulting demands for reform from the intelligentsia and some elements of the Party apparatus. Ulbricht maneuvered skillfully, joining the attack on Stalin while attempting to divert energies from the criticism of past errors to the accomplishment of economic tasks. He was particularly disturbed by the ouster of Rakosi in July and by the restraints placed on the political police in both Hungary and Poland. Dissident German Communists released from Soviet prison camps began returning to East Germany; some of them charged bitterly that Ulbricht had survived Stalin's purges by denouncing his rivals to the Soviet political police. Once again, as in the months following Stalin's death,

[42] Hoxha speech, November 7, 1961; trans. in Dallin, p. 115. (See note 19, above.)
[43] *Ibid.*

rivals in the top leadership began plotting to take advantage of disaffection in the Party and in German society in order to challenge Ulbricht.

The main rival to emerge in this secretive maneuvering was Ulbricht's chief deputy, Karl Schirdewan. He had replaced Franz Dahlem as the second in power (as the secretary for organization and cadres) after Ulbricht purged Dahlem in May 1953. Schirdewan and Ernst Wollweber, the purged Zaisser's successor as minister for state security, began to voice criticism of conditions in the country, and in particular of Ulbricht's leadership.[44] The two were later accused of seeking "to alter the party leadership," and of advocating a " 'relaxation' of our state organs of power and the use of the tactic of the 'safety valve.' " According to Heinz Brandt, who knew Schirdewan and some of his close friends, Schirdewan had solicited Khrushchev's support against Ulbricht on a visit to Moscow after the Twentieth Congress. "There is no doubt that for a brief period Khrushchev agreed that Karl Schirdewan was to be promoted to first secretary of the SED [the Communist Party of East Germany] . . . [and] made efforts in that direction so that he might establish a new Politburo." [45] On this basis, Schirdewan was able to attract support from other key leaders during 1956, including Otto Grotewohl, Fritz Selbmann, Fred Oelssner, and Gerhart Ziller. The opposition became particularly dangerous to Ulbricht after Gomulka succeeded, on October 20, in coming to power in Poland on a program of reform. The outbreak of revolution in Hungary in the next few days, however, compromised Khrushchev's de-Stalinization campaign and, according to Brandt, obliged him to withdraw his support from Schirdewan. As a result, Ulbricht easily survived the crisis.

It is difficult to judge the accuracy of Heinz Brandt's third-hand account of Khrushchev's involvement in the campaign to oust Ulbricht. Certainly Khrushchev had no objection in princi-

44 Stern, *Ulbricht*, pp. 158 ff.
45 Brandt, *Search for a Third Way*, p. 292.

ple to intervening against opponents of his de-Stalinization policies and was, in fact, so engaged at this time in Bulgaria, replacing Chervenkov with Zhivkov, a more pliant, not a more able,
leader. If Khrushchev did oppose Ulbricht in 1956, it may have
been on the ground that he was an inveterate Stalinist, but it
may also have been because Khrushchev feared that Ulbricht
was in league with his factional opponents inside the USSR. In
any case, once Khrushchev succeeded in purging opponents of
de-Stalinization in the USSR (the so-called anti-Party group), he
did not offer his support to Schirdewan, who was still engaged in
factional activity against Ulbricht. On the contrary, Khrushchev
permitted Ulbricht to purge the Schirdewan faction from the
East German politburo, an action carried out in February 1958.
By then stability in Eastern Europe had priority over reform for
Khrushchev, while his ascendancy in the USSR, on the other
hand, left Ulbricht no choice but to reach an accommodation
with him.

Following the Twentieth Congress, the chief candidate for rehabilitation in East Germany was Franz Dahlem. His name appeared, however, together with Schirdewan's, in oppositionist
speculation about a possible successor to Ulbricht. In a brilliant
stroke, Ulbricht set the two candidates for the succession against
each other. He compelled Dahlem to *earn* his rehabilitation by
attacking Schirdewan in the crucial battle in February 1958 and
by giving servile praise to Ulbricht. The outcome was the political destruction of Schirdewan and the rewarding of Dahlem
with an obscure place in the central committee. Ulbricht had
routed his opponents and would not face another challenge to
his leadership for a dozen years.

The consequences of de-Stalinization in 1956 were least in
Czechoslovakia. Novotny was able to protect his power and to
avoid the rehabilitation of either the Jewish or the Slovak victims
of Stalin's repression. The Slansky group's guilt in the crimes for
which it had been tried in 1952 was reaffirmed on April 13, 1956,
although the anti-Yugoslav and anti-Semitic implications of the

trial were disavowed. In fact, far from rehabilitating Slansky and his associates, Novotny took advantage of the de-Stalinization campaign to charge them with complicity in Stalin's evil deeds. Although the large Jewish element of the leadership had been wiped out by the Slansky trial, the Slovak nation and its nationalism remained a serious problem for Prague. Repression of Slovak Communists who emphasized their nationality was actually stepped up after Stalin's death and continued for several years after Khrushchev's secret speech. That speech did not weaken Novotny's position or seriously unsettle Czechoslovak politics, although he was still engaged at that time in the struggle to succeed Klement Gottwald. Novotny even turned Khrushchev's speech to advantage by demoting his most dangerous rival, Alexis Cepicka (the husband of Gottwald's daughter), for practicing a "cult of personality."

The credibility of Moscow's hints that it might intervene has been a crucial but variable factor affecting political disturbances in Eastern Europe. Disbelief in Soviet intervention made possible the East German uprising of 1953 as well as the 1956 revolution in Hungary. Moscow's demonstration of a willingness to use force to remove the Nagy government in November 1956, however, brought the year of successions to a close. Not until 1968, a dozen years later, did Moscow again have to cope with a problem of succession in Eastern Europe brought on by indigenous political developments.

5

Plots against Rulers
(1960–1965)

Khrushchev defeated his opponents in the Party presidium in July 1957 and consolidated his power, thereby resolving the succession in the USSR. The resulting stability in Moscow helped stabilize politics in Eastern Europe as well. In Czechoslovakia, by 1957, Novotny had fully resolved the Gottwald succession. In Bulgaria the succession was not resolved until 1962 because of Zhivkov's difficulty, even with Soviet support, in coping with Chervenkov and Yugov. Finally, however, Zhivkov purged both rivals and established personal rule.

During these years Khrushchev made several efforts to intervene against leaders of whom he disapproved, but Moscow's capacity to effect its will was substantially reduced from what it had been in the early post-Stalin period. Soviet prestige, an important source of Moscow's influence in Eastern Europe, had been seriously damaged when the Twentieth Congress revealed Stalin's crimes. Direct control of the political police in Eastern Europe had been lost or surrendered by Moscow in the months following Stalin's death and the purge of Beria and his allies. The utility of Soviet military forces in Eastern Europe as instruments of political control declined subsequently—not only in Romania, where Soviet troops, through a miscalculation, were withdrawn in 1958, but even in Poland, where they remained. Nevertheless, Moscow's capacity to influence the various currents of Eastern

European politics, though reduced, remained substantial. Moscow could still prevent the ouster of rulers of whom it approved, but, as Khrushchev was to discover, it lacked the capacity to order the removal of rulers who displeased it. After the year of succession, 1956, the reasons for Moscow's interventions against particular leaders also changed. Interventions no longer were motivated chiefly by Khrushchev's de-Stalinization campaign, but now served Soviet foreign policy goals more directly.

Soviet Plots That Failed

Successful Soviet attempts to change the leadership in Eastern Europe are of course easier to recognize than attempts that failed. Nevertheless, there is strong evidence of two unsuccessful Soviet plots, in Albania and Romania, as well as evidence pointing to a third, in Czechoslovakia.

Khrushchev attempted a coup in 1960 against Hoxha (who had resisted his rapprochement with Tito), relying on pro-Soviet leaders in the Albanian Party. The plot was discovered, however, and they were purged. For the first time since 1948, a Soviet attempt to replace an Eastern European leader failed. A year later, at the Twenty-second Party Congress, Khrushchev called openly for the Albanian leadership's replacement: "To put an end to the personality cult means essentially for Mehmet Shehu, Hoxha, and others to give up their command posts in the Party and state. But they do not want to do this." [1] By then, however, the USSR lacked means to effect the leaders' replacement easily and could only hope "the Albanian people" would do the job; the Albanian people, whatever their sentiments in the matter, also were in no position to do much about it.

In Romania too an unsuccessful effort was made to remove the leader. Taking advantage of the withdrawal of Soviet troops in

---

[1] Hoxha quotes this passage to ridicule it in his speech delivered November 7, 1961; trans. in Dallin, *Diversity in International Communism*, p. 129. Mehmet Shehu, the head of state, has long been the number-two leader and Hoxha's closest lieutenant.

1958, Gheorghiu-Dej subsequently had taken an independent line in resisting Moscow's efforts to integrate the economies of the Soviet bloc. "According to reliable reports, Khrushchev tried to suborn certain Party leaders in order to overthrow Gheorghiu-Dej in 1963. The main target of Soviet efforts was unofficially reported to be Emil Bodnaras. . . . But Bodnaras refused to be subverted." [2] Since he was responsible for supervising Romania's armed forces, Bodnaras might have proved a dangerous opponent of Gheorghiu-Dej if his patriotism had not proved stronger than his loyalty to Moscow.

The failure of Khrushchev's efforts to replace leaders in Albania and Romania in the early sixties foreshadowed the Soviet difficulties in attempts at political intervention in Romania and Czechoslovakia later in the decade.

There was a third unsuccessful plot against a personal ruler in the Khrushchev period, directed against Antonin Novotny, in Czechoslovakia, by Rudolf Barak. Barak was brought into the top leadership by Novotny immediately after Gottwald's death and served as a trusted subordinate during Novotny's rise to power. As minister of the interior, Barak played a key role in the investigation of Czechoslovakia's political trials and in decisions regarding the rehabilitation of their victims. Barak's relationship with Khrushchev is unclear, although he apparently performed an important mission for Khrushchev at the Albanian Party Congress in February 1961. Subsequently, an Albanian leader spoke ironically of "the 'marvelous' and 'preferred' men of N. Khrushchev like Rudolf Barak." [3] Khrushchev's favoritism, together with Barak's considerable personal popularity in the Party, may have awakened Novotny's suspicions, however, for in June 1961 he removed Barak from his post of minister of interior, and Barak began to fade from prominence. By the end of January 1962, accord-

[2] J. F. Brown, *The New Eastern Europe* (New York: Praeger, 1966), pp. 67–68.
[3] Speech of Hysni Kapo, in *Zeri i Popullit*, February 28, 1962; trans. in Griffith, *Albania and the Sino-Soviet Rift*, p. 141.

ing to the report of the 1968 Czechoslovak commission that investigated the political trials and the subsequent cover-up, Barak and Novotny were engaged in an intense personal struggle, and Barak was preparing for a political confrontation with his former patron:

He intended, for his own political advancement, to attack Novotny's policies at the forthcoming meeting of the Central Committee in February [1962]. Just at that time Novotny had discovered that, when leaving the Ministry of the Interior [six months previously], Barak had failed to account for a sum of money in foreign currency and that he had taken from the archives documents on the political trials, transferring them to his office in the Government building. Novotny, therefore, gave orders for the safe in charge of Barak's secretary, Jenys, to be searched. . . . Barak had in his hands a number of documents concerning the part played by top politicians in staging the trials, as well as intelligence reports on the conduct and former attitudes of certain members of the Politburo; in all probability he intended to use them in his criticism of Novotny's regime. . . . This was confirmed by Hendrych [the Party's number-two man] at a subsequent Politburo meeting on 27 November [1962], when he said: "Barak kept the documents so that he could produce them whenever it suited him. He counted on becoming head of the State—such were his ambitions." [4]

The struggle between Barak and Novotny came to a head at a time when Barak's position in the Czechoslovak leadership was deteriorating but when Novotny himself had been placed on the defensive by Khrushchev, who had just initiated at the Twenty-second Congress a new campaign aimed at de-Stalinization. No doubt Barak was trying to capitalize on this circumstance in his showdown with Novotny, but whether he was encouraged or deliberately assisted by Khrushchev is not known. In any case, Novotny, having learned that Barak had secreted the documents in the safe of the latter's secretary, had them seized and took the offensive. Barak was expelled from the Party and arrested.

Novotny subsequently charged, in a radio speech (February 22, 1962), that Barak had "tried to seize power in the govern-

[4] Pelikan, *The Czechoslovak Political Trials*, pp. 218–219.

ment"—presumably to replace Novotny as president—but when
the speech was published the next morning, the charge was not
to be found.[5] The political charges against Barak were further
watered down in the next weeks—an indication that opposition
in the leadership had compelled Novotny to abandon his aim
of staging a new political trial. Khrushchev's role in Barak's
struggle against Novotny remains obscure. Whether or not
Khrushchev plotted to unseat Novotny in 1961 and 1962, the
two men subsequently were reconciled. By October 1964, when
Khrushchev was unseated, Novotny was his strong supporter.

An Indigenous Plot That Failed

Four indigenous campaigns to oust an incumbent have met
with success: in Hungary in 1956, against Rakosi; in Czechoslovakia in 1967, against Novotny; in Poland in 1970, against
Gomulka; and in East Germany in 1971, against Ulbricht.[6] At
least one such attempt met with failure: the indigenous conspiracy against Bulgaria's Todor Zhivkov.

In the spring of 1965, after Zhivkov had finally established
personal rule, several high-ranking army officers and wartime
partisan leaders, perhaps influenced by the fact that Zhivkov's
patron, Nikita Khrushchev, had just been removed from office,
plotted a coup against Zhivkov.[7] So far as is known, this is the only
indigenous military coup ever organized within a European Communist state.[8] When the plot was discovered, its leading figure,
Ivan Todorov-Gorunya, a member of the central committee, committed suicide to avoid arrest. Two months later, in June 1965,

[5] *Rude Pravo*, February 23, 1962.

[6] The campaigns against Rakosi and Ulbricht at certain stages received
active Soviet support.

[7] The factual basis of my treatment of this conspiracy is J. F. Brown's
careful account in *Bulgaria under Communist Rule*, pp. 173–189.

[8] However, in Yugoslavia (1948) and in Albania (1960), Moscow tried
to turn the local military forces against the ruler. There was also an abortive
attempt by Novotny in December 1967 to use the Czechoslovak army
against his opponents. In China, Lin Piao was accused of planning a military
coup against Mao,

nine defendants were tried as "power seekers" and found guilty of crimes against the state. Political repercussions of this plot were still being felt three years later, but finally subsided.

Information about the plot released by the government is tantalizing but inconclusive. Two of the plotters had worked in the sensitive political administration of the army. Higher-ranking Party officials responsible for the work of the political administration were removed from their posts after the plot's discovery, presumably for lack of vigilance. It was rumored in Sofia that Soviet security officials, not the responsible Bulgarians, uncovered the plot. The conspiracy was somehow closely linked with the Vratse district, one of twenty-eight in Bulgaria. Many of the plotters had served in World War II partisan detachments that operated in the Vratse area; subsequently, two high-ranking conspirators worked together in the district's Party apparatus. After the plot's discovery, the district was subjected to a far-reaching purge.

The conspiracy was widespread and involved some of the most sensitive control points in the regime. It evidently aimed at removing Zhivkov from power, yet the men arrested were not themselves capable of governing. Who was to rule and what sympathy they had in the highest Party organs are not known. While the plotters may have sought greater independence from the Soviet Union, the authorities' charges of Maoist tendencies were not substantiated. (One plotter had formerly headed the Asian department of the foreign ministry and had served as ambassador to North Korea.) Presumably, the plotters believed that if they succeeded, the Soviet authorities would accept the result; initially, at least, the conspirators probably would not openly have opposed Soviet influence in their country. Although the plot proved abortive, it is striking that so many experienced officials were prepared to engage in it. Their resort to conspiracy is a reminder that opposition elements within Communist parties of the Soviet bloc may have no other means of changing rulers. Such an undertaking requires a strong will and much courage. It is doubly hazardous, for it may not only be discovered and forestalled, but, even if it succeeds, it may be disavowed and its results overturned by Moscow.

A Soviet Plot That Worked: The Khrushchev Succession

Khrushchev, who had plotted to oust various leaders in Eastern Europe with whom he was dissatisfied, was himself the victim of an indigenous plot in October 1964, which brought a new instability to Soviet politics.[9] The plot's organizer and chief beneficiary was the heir presumptive and second secretary, Leonid Brezhnev. Complete surprise was achieved because the two key officials charged with protecting the victim's person and power—the head of the State Security Committee (KGB), Vladimir Semichastny; and the Party secretary responsible for supervising the state security organs, Aleksandr Shelepin—participated in the conspiracy. (They were amply rewarded in the following weeks.) Brezhnev himself immediately succeeded to Khrushchev's post of first secretary, but in accordance with the resurrected doctrine of collective leadership, he was denied Khrushchev's former post of head of the government.

In his efforts to aggrandize power and establish personal rule, Brezhnev followed the classic political strategy of candidates for the succession in Communist states, which involves using the post of senior secretary to gain primacy in the secretariat of the central committee, using the secretariat to win control over the Party apparatus throughout the country, and using the Party apparatus to establish dominance over the other institutions of the regime. The strategy also required Brezhnev to bring supporters into the central committee (CC) and to purge opponents from that body, and then to employ his increased influence in the central committee to change the composition of the politburo—that is, to add partisans and (what is more difficult) remove opponents. While

[9] The Khrushchev succession is treated at length in this author's *Political Succession in the USSR* (rev. ed.; New York: Columbia University Press, 1968) and in a subsequent article, "Brezhnev and the Succession Issue," *Problems of Communism*, July–August, 1971.

his basic strategy followed this pattern, Brezhnev had to adapt the tactics, style, and timing to his special circumstances. In applying a time-worn strategy whose required maneuvers were familiar to his opponents, Brezhnev found it necessary to move slowly and cautiously. Beginning in the spring of 1965, his rise proceeded by a long series of small steps forward, with relatively few setbacks.

Unlike Stalin and Khrushchev, each of whom enjoyed the initial advantage of being the only politburo member in the secretariat, Brezhnev at the outset had to deal with four powerful secretaries who were also in the politburo: Mikhail Suslov, Andrei Kirilenko, Nikolai Podgorny, and Aleksandr Shelepin. In the first weeks after Khrushchev's downfall, several of them evidently combined forces, particularly at the December 1964 central committee plenum, to prevent Brezhnev from exercising paramount power as first secretary. By the end of 1965, however, Brezhnev had isolated and removed Podgorny from the secretariat; subsequently, in the wake of the Middle East crisis of mid-1967, he managed to expel Shelepin from the secretariat and to oust Shelepin's partisans from leading positions. Kirilenko and Suslov remained in the secretariat as potential opponents, but the first was a temporary ally and the aging Suslov had limited ambitions.

Thus, with the passage of time, Brezhnev succeeded in eliminating his most dangerous colleagues from the secretariat and neutralizing or gaining the support of the rest. Since the secretariat was already powerful and authoritative when Khrushchev was forced from power, Brezhnev did not have to fight some of the early battles that Khrushchev had waged to make it so. The presence of several politburo members in the secretariat gave this body, from the beginning, a prominence and authority second only to those of the politburo itself.[10] The council of ministers,

---

[10] Brezhnev subsequently spoke of these top Party bodies in terms that elevated the prestige and authority of the secretariat in relation to the politburo. For example, in his 1971 report to the Twenty-fourth Party Congress (delivered in the name of the central committee), he no longer

while more authoritative than before, probably was not a serious competitor.

Much criticism of the "cult of personality" and frequent injunctions to observe "collective leadership" accompanied Khrushchev's removal; consequently, Brezhnev generally advanced his own cult by modest increments. One of his few bold moves was to have the title general secretary (instead of first secretary) of the central committee conferred on himself in 1966. This title was the one under which Stalin had exercised authority during the period of his limited personal rule, from 1928 to 1937.

Initially, Brezhnev also faced difficulties in advancing his own men to key positions. Stalin and Khrushchev had both profited from the personnel practices of the oligarchies they were subverting. The post-Lenin oligarchy had undertaken to expand the Party organization, while the post-Stalin oligarchy had decided to replace the most loyal partisans of Stalin and of Beria. In each instance, the Party secretary made good use of the numerous posts to be filled. But the watchword of the post-Khrushchev oligarchy was "confidence in cadres." Khrushchev's method of rotating leaders and shaking up middle-level personnel in order to breed a sense of insecurity and of dependence on his good opinion had led to widespread dissatisfaction.[11]

To restore morale and win support, the post-Khrushchev oli-

---

spoke of the politiburo as "the supreme political body of our Party," as he had done at the previous Party congress in 1966. His 1971 report referred only once to the politburo, and in that instance, it imparted the information that the politburo and the secretariat hold regular meetings (*zasedaniia*) once a week. In coupling the politburo with the secretariat, Brezhnev tended to diminish the politburo's importance as the organ of collective leadership.

[11] Brezhnev alluded to this discontent in his report to the Twenty-third Party Congress (1966): "The frequent reorganizations of Party, government and economic bodies that have taken place in recent years [i.e., under Khrushchev] have had an adverse effect on the . . . selection, promotion and training of cadres. As a rule, these changes were accompanied by an unjustified shifting and changing of officials, and this resulted in a lack of confidence among them, prevented them from making full use of their abilities, and gave grounds for irresponsibility" (*Pravda,* March 30, 1966).

garchy found it expedient to express confidence in the middle ranks of the Party and to give assurances that officials would not be replaced without good cause. (Indeed, the turnover of cadres was reduced to a point at which the bureaucracy began to be less responsive to the leadership.) Hence, Brezhnev had to move slowly in performing the crucial function of making appointments to policy-making bodies in the provinces and at the center. Not until the December 1969 central committee plenum was he able to renew demands for discipline and good performance on the part of officials and to step up the replacement of unsatisfactory ones. The latter process culminated at the Twenty-fourth Party Congress in April 1971, when 47 members of the previous central committee were replaced by newcomers. Those individuals who were returned to the central committee also suffered a dilution of their power, because of the designation of 46 additional members. Thus, of the 241 members in the central committee chosen at the congress, 93 were newly elected—approximately 4 new members for every 7 old ones. The opportunity existed for Brezhnev to expand his influence in the central committee considerably, and there is indirect evidence that he did so.

When the central committee met to elect its executive organs, including a new politburo, all the incumbents won re-election, but their ranks were expanded by the promotion of three candidate (i.e., nonvoting) members (Vladimir Grishin, Dinmukhamed Kunaev, and Vladimir Shcherbitsky) and a Party secretary not hitherto a candidate member (Fedor Kulakov) to full membership. At least three of the new members were Brezhnev's partisans, and probably the fourth (Grishin) as well. Thus the politburo, which throughout its history normally had had between nine and twelve members, acquired fifteen, making it easier for Brezhnev to manipulate.

Brezhnev took another important step toward personal rule in April 1973 at a meeting of the central committee, when two figures who had crossed him, Petr Shelest and Gennady Voronov, were dropped from the politburo. Both men were vulnerable to such action, having previously lost the offices that usually confer membership in the politburo: Shelest had been first secretary in the Ukrainian Republic until May 1972; Voronov had headed the government in the Russian Republic until July 1971. What previously had saved their places in the politburo was the implicit principle of collective leadership that politburo members retain membership in that body so long as they do not employ proscribed methods in the leadership struggle. The abandonment or disregard of this rule, which imparts stability to an oligarchical body and which had been observed for nine years after Khrushchev's ouster, was a victory for Brezhnev. Moreover, in making new appointments to the politburo, Brezhnev was able to pass over the economic bureaucracy, whose influence had declined after 1968.

Brezhnev did not have things all his own way, however. The three new members of the politburo, though allied with Brezhnev, were not members of the Party apparatus. Two were experienced specialists who headed politically sensitive institutions: Yuri Andropov was chairman of the State Security Committee (KGB), and Andrei Grechko headed the defense ministry. The third, Andrei Gromyko, head of the foreign ministry, commanded specialists only, not military force like the other two. The three institutions thus acquired spokesmen at the highest level. It was not apparent whether, in the long term, their enhanced status would make these men better agents of political control over the bureaucracies they headed or whether, on the contrary, it would induce them to act as these bureaucracies' representatives in opposing the Party apparatus and in checking the growth of Brezhnev's personal power.

The immediate effect of placing the bureaucracies' representatives in the politiburo and of further enlarging its size (to sixteen members and eight candidates) was probably to reduce the effectiveness of the politburo as a collective decision-making body and, consequently, to enhance Brezhnev's personal authority within it. If a majority vote prevailed in the politburo (as Brezhnev, like his predecessors, asserted), the votes of Gromyko and Grechko, who were unaccustomed to dealing with many of the matters discussed there, may have been readily influenced by Brezhnev and his partisans. Brezhnev probably was strong enough to keep the politburo from acting contrary to his wishes in most instances. However, as long as his opponents remained in the politburo, they could prevent the adoption of major measures he favored, deprive his existing programs of the resources needed for success, and even on occasion make policy decisions of which he disapproved. Furthermore, by capitalizing on crises that arose, they might attack him at vulnerable points, thereby endangering his primacy in the leadership.

Since a major crisis would probably upset the political balance, Brezhnev doubtless was tempted to try to increase the leadership's stability by removing more of his opponents from the politburo. The ouster of Shelest and Voronov from the politburo in the spring of 1973 set a useful precedent, but it did not clear the way for Brezhnev simply to purge the politburo. An attempt to deprive the army and the political police of their recently acquired spokesmen in the politburo, for example, might prove difficult to accomplish, and the Party apparatus might hesitate to support it.[12] Brezhnev's best tactic for ridding himself of politburo members on whom he could not rely was probably to justify their expulsion by the need to reduce the size of the bloated politburo. Such a maneuver would require careful preparation and sophisticated execution, however, and would entail a significant risk that Brezhnev's endangered opponents might combine against him.

The course of the Khrushchev succession to date, particularly the progress Brezhnev has made in arrogating power, corresponds to developments in the Lenin and the Stalin successions, although the pace of events has been markedly slowed: Brezhnev, after ten years, is approximately where Khrushchev was after

---

12 It should be recalled that Khrushchev did not move to oust Marshal Khukov from the Party presidium until October 1957, three months after Khrushchev had purged his chief rivals from that body.

four. If allowance is made for this significant difference in time, the correspondence is reasonably close. This parallel raises a question about the current argument that, in the changed circumstances in which the Soviet leadership now operates, it may no longer be possible for one man to concentrate authority in his own hands. According to this argument, the evolution of Soviet society, since it is no longer the relatively inert mass it was in the years immediately after the October revolution and again after the trauma of Stalin's imposition of several revolutions from above, facilitates rule by a stable oligarchy or collective leadership. In short, the increasing differentiation in Soviet society— with middle strata made up of the technical intelligentsia, the bureaucracy, the managers, and the creative intellectuals—will effectively counter the tendency for power to concentrate in the hands of a single leader.

This factor does make unlikely the emergence of a new autocrat like Stalin, before whom each individual, group, and stratum of society stood powerless as before the elements. Whether this increased differentiation in Soviet society will act to preserve the present collective leadership, however, remains a question. Certainly, to date it has not enabled broad social strata or even organized groups to participate openly in higher politics. In this connection, the outside observer is struck by the efficiency with which the Khrushchev succession crisis has been insulated from public scrutiny and concern. Unlike other, more open political processes in the Soviet Union, this most important struggle for power has been virtually closed to observation by anyone outside the inner circle; and its reverberations have been even less manifest than those of the Stalin succession. Soviet society is no longer inert, but its impact on the Khrushchev succession hardly sustains the view that the structure of Soviet politics must inevitably accommodate to it.

No doubt Brezhnev, in arrogating to himself such a high degree of personal power, found it necessary to appeal to particular institutions and to broad social groups. The shift in economic priorities to satisfy consumer demand reflects in part this imperative. Nevertheless, it would be a mistake to suppose that the USSR has become pluralist, that society has escaped from the regime's ultimate control. The Party apparatus, in particular, has repeatedly proved its capacity to exercise authority over other institutions and groups, and over Soviet society as a whole, and has done so again during the Khrushchev succession. Major functional groups and the institutions in which they are represented did succeed in winning significant concessions from the Party, including a measure of independence. This was particularly true of the economic bureaucracy in the first years after Khrushchev's removal. In the end, however, the economic bureaucracy failed to forge the kind of political alliance with other key institutions that alone could deprive the Party apparatus of decisive control.

The *apparat*'s staying power is impressive, at least in the states within the Soviet sphere. The only force inside the Soviet bloc that succeeded in subordinating the *apparat* was the secret police under the command of Stalin; this threat the *apparat* no longer has reason to fear. No doubt institutions and interest groups in future successions will challenge the *apparat*'s sovereignty; their prospects, based on the historical record, are uncertain at best.

On learning that Khrushchev had been ousted by a plot of his lieutenants, the rulers in Eastern Europe were understandably concerned about its bearing on their own positions. Several of them—particularly Gomulka, Kadar, and Zhivkov, and later Novotny as well—had established close personal ties with Khrushchev. Once they were reassured that their own positions would not be affected and that the new leaders in Moscow did not plan to alter Soviet policy radically, it was not difficult for them to accept the change.[13]

[13] General works used in treating succession in the post-Khrushchev period include the following: Brown, *The New Eastern Europe;* H. Gordon Skilling, *Governments of Communist East Europe* (New York: Crowell, 1966); Richard F. Staar, *The Communist Regimes in Eastern Europe* (rev. ed.; Stanford, Calif.: Hoover Institution, 1971); and Richard F.

The Khrushchev succession did not produce political instability in the Communist countries of Eastern Europe. They were not so closely tied to Moscow as when Stalin died, and were therefore less immediately affected by Soviet developments. Moscow, for its part, was less inclined than in 1953 to initiate changes in the domestic policy and leadership of the Communist states. Consequently, the Khrushchev succession did not lead to a series of succession crises in Eastern Europe, as happened after Stalin died. This time when succession occurred, it was a result of indigenous developments which Moscow could not readily control. Because of its reduced influence in the ordinary politics of these states, it was crucial for Moscow to control the incidence and outcome of successions in Eastern Europe. But this was not easy, particularly at a time when the Soviet leadership was trying to cope with its own succession. In the early post-Khrushchev successions in Eastern Europe, in Romania (1965) and Czechoslovakia (1967–1968), Moscow was inclined to stand aside, perhaps because of its awareness of the unfortunate consequences of excessive intervention in 1956. The initial Soviet restraint in Czechoslovakia had consequences that were unacceptable to Moscow, and they finally were opposed by force. This episode may have induced in the Soviet leaders a greater willingness to participate more actively in the process whereby Communist states in Eastern Europe change their rulers. During Gierek's succession to Gomulka (December 1970), Moscow was careful to monitor the transfer of power very closely, and during Honecker's succession to Ulbricht, it played a highly active part.

Staar, ed., *Yearbook on International Communist Affairs* (Stanford, Calif.: Hoover Institution, 1968–1973).

6

Romania's Arranged
Succession (1965)

Death took Gheorghiu-Dej in March 1965, thus bringing on
the succession in Romania that Khrushchev's 1963 plot against
him had failed to accomplish.[1] Moscow had a new opportunity to
try to modify Romania's policies, while Romania faced a new
danger. Actually, as it turned out, the dispute with the USSR
probably facilitated a solution to Romania's crisis of succession.
It helped to solidify the leadership after Gheorghiu-Dej died, just
as earlier it had motivated Gheorghiu-Dej to take far-reaching
measures to assure an orderly succession. He was able to take
such measures because at the time of his death his power was
unchallenged. This was also why he had been able to move toward a position of independence from Moscow, first cautiously,
then with breathtaking boldness. If Gheorghiu-Dej had not made
his position impervious to challenge in the early post-Stalin years,
he could neither have opposed Moscow nor persisted in the bold
steps he took to assure an orderly succession by grooming an
heir, Nicolae Ceausescu.

Ceausescu's relationship to Gheorghiu-Dej was not a simple

[1] This chapter, in addition to primary sources, draws upon the following
secondary sources: Fischer-Galati, *The New Rumania*, especially chap. iii;
Ionescu, *Communism in Rumania;* Kenneth Jowitt, *Revolutionary Break-*
throughs and National Development (Berkeley, Calif.: University of California Press, 1971); and Paul Lendvai, *Eagles in Cobwebs* (Garden City,
N.Y.: Doubleday, Anchor Books, 1969).

121

one, according to Ceausescu's subsequent account. After coming to power, he rehabilitated several of Gheorghiu-Dej's victims and denied his own involvement in the injustices that had been done them. Yet Ceausescu obviously benefited from his early association with Gheorghiu-Dej while in prison during World War II, and from his patronage in the early years of the Communist regime. Ceausescu performed important functions for the Party *apparat,* particularly in carrying out sensitive tasks in the re-cruitment of new Party members and in the Party's indoctrina-tion and supervision of the armed forces. Certainly he benefited from the purge of Gheorghiu-Dej's enemies from office, even if we credit his claim that he opposed their subsequent disgrace and punishment. In 1952, when Ana Pauker, Vasile Luca, and Teohari Georgescu were ousted from power, Ceausescu became a full member of the central committee and entered the Party's organizational bureau. When Gheorghiu-Dej downgraded Miron Constantinescu and Iosif Chisinevschi in 1956, Ceausescu, at age thirty-seven, became a full member of the Politburo; when, the following year, Gheorghiu-Dej removed the two men from the leadership, Ceausescu became the second-rank secretary after Gheorghiu-Dej himself.

Ceausescu's rise was not without interruption, for Gheorghiu-Dej was careful to circumscribe his power with that of powerful rivals. Ceausescu's chief rival was Alexandru Draghici, a top official in the state security forces.[2] Ceausescu subsequently em-

---

[2] At particular junctures, Gheorghiu-Dej balanced the power of the two rivals so carefully that from moment to moment the advantage shifted from one to the other in rank-order listings of the top leaders: "Throughout 1955 their relative positions in the hierarchy shifted. In April and May Ceausescu preceded Draghici; in June the two alternated in terms of precedence; and through the late summer Ceausescu was conspicuous by his absence and Draghici was promoted in the ranks of the security forces (*Scinteia,* August 25, 1955). Immediately prior to the Congress [of Ro-mania's Communist Party, in December 1955], Ceausescu appeared again before Draghici, but at the Congress itself Draghici was listed above Ceausescu, in the announcement of the Politburo's membership (*Scinteia,* December 29, 1955)" (Jowitt, p. 151n).

phasized Draghici's closeness to Gheorghiu-Dej: the security official believed "he could do anything because of his connections with Gheorghiu-Dej." When the politburo decided, in April 1956, to remove Draghici as head of the ministry of interior, the measure, according to Ceausescu, could not be carried out because of opposition from Gheorghiu-Dej and from Draghici himself.[3] No doubt Draghici was close to Gheorghiu-Dej, but Ceausescu was much closer, and his succession was taken for granted by knowledgeable Romanians.[4] In the rivalry between the two men for the favor of their common patron, Ceausescu had a crucial advantage: he was the presumptive heir, while Draghici was assigned the secondary role of counterheir: i.e., he was granted important powers in order to prevent the heir from seizing the supreme office prematurely. The head of state security has considerable power of a specialized kind, of course, but the fear inspired by its exercise makes him vulnerable to attack once his patron is gone. Ceausescu, on the other hand, was the second secretary charged with the assignment of cadres, an office and a task which repeatedly have proved decisive in a Communist leader's rise to power. In exercising this responsibility for almost a decade before his patron died, Ceausescu succeeded in building up a personal political machine that served him well at the critical moment. Nevertheless, while Gheorghiu-Dej favored Ceausescu in his contest with Draghici, he did not allow their rivalry to reach a decisive outcome. It continued into the period of succession, making it necessary for Ceausescu to find the means of removing Draghici from his key post in state security. Ceausescu's problem was complicated by the fact that he had still to deal with a number of senior figures, including Gheorghiu-Dej's contemporaries and close associates Gheorghe Apostol and Chivu Stoica.

When Gheorghiu-Dej died at the age of sixty-three on March 19, 1965, Ceausescu, probably by previous arrangement, im-

[3] *Scinteia*, April 28, 1968; quoted by Jowitt, p. 192.
[4] Fischer-Galati, *The New Rumania*, p. 112.

mediately replaced him as head of the secretariat. At first, however, he did not receive Gheorghiu-Dej's post as head of the
state council, presumably owing to the efforts of powerful opponents in the leadership to deny him Gheorghiu-Dej's full
powers. Instead, a nominal triumvirate seemed to take shape,
consisting of the heads of the Party, state, and government
(Ceausescu, Apostol, and the jurist Ion Maurer). Nevertheless,
taking advantage of the substantial powers Gheorghiu-Dej had
conferred upon him, Ceausescu moved quickly to make himself
master of the secretariat, and on this basis to consolidate his
position in the Party.

A Party congress was quickly scheduled for July 1965, and
other measures were taken to mark the ending of the old era
and the beginning of a new one. The Workers Party, as it had
been known, became the Romanian Communist Party, and the
state was raised in rank to become the Romanian Socialist, instead of People's, Republic. When the congress met, no portrait
of Gheorghiu-Dej was in evidence, and after a silent tribute was
paid him, no Romanian speaker again mentioned his name.[5] This
downgrading of the cult of Gheorghiu-Dej doubtless was to
Ceausescu's advantage. It at once removed an obstruction to his
own image and deprived his senior rivals of the opportunity to
stress their long association with the dead dictator. The spot-
light was now on Ceausescu, and he used the occasion to emphasize his pre-eminence. "He alone appeared at the rostrum and
received a standing ovation from the nearly four thousand delegates and guests, while the other Politburo members remained
for a few minutes in the background." [6] The congress gave
Ceausescu the more ambitious title of general secretary (instead
of first secretary) of the central committee, which had not been
used in Eastern Europe in the post-Stalin period. (Leonid
Brezhnev aped this move a year later, in the USSR, in his campaign to succeed Khrushchev.)

[5] Lendvai, p. 391. In the following discussion I have availed myself of
Lendvai's perceptive account.
[6] *Ibid.,* p. 393.

The congress also introduced major organizational changes which gave Ceausescu an opportunity to make important political gains. The politburo was replaced by two bodies, a presidium of seven members, from which two veteran leaders, Petre Borila and Alexandru Moghioros, were denied membership; [7] and an executive committee of twenty-five members and alternates, to which Ceausescu was able to add several close supporters. The central committee was increased in size by over half (from 79 to 121), providing Ceausescu with an opportunity to promote many of his middle-level supporters. In the following months, Ceausescu extended his influence over the government, the army, and the central Party apparatus by promoting into them men whom he had earlier placed in regional Party positions. At the same time, he consolidated his control over the provincial Party apparatus by replacing 85 of 150 district Party secretaries. A cult of Ceausescu began to emerge, as he became virtually the regime's sole spokesman on major questions of policy, and was increasingly praised by junior colleagues for his personal initiative and his constant leadership in the work in which they were engaged.

A new step in Ceausescu's advance toward power. was taken at the national Party conference in December 1967. Reversing his previous call for the separation of government and Party posts, Ceausescu now proposed their fusion, thereby necessitating a new reorganization of both institutions. In the resulting shakeup, general secretary Ceausescu acquired the office of president of the state council. Stoica, who lost this post to Ceausescu, was required to introduce the proposal that Ceausescu hold the top Party and state posts jointly: "The carrying out by the same person of the function of Secretary-General of the Party Central Committee and of President of the State Council will ensure the implementation of the unitary leadership by the Party Central Committee of all social and state activity." [8] This

---

[7] A year later, at the June 1966 meeting of the central committee, two new members were added to the presidium, Ilie Verdet and Paul Niculescu-Mizil, both key supporters of Ceausescu.

[8] Trans. in *Yearbook on International Communist Affairs, 1968*, p. 509.

formulation, by suggesting that Ceausescu's occupancy of the regime's two leading posts would enable *the central committee to rule the country*, went far toward acknowledging his *de facto* personal rule.

Ceausescu took the decisive step in his struggle for the succession in April 1968. Gheorghiu-Dej had refused to implement seriously Khrushchev's de-Stalinization policies because they had unfavorable implications for his own power; instead like Novotny in Czechoslovakia, he simply accused his purged rivals (Pauker, Luca, and Georgescu) of responsibility for Stalinism in Romania.[9] Now, with Gheorghiu-Dej dead and Khrushchev no longer in power, Ceausescu finally enacted in Romania a program of de-Stalinization, including posthumous rehabilitations and charges of political repression directed at the previous ruler. Moreover, by implicating his rivals in the Stalinist practices of the past, Ceausescu's de-Stalinization policy furthered his campaign to succeed Gheorghiu-Dej, just as Khrushchev's de-Stalinization program had served his efforts to succeed Stalin.[10] The Romanian central committee, at Ceausescu's bidding, posthumously rehabilitated several top leaders whom Gheorghiu-Dej had executed, including Stefan Foris (1946) and Lucretiu Patrascanu (1954), and rehabilitated many others whom he had only disgraced. Ceausescu's opponents were accused of complicity in these unjust actions. The accusations against Draghici were particularly serious, and he was purged from the leadership, but Stoica, Apostol, and Bodnaras were disgraced also, rendering them impotent to oppose Ceausescu.

The death of Gheorghiu-Dej probably encouraged the Soviet leaders to hope that a new start might be made in relations with Romania now that the feuding leaders of both countries were out of the way. If the new Romanian leadership would not change its

[9] Novotny had blamed Rudolf Slansky and his fellow conspirators for Stalinism in Czechoslovakia.

[10] Needless to say, de-Stalinization meant more to both men than simply a means of waging the struggle for power.

policies willingly, perhaps it would be sufficiently weakened for the USSR to acquire means of influencing its composition and deliberations. Although the struggle for the succession to Gheorghiu-Dej did weaken the Romanian leadership for a time, this did not lead to an alteration of the country's policies toward the USSR or to an incapacity to carry them out.[11] Fear of the USSR no doubt limited the severity of the struggle for succession and thus helped to stabilize the leadership, but it did not freeze the country's political processes. If it had, or if the candidates for the succession had been more evenly matched, there might have been an extended period of stalemate that would have made it difficult to respond to Soviet pressures and initiatives. As it was, the struggle went forward, but without causing serious disruption, and Ceausescu showed himself far superior to his rivals. His shrewdness and skill, reinforced by the advantages that Gheorghiu-Dej had conferred upon him, enabled Ceausescu to wage his campaign for power with hardly a serious misstep or a major setback. As a result, three years after the death of Gheorghiu-Dej the crisis of his succession was resolved and the USSR had lost its opportunity to change Romania's course. Once Ceausescu had established his personal rule, the cost of Soviet intervention rose sharply and could not reasonably be incurred unless Romania's policies directly threatened vital Soviet interests.

The relatively orderly transfer of power to Ceausescu not only averted great dangers, but it also brought positive benefits. It conferred power upon a new generation of leaders who were less encumbered by the deep fears and limited methods of Stalinism.[12] It was a generation that was better educated than

[11] Presumably none of the protagonists sought Soviet assistance during the succession struggle, although Ceausescu sharply warned at one point that no member was allowed "to maintain contacts with other parties without the knowledge of the leadership" (Lendvai, p. 397).

[12] Jowitt goes so far as to speculate that only "Gheorghiu-Dej's 'timely' death in 1965 prevented the appearance of a critical intra-elite conflict over the 'political meaning' of the Romanian independent course," although he

its predecessors and had more confidence in the technicians upon whom it relied, and therefore allowed them to exert greater influence in the making of policy. In some measure, perhaps, the new leadership had more confidence in the people as a whole. The new leaders were no less nationalistic than the old, but they appeared less disposed to force Romanian culture on the country's ethnic minorities. While Gheorghiu-Dej had had no difficulty in tapping the old reserves of popular anti-Russian feeling, Ceausescu and his associates probably were better able to commit the generation that had grown up under Communism to new and more basic departures from the Stalinist notion of what socialism entailed.

Gheorghiu-Dej's success in arranging the succession before his death was a remarkable achievement, unmatched as yet by any other Communist leader. Since the succession was not engineered by an outside agency (as, for example, the succession to Georgi Dimitrov was), it is evident that the Communist system does permit the ruler to impose order upon the succession, at least when circumstances are favorable. Gheorghiu-Dej's fatal illness (skin cancer, apparently) [13] may at once have forewarned him of the need to prepare a successor and obviated his fears that an heir presumptive might deprive him of power prematurely. At the same time, Gheorghiu-Dej showed acute judgment of political character and ability in his choice of Ceausescu, who possessed the tactical skill to overcome his colleagues' opposition and make himself personal ruler, and who possessed the statesmanship to carry forward Gheorghiu-Dej's program of independence from Soviet control. The two men share credit for the smooth transfer of power, which deprived Moscow of an opportunity to intervene in order to reverse Romania's policy of independence.

---

provides little evidence for this view (p. 213n). Not too much should be made of Ceausescu's subsequent criticism of Gheorghiu-Dej; Communist rulers, on coming to power, have made a practice of criticizing their predecessors.

[13] A skin cancer specialist from the West, while traveling to Romania, reportedly revealed this diagnosis to a journalist.

Gheorghiu-Dej did not succeed, however, in forestalling strong criticism of his own rule. Perhaps, in arranging the succession, a prudent ruler will anticipate that he will be criticized. If his aim is the good of the regime rather than the protection of his own reputation, he may even find it expedient to counsel the heir presumptive to be ready to engage in such criticism when the time comes.

7

Czechoslovakia's Mismanaged
Succession (1967–1969)

After a decade of personal rule, Antonin Novotny was ousted by the central committee of the Czechoslovak Communist Party on January 5, 1968.[1] This event is unique in the history of the Communist movement: Novotny's ouster was not the result of a conspiracy (as Khrushchev's was), but was the outcome of an intensive campaign in the top circles of the leadership that began in the fall of 1967 and culminated in the first days of January 1968. Moreover, while it was not waged openly in the mass media (the public knew little of what was going on), it was waged openly in the restricted arena of Communist politics, which engages hundreds of participants. Novotny knew the depth of the opposition and its identity, but he could no longer employ re-

[1] This account has used the following main sources: Zdenek Elias and Jaromir Netik, "Czechoslovakia," in Griffith, ed., *Communism in Europe,* Vol. II; Paul Ello, ed., *Czechoslovakia's Blueprint for "Freedom"* (Washington, D.C.: Acropolis Books, 1968); Galia Golan, *The Czechoslovak Reform Movement* (Cambridge, Eng.: Cambridge University Press, 1971); Galia Golan, *Reform Rule in Czechoslovakia* (Cambridge, Eng.: Cambridge University Press, 1973); Barbara Jancar, *Czechoslovakia and the Absolute Monopoly of Power* (New York: Praeger, 1971); Richard Lowenthal, "The Sparrow in the Cage," *Problems of Communism,* November–December, 1968; Vojtech Mencl and Frantisek Ourednik, "What Happened in January," *Zivot strany* (Prague), Nos. 16–19, trans. in Remington, ed., *Winter in Prague,* pp. 18–39; Jiri Pelikan, ed., *Le Congrès clandestin* (Paris: Editions du Seuil, 1969); Jiri Pelikan, ed., *The Czechoslovak Political Trials,*

pression to defeat it. Like Rakosi in 1956, he had to defend himself with limited means, and these proved inadequate. But while Rakosi was removed by his own supporters (including the Soviet leaders) when they became convinced he was a liability, Novotny was defeated by his opponents, who were helped by the defections of close associates (for example, Jiri Hendrych). The opposition was motivated more by policy concerns than by a thirst for naked power. The movement to oust Novotny, then, resembled a conspiracy far less than it did secret parliamentary maneuvering to remove a party leader. That this quasi-parliamentary removal of the leader happened in Czechoslovakia—which alone among the Communist states of Eastern Europe had experienced parliamentary democracy as late as 1948—and in a Communist Party whose leaders had themselves engaged in the parliamentary game doubtless was no accident. Nevertheless, Novotny's defeat after a long period of rule was not owing to the rising strength of his enemies but to the perceptible decline of his own.

Novotny's troubles in the mid-sixties were a direct consequence of both his failures and his successes in the previous decade. One of his great achievements, as noted earlier, had been to shield politics in Czechoslovakia from the unsettling effect of Khrush-

1950–1954; Michael Platzer, "1968 Czechoslovak Reforms," M.A. thesis, Cornell, 1972; Jan Provaznik (pseudonym), "The Politics of Retrenchment," *Problems of Communism,* July–October 1969; Radio Free Europe, *Czechoslovak Press Survey;* Robin Remington, ed., *Winter in Prague;* Harry Schwartz, *Prague's 200 Days* (New York: Praeger, 1969); William Shawcross, *Dubcek* (New York: Simon and Schuster, 1970); H. Gordon Skilling, "The Fall of Novotny in Czechoslovakia," *Canadian Slavonic Papers,* Fall 1970; Tad Szulc, *Czechoslovakia since World War II* (New York: Viking, 1971); Michel Tatu, *L'Hérésie impossible* (Paris: Grasset, 1968); Pavel Tigrid, "Czechoslovakia: A Post-Mortem," *Survey,* Autumn and Winter 1969, also published as *Why Dubcek Fell* (London: Macdonald, 1969); Deryck Viney, "Alexander Dubcek," in Rodger Swearingen, ed., *Leaders of the Communist World* (New York: Free Press, 1971); Philip Windsor and Adam Roberts, *Czechoslovakia, 1968* (London: Institute for Strategic Studies Paperback, 1969); and A. A. Zeman, *Prague Spring* (Middlesex, Eng.: Penguin, 1969).

chev's de-Stalinization policies. Intellectual ferment proved less dangerous than in Poland or Hungary, and was successfully treated, at least for a time, as a mild disease that need not be cured but only prevented from spreading, since it would not impair the social organism's vitality. In the end, however, by resisting the pressures to de-Stalinize (particularly by rehabilitation of the victims) and by engaging in continuing repression of volatile political forces, Novotny succeeded only in increasing their explosive power once these forces could no longer be contained. In general, Novotny's success in suppressing problems rather than solving them, in preserving political stability when what was needed was political movement, only deepened Czechoslovakia's crisis once the festering sores broke open.

Ultimately, of course, what deprived Novotny of the fruits of his limited successes was the massive failure of his policies. From the early sixties onward, the economy stagnated and failed to respond to the timid reform measures that were attempted. The problem of an intractable economy, unlike the discontent of intellectuals and nationalists, could neither be ignored nor treated with superficial remedies. When Novotny was tempted to adopt fundamental economic reforms, however, he found that they could not be carried through effectively without fundamental political reforms, and from these, understandably, Novotny drew back.

Novotny's decline began about 1961. His power had been at its zenith from the fall of 1957, when after President Antonin Zapotocky's death he added the office of head of state to that of Party head, to 1960, when Czechoslovakia became the second state (after the USSR) to declare itself a *socialist* republic. The descent from this plateau in the next half-dozen years was neither sustained nor precipitous, but was marked by several crises. Novotny surmounted each of them, but at the cost of a weakened position. Three crises in particular reveal the narrowing limits of Novotny's power.

The first was the Barak affair in 1961 (discussed in Chapter 5, above). While Novotny succeeded in overcoming the challenge and in having Rudolf Barak imprisoned, he was rebuffed in the effort to have Barak condemned for political treason.

The second crisis came in 1963, a bad year for Novotny. He remained under pressure from Moscow to investigate and rectify past acts of repression, and finally had to acknowledge that Slansky was innocent of the charges that led to his execution. Novotny accomplished this enforced retreat with his usual dexterity, but was compelled to sacrifice several of his closest supporters, including Karel Bacilek, first secretary of the Slovak central committee, and Bruno Kohler, a key secretary of the central committee. Even so, pressure for de-Stalinization continued, particularly from Slovak intellectuals who publicly linked Viliam Siroky, then head of the Czechoslovak government, with Stalinist political repression in Slovakia a decade earlier. As a result, it became necessary, in September 1963, to throw this new victim to the wolves. That Novotny, by purging these supporters, was able to avert public criticisms of his own responsibility for the political trials of the early fifties is of course evidence that considerable power remained to him; but that he was *compelled* to do so suggests how much his power had eroded.

Striking evidence emerged several years later that Novotny's crucial power of appointment had already been questioned in 1963. When Novotny was compelled to sacrifice Bacilik as first secretary of the Slovak central committee the man who replaced him, Alexander Dubcek, was apparently not trusted by Novotny. According to a speech delivered to the Czechoslovakia central committee in December 1967 by a secretary of the Slovak central committee, Vasil Bilak,

[Novotny's] reservations vis-à-vis the CPSL CC [Central Committee of the Communist Party of Slovakia] aimed chiefly against Comrade Dubcek, have been sensed by many members of the CPSL CC from the time when Comrade Bacilek had to be dismissed from his post as First Secretary of the CPSL CC. . . . From that time [April 1963] it appeared as if all of a sudden Comrade Novotny regarded Slovakia as the weak spot in the Republic. . . . . Many members of the CPSL cannot understand why Comrade Novotny, who attended the Plenum of the CPSL at which Comrade Bacilek was removed from his post of First Secretary and Comrade Dubcek nominated to replace him, went to such great lengths to exculpate and even justify Comrade Bacilek and left the meeting before Comrade Dubcek was elected. The fact that Comrade Dubcek had been elected First Secretary of the CCSL CC could not be published for several months.[2]

Bilak strongly hints that Novotny opposed Dubcek's appointment as Party first secretary in Slovakia: Novotny had "reservations" about Dubcek, left the central committee meeting before Dubcek was elected, and subsequently regarded Slovakia as a "weak spot." That Novotny had unsuccessfully protested Dubcek's nomination for the post and then demonstratively left the meeting was asserted explicitly by Lubos Kohout, a dissident writer and public figure.[3] If this account of Dubcek's replacement of Bacilek is true, then as early as 1963, Novotny's position had been seriously weakened and he was vulnerable to further attack.

If Novotny objected to Dubcek's appointment, one wonders how it happened that his views did not prevail. The most likely explanation is that Moscow (perhaps in the person of Khrushchev) took a hand in the matter. Shortly after Dubcek replaced Bacilek as Slovak first secretary, Jozef Lenart replaced Siroky as head of the Czechoslovak government, and it is noteworthy that both men had attended Soviet Party schools in Moscow, Lenart from 1953 to 1955 and Dubcek from 1955 to 1958. Possibly the two *apparachiks*, then at a mid-point in their careers, sufficiently impressed the Kremlin with their ability and trustworthiness that Moscow sponsored them at important junctures in their later careers. It would be ironic if Dubcek was forced

[2] Quoted by Vojtech Mencl and Frantisek Ourednik in "What Happened in January," *Zivot strany*, No. 19, September 11, 1968; trans. in Remington, ed., *Winter in Prague*, p. 34.

[3] *Pravda* (Bratislava), April 14, 1968, as cited by Deryck Viney, "Alexander Dubcek," in Swearingen, p. 282.

on a reluctant Novotny in 1963 by Soviet leaders who had misjudged Dubcek's true character.

Aware of the danger to his position in Slovakia, Novotny maintained close control over the operations of the Slovak Party organization after 1963, particularly its personnel appointments, so that on major questions Dubcek could act only with Prague's consent.[4] Not satisfied with this limitation on Dubcek's authority, Novotny tried to replace him with a trusted supporter, Michal Chudik.[5] The attempt failed; even if it had succeeded, it might not have saved Novotny, though it perhaps would have deprived Dubcek of his crucial role in the Prague Spring. As things turned out, Dubcek was able to use the Slovak Party organization as his chief base of power in the climactic struggle against Novotny in the fall of 1967.

Resistance to Novotny, between 1963 and 1966, though present, was not very effective. Near the end of his term as president (November 1964) he was criticized, perhaps at a central committee plenum, by Jan Piller, a high government official, but evidently no serious attempt was made to deny him re-election. Again, during preparations for the Thirteenth Party Congress (May 1966), a number of concessions were forced from Novotny, but he nevertheless succeeded in controlling the congress sufficiently to pack the central committee and its presidium with conservatives.

The challenge to Novotny's leadership during the third and final crisis, in 1967, took shape in two arenas: in the central committee and in a larger group involving the special interests and patriotic concerns of writers and academicians and of Slovaks—men, for the most part, active in the Party—as well as of students. In the second arena there was a series of small crises from June to December: (1) Speaker after speaker at the writers' congress

---

[4] Mencl and Ourednik, in Remington, p. 19. If, as it appears, his power over top-level appointments was reduced after 1963, Novotny evidently tried to compensate by heightened central control.

[5] Viney, "Alexander Dubcek," in Swearingen, p. 282.

in June rose to criticize the state of the nation and of its literature, and the political leadership which lay heavily on both.
Knowledge of this defiance of political authority and, in particular, of Hendrych, who was present to keep the writers in line,
did not reach the public, for the speeches were not published,
but the challenge was clear, and Novotny reacted sharply. (2)
At a Slovak celebration in August 1967, Novotny offended his
hosts, and when challenged by Vasil Bilak, he departed in anger.
(3) Students engaged in a peaceful protest, in late October,
against poor dormitory conditions were set upon by the police.
Public reaction was strong, and after a month of agitation the
government conceded that the police had been in the wrong.
None of these crises was serious in itself, though each in turn
revealed a further weakening of Novotny's political authority.

Repercussions of these crises were felt in the central committee. Because of the secrecy that is normally obligatory for Communist regimes, the situation in the central committee during
1967 is obscure. But some light penetrated these dark recesses
during the Prague Spring, making it possible to reconstruct developments, at least in broad outline.[6] What happened in the
crucial meetings of the central committee's executive body, its
presidium, is even more obscure. Even the central committee at
first knew little of what went on there, but by autumn, controversy inside the presidium had become so intense that it occasionally spilled over into dramatic confrontations at meetings
of the central committee.

Although the central committee had been chosen under Novotny's strong influence in mid-1966, within a few months it was
causing him difficulty. Criticism of the conduct of Party affairs at

[6] The following discussion relies heavily on the remarkably informative
articles, previously cited, of Mencl and Ourednik in *Zivot strany*, translated
in Remington, *Winter in Prague.* They provide a semiofficial Party history
of Novotny's decline and fall. Another valuable source is Pavel Tigrid's account, based on documents and testimony provided by several Party officials,
"Czechoslovakia: A Post-Mortem," *Survey,* Autumn and Winter 1969; also
published in *Why Dubcek Fell.*

the plenum in February 1967 was so unsettling to Novotny that he afterward told the presidium that "the February Plenum must never be repeated." After this plenum Novotny's chief lieutenant, Jiri Hendrych, and his growing group of followers in the Party leadership "gradually began to disassociate" themselves from Novotny's policy.[7]

Development of the anti-Novotny movement in the central committee was due to the convergence in that body of several groups that were opposed to certain of his policies: Slovak federalists (particularly Dubcek and Bilak), who opposed Novotny's centralism; advocates of economic reform (Ota Sik in particular), who blamed him for not backing it more energetically; de-Stalinizers, who resented his failure to carry forward the rehabilitation of purge victims; and critics of his cultural policies, which had provoked writers into open opposition that in turn led to a demand by Novotny for renewed repression.[8] Finally, there were the provincial *apparachiks*—a group strongly represented in the central committee—whose disaffection with Novotny has received relatively little attention from Western observers, but whose early opposition, according to Mencl and Ourednik, was crucial:

The Presidium of the . . . CC [central committee], which had centralized decision-making on an enormous number of issues, was in fact losing control of the lower organs in the party system by doing so. . . . This sharpened the conflict inside the party organization itself between the regime of personal power in the party and some of the regions. . . . This discord with the center . . . was [the] factor which ignited the chain reaction that finished with the fall of Novotny's leadership.[9]

The two meetings of the central committee that followed the February plenum gave rise to little excitement, although they could hardly have proved satisfactory to Novotny. The May meeting discussed the working of the New Economic Model, a

[7] Mencl and Ourednik, in Remington, p. 23.   [8] *Ibid.*, p. 25.
[9] *Ibid.*

market-type reform measure designed to improve economic efficiency and promote growth, which had finally been inaugurated on January 1, 1967. It was already clear that the Model was not achieving its primary objectives, partly because of Novotny's failure to override resistance in the middle levels of the economic and Party bureaucracies. At the September plenum Novotny demanded repressive measures against the writers who had spoken out at the June congress, but met with some opposition. "The Plenum finally approved the proposals that had been submitted to it, but only after Novotny had declared at the end of the discussion that he had proof that the 'Writers' Congress had been prepared in Paris' "—i.e., that Czechoslovak émigrés in Paris had directly influenced the content of speeches delivered at the writers' congress.[10] Such proof was never provided.

The evolving challenge to Novotny's position finally came into the open when the central committee next met, on October 30, to discuss the role of the Party in the "current stage of socialist development." A number of papers presenting research findings and new proposals had been solicited from Party organizations and scientific institutes, but they were largely disregarded because the majority of the presidium, which Novotny still controlled at this point, found them too "daring." Nevertheless, fundamental criticism of the Party's work was voiced, particularly by Alexander Dubcek, who now, at the eleventh hour, made his appearance as a leader of the opposition to Novotny. The burden of his talk was that the Party should not fear the people and the supposed class enemies among them, and should not "manage society, but lead it." [11] The country was entering "a new stage" in its development. This made it necessary for the Party to change fundamentally its methods of work.

Dubcek now also raised the question of the "accumulation of functions" at the highest level—that is, of Novotny's excessive powers resulting from his position at the head of both the Party and the state. Dubcek was immediately attacked by one of

[10] *Ibid.*, p. 23.   [11] *Ibid.*, pp. 26–27.

Novotny's closest supporters, Martin Vaculik, for raising questions in the central committee that he had not previously raised in the presidium—apparently an effort on Novotny's behalf to maintain discipline in the presidium, to prevent its members from appealing decisions of the presidium to the central committee. Novotny himself launched a personal attack on Dubcek, speaking "extemporaneously, very excitedly and sharply." [12] He made the tactical mistake, however, of accusing Dubcek of having been influenced by "narrow and national interests," thus hinting that he was a Slovak nationalist. This led several speakers, including Bilak, to recall that such charges had unjustly kept men in prison until 1960, as the central committee had acknowledged in 1963 in its self-criticism.

Novotny succeeded a last time in staving off the attack, but now the division in the presidium had been revealed to the central committee, and the personal rivalry of Dubcek and Novotny had emerged to view. In this new situation Novotny evidently decided to invite Leonid Brezhnev to Prague. Novotny's decision to invoke Soviet intervention on his behalf represented a considerable gamble, for it revealed the weakness of his position in the Czechoslovak leadership and also threatened to intensify anti-Soviet feelings directed against himself. Brezhnev, after visiting Prague and being apprised of the situation, wisely decided against giving full support to Novotny. Thus, ironically, the outcome of Novotny's appeal to Moscow was to make it clear that the Czechoslovak leadership was free to oust Novotny if it so desired. [13]

When the central committee next met, on December 19, 1967, after a postponement necessitated by Brezhnev's visit, Novotny clearly was on the defensive. He found it necessary to engage in

[12] According to Tigrid, Novotny's anger was customary "on the infrequent occasions when he was criticized" ("Czechoslovakia," *Survey*, p. 133).

[13] There are some reports that Brezhnev asked that there be a delay before action was taken on the matter.

self-criticism for his unfortunate remarks about the work of the Slovak Party leadership.[14] What was now at issue was Novotny's position as first secretary of the central commitee. After two days of discussion in the plenum, followed by an evening meeting of the presidium, Novotny placed his post "at the disposal of the plenary session." He and his followers apparently believed that immediate debate on the question might enable him to keep the post—a realistic hope, according to Mencl and Ourednik, since "no alternative candidate existed." [15] Novotny's formula thus had advantages: by placing his office merely at the disposal of the central committee, he caused the central committee to contemplate the difficulties of finding a successor without actually having to choose one; if Novotny had simply resigned, the central committee, being compelled to find a replacement, no doubt would have found one.[16] After some discussion, however, the central committee decided to charge the presidium and a consultative body of regional Party officials to present their recommendations to a central committee plenum in the first days of January.

When the central committee met on January 3, 1968, "it was clear that neither the Presidium nor the consultative body had been able to take a definite stand since the end of the December Plenum. . . . Thus the decision remained with the . . . Plenum." Novotny continued the fight, rejecting "in principle the criticism of his work as First Secretary." After some debate in which Novotny was attacked and defended, Josef Smrkovsky gave a crucial speech in which he seemed to warn those who opposed Novotny that they now had gone too far to turn back, that if they failed to remove Novotny, they would be subject to his reprisals.

---

[14] Mencl and Ourednik, in Remington, pp. 30–32.   [15] *Ibid.*, p. 35.

[16] Tigrid quotes Smrkovsky in a speech to the central committee on this point: "To put your office at the Committee's disposal, comrade Novotny, is one thing. To lay it down and say, 'For various good reasons I will not hold it any more and I want the Central Committee to appoint a successor' —that would be quite different" ("Czechoslovakia," *Survey,* p. 143).

Among our comrades prevails a feeling of uncertainty as to what would happen if, after all the criticism that has been expressed, everything remained as it was. I say openly—and I feel that someone has to say it without mincing matters—that many comrades are afraid— and in view of certain experiences they may not be entirely wrong— that there could be, to some extent at least, a return to the fifties, to harsh repression of opponents within the party, and that such a struggle might lead to the use of the instruments of power, especially those of the security organs, to resolve internal party problems. Of course, this would be of the most serious danger for the whole republic. All this has convinced me that it is imperative for the decision about the office of First Secretary to be made at this Plenum.[17]

By this time it had become clear to the presidium and the consultative group that opinion in the central committee had finally hardened against Novotny, making it necessary to take action against him.

It is important to understand the interaction of the presidium and the central committee in the campaign to remove Novotny. The central committee was reluctant to take up the question, even when it first learned of the split in the presidium. By then the presidium was too evenly divided for it to undertake any major initiative against Novotny or, by the same token, to provide him with the cohesive support from the inner circle that he so desperately needed. It was chiefly to overcome the effects of this division that a consultative group had been set up, but it too was divided and therefore could not serve its purpose. Because the presidium could not act itself, it became responsive to swings of sentiment in its parent body, the central committee. At its December plenum, the central committee was still divided on the question of Novotny. However, "events at the January Plenum demonstrated that a considerable shift had taken place in the mood and attitude of most members of the Plenum since December. Even those members who in the face of the surprising and dramatic development had hesitated in December now

17 Mencl and Ourednik, in Remington, p. 38.

took a more determined stand." [18] Once the central committee had finally arrived at a consensus on the need to choose a successor to Novotny as first secretary, the presidium had no alternative but to do so.

The presidium and the consultative group met the night of January 4, 1968, to decide who should replace Novotny. Unfortunately, there is no authoritative account of the deliberations that led to the choice of Alexander Dubcek, and the accounts that have appeared are conflicting. We can only try to reconstruct the situation in which the choice was made and speculate on some of the considerations that influenced the designation of Novotny's successor. The small group of about twenty-five men who made the decision was divided rather evenly into pro- and anti-Novotny factions. Moreover, since no single figure had led the movement against Novotny, there was no leader of the opposition to turn to for his successor. No candidate would be acceptable, according to Mencl and Ourednik, who did not carry "an overwhelming majority" of the central committee, but in view of the deep divisions in that body, this meant merely that a candidate who was unacceptable to a large minority in the central committee would be rejected. [19]

Three kinds of choices were possible. First might be someone outside the current leadership, like Gustav Husak, who had suffered at Novotny's hands. Even after his rehabilitation in 1963, Husak had held no political office and therefore bore no responsibility for the unsatisfactory state of affairs. [20] A choice of this kind was made in October 1956 in both Poland and Hungary, when Gomulka and Nagy, respectively, were placed at the head of the leadership. This was done, however, under strong popular pressure, which supported Gomulka and Nagy because they had

[18] *Ibid.*, p. 37.   [19] *Ibid.*, p. 39.

[20] At this time Husak advocated basic reform. (See his speech of April 21, 1968, in Remington, pp. 142–146.) Husak's initial liberalism and popularity with youth have generally been lost sight of, since he replaced Dubcek following the Soviet occupation.

been victims of the existing leadership and therefore symbolized radical alternatives to it. In Czechoslovakia, on the other hand, the decision to replace Novotny was not made in response to an articulate and effective public opinion or to strong popular pressure. No candidate from outside the narrow circle of men who made the decision, apparently, was seriously considered.

A second type of candidate that might have been chosen was someone close to Novotny, like Josef Lenart, then head of the government. This was the kind of choice made in Hungary in July 1956, when Matyas Rakosi was replaced by Erno Gero. (A comparable successor in Czechoslovakia would have been Jiri Hendyrch, who had been Novotny's closest lieutenant but in the end opposed Novotny.) Lenart's close association, as head of government for four years, with Novotny may not of itself have disqualified him, but together with his last-ditch defense of Novotny, it doubtless hurt Lenart when his candidacy was considered.

Finally, a third category of potential successors to Novotny consisted of those who had opposed him from within the leadership. Persons in this category were at least partially responsible for the situation that the new leadership was meant to remedy, but they had the virtue, in the eyes of the men making the choice, of being tied to the existing system and were therefore unlikely to try to change it radically.

Two candidates were prominent in this category, Oldrich Cernik, a deputy head of the Czechoslovak government, and Alexander Dubcek, first secretary of the Slovak central committee, and both were considered. Since a Slovak, Jozef Lenart, was then head of the government, it would seem that Dubcek, also a Slovak, was less likely than Cernik, a Czech, to be chosen Party first secretary. Why Dubcek nevertheless was chosen is unclear, although two circumstances may be relevant. First, the liberals may have feared that Lenart, who was favored by the Novotny faction, as a Slovak might succeed in getting sufficient support from fellow Slovak members of the central committee to win the top Party office.[21] Conceivably, then, it was to win Slovak support away from Lenart that the anti-Novotny faction backed Dubcek.[22] Second, Novotny, still hoping to regain power, may have preferred Dubcek for the post because, as a Slovak, he was more vulnerable and because Novotny considered him less effective than Cernik as a political leader. Dubcek, then, may have been preferred to Cernik by the liberal faction as better able to win approval from the Slovaks in the central committee, and by the Novotny faction as less able to survive, once in office.

What did Moscow think of the appointment? Soviet involvement in the choice of a successor to Novotny is a crucial question for a study of succession in Eastern Europe, but there is little direct information bearing on the subject. Soviet views about the small circle of candidates for Novotny's post may have been known, in broad outline, to those who made the decision in the early morning of January 5, 1968, but it is unlikely that Moscow participated in their deliberations. His public record certainly should have won Dubcek Soviet approval. He was reared in the Soviet Union as a child and had returned to Moscow in the mid-fifties to study at a Party school of the central committee.[23]

[21] Whether Lenart in fact was looked on favorably by Slovaks in the central committee is not known.

[22] The account of Harry Schwartz, based on interviews in Prague, is consistent with this reconstruction: "The liberals advanced the name of Olrich Cernik. . . . The Novotnyites countered with Josef Lenart. . . . Understanding his opponents' strategy, Cernik played a master move. He withdrew from the race and proposed the Slovak party chief, Alexander Dubcek, as the liberal candidate (*New York Times Magazine,* March 31, 1968, p. 80). On the other hand, according to Tigrid, when "Cernik's name cropped up, the candidate was himself disinterested— he was more keen to be premier, and a combination of both jobs was after all no longer possible. So Cernik put forward a name that had not been considered till then: Dubcek" ("Czechoslovakia," *Survey,* p. 148.) The two accounts agree that it was Cernik who, rather late in the discussion, first proposed Dubcek.

[23] Dubcek's designation as first secretary of the Slovak Party in 1963 despite Novotny's evident coolness toward him, as noted earlier, may have been due to Soviet support.

Moreover, because Dubcek had lived so long in the USSR and, for a foreigner, so close to the center of its politics, Moscow did not have to rely on the public record alone: the KGB doubtless had a fat dossier on Alexander Dubcek. Both the public and the secret records were available to Brezhnev, who as first secretary had a special responsibility for watching over succession in the Czechoslovak Party.[24] He would surely have supplemented these records with his own personal judgment of Dubcek. Brezhnev had looked him over as a potential candidate for the succession on his visit to Czechoslovakia the previous month, as well as on other occasions, perhaps even while Dubcek was attending the Soviet Party school a full decade before. While, in retrospect, Brezhnev's failure to head off the appointment was a disastrous mistake, in extenuation it should be said that he had to make his decision without knowing in advance Dubcek's programmatic views—for the simple reason that Dubcek had announced no program.

One group sought to play a role in the crisis involving Novotny's position as Party leader, but was too sharply divided to influence the outcome. This was the military leadership, particularly the political officers in the defense ministry, led by Miroslav Mamula, head of the department in the Party secretariat that is responsible for supervision of the military and the political police, and General Jan Sejna, a high Party official in the defense ministry. In the last weeks of December secret discussions took place about the role the army might play in the crisis. It is not clear whether the discussions considered the actual use of military force to prevent Novotny's removal from Party office or only an official presentation of the views of the military (more precisely, the views of the Party organization in the defense ministry). In any case, it seems doubtful that the *threat* of force would be wholly absent from an expression of political views

[24] Brezhnev was exercising this responsibility for the first time. The only other political succession in Eastern Europe since Khrushchev's ouster had been in Romania, where Moscow's views had no weight.

emanating from the defense ministry and directed to the central committee on a crucial question the latter was about to decide. Whatever the aim of these discussions, their only outcome was a letter to the central committee from Party members in the defense ministry opposing the removal of Novotny from his post as first secretary. Because of extended debate about what its contents should be, the letter reached the central committee only after Novotny had already resigned.

The consultative group arrived at its conclusion that Dubcek should replace Novotny only after a drawn-out session lasting into the early hours of January 5. Later that morning, according to Tigrid's account based on unpublished documents, Novotny addressed the plenum of the central committee when it reconvened to consider the consultative group's proposals:

Right from the start of our talks in the Presidium . . . I declared that I was in favour of separating the functions of First Secretary and President of the Republic. And I stress, comrades, that I am still of this opinion. . . . I ask, in line with our discussions in the Presidium and with my own conviction, that I should be relieved of the office of First Secretary, and I say quite frankly that I do so in the interest of Party unity and I hope my decision will be understood in this spirit.[25]

By these remarks Novotny wished to make it appear that he was resigning voluntarily, "in the interests of Party unity," and was not being forced out by his enemies. Then, in accordance with the Communist custom whereby the first secretary, on behalf of the presidium, proposes to the central committee the names of candidates for the top posts in Party, government, and state bodies, Novotny proceeded to nominate Dubcek:

I also wish to put forward in the Presidium's name and in accordance with the view of the consultative group and with my own preference the unanimous proposal that comrade Dubcek should be chosen as First Secretary. . . . My own feelings, comrades—and I know a good deal of thought was given to these appointments—is that a good

25 Tigrid, "Czechoslovakia," *Survey*, p. 149.

and happy choice has been made, that in comrade Dubcek's person we have a guarantee that . . . his work will lead to a reinforcement of unity.[26]

In proposing Dubcek's name, as directed by the consultative group, Novotny says nothing of Dubcek's merits and gives no reason why he was chosen.

After the central committee elected him first secretary, Dubcek, in his acceptance speech, expressed reluctance (probably sincere) to assume the post. He also tried to heal the wounds left by the campaign that had ousted Novotny.

I should like to say, comrades, what I have said in the Presidium and to the consultative group when I was proposed as a candidate . . . : anyone who knows me will realize this is one of the hardest decisions I have ever had to make. . . . I shall exert every possible effort to work towards the aims which the Central Committee has always had under the leadership of comrade Novotny. . . .

We talked in the Presidium . . . [of] the most important thing a man can rely on in his work: the collective. And that includes, last but not least, the assistance of comrade Novotny which he has promised me—and that of course is something I value. . . .

I should like to thank comrade Novotny for the work he has done . . . all these years; there is no doubt he has tried to the best of his conscience to make his contribution to the fulfilment of our Party's policy.

Comrades, thank you for your expression of confidence.[27]

There is no hint here that the change in leadership would lead to a marked change in the Party's policy.

Once Dubcek was chosen first secretary, the crisis that had produced his election subsided, but the Prague Spring did not begin immediately. The announcements to the Party and the nation of the plenum's decisions were a product of compromise and were fashioned to avoid giving an unnecessary shock to the Party as well as the public. Dubcek's remarks to the central committee expressing appreciation of Novotny's past work gave an impres-

[26] *Ibid.*   [27] *Ibid.*, p. 150.

sion of continuity in the Party's leadership. Quite apart from this deception of the Party and the public, the succession to Novotny, because of the way it had come about, failed to bring into being a program of reform. The struggle to unseat Novotny had not been waged by a coherent opposition with its own program but was, rather, an inchoate movement within the central committee that increasingly became focused on the deficiencies of the personal ruler. As Dubcek later put it in an apologia, "The system of personal power did not allow us to plan ahead in a democratic, gradual and rational way. . . . We were simply unable to make preparations." [28]

No doubt the absence of a tradition of legitimate opposition in Communist states makes it difficult, at times even dangerous, to prepare a set of alternative policies to be put into effect once its authors come to power. But it is also probably true that the men who unseated Novotny initially saw little need for radically new policies. From their viewpoint, important reforms, like the New Economic Model, were already in operation and doubtless required only proper implementation under a new leadership to remedy the country's ills. Nevertheless, Dubcek brought with him to his new office one idea that was deceptively simple: that the Party must have a new relationship with society. Since the problems of Czechoslovak society were far more profound than the leaders realized, this simple idea was to have dangerous consequences. In Dubcek's own terms, the Party, having "managed" the society for so long, would discover that it lacked the capacity to "lead" it.

The Party's difficulty in leading the society was compounded by the Party's lack of an effective head. In his last years in office Novotny had continued to dominate the leadership, even while dissatisfaction with the Party's performance and with his own leadership grew. To compensate for the decline in his authority, Novotny concentrated more and more power "in the hands of a

[28] Speech to the central committee, September 26, 1969; in Shawcross, *Dubcek*, pp. 275, 277.

very small circle of people," especially in his own.[29] That power rapidly disintegrated in the last two months of 1967. With Novotny's removal as Party head in early January, Czechoslovakia slipped deeper into a crisis of succession that was to last for many months. In place of Novotny's repressive will there was now a vacuum, a vacuum that was to be filled in the months ahead by the strongly held convictions of intellectuals and by the long suppressed passions of all those who had suffered physically and morally under Gottwald and Novotny.

Dubcek, by taking Novotny's place as Party first secretary, did not resolve the crisis of succession. He took office not as supreme leader but, according to his own phrase, as "first among equals" in a collective leadership in which his supporters lacked decisive authority. Several of the men who had been associated with him in the campaign against Novotny did not at first share his objectives, and the disparity in their views widened as Dubcek shifted with the currents of popular opinion. Moreover, Novotny, though he was largely discredited within the leadership, remained a force to be reckoned with. He was not criticized officially for his responsibility in the political trials of Slansky or Husak and he remained president of Czechoslovakia. More important, many of his partisans remained, at least for a time, in crucial positions under the new leadership: for example, the head of government was Jozef Lenart (not till April 1968 did Cernik establish a new government); the first secretary of the crucial Prague Party organization was Martin Vaculik; the chief editor of the Party newspaper was Oldrich Svestka. Besides feeling the effects of Novotny's continuing influence, Dubcek never really succeeded in taking hold of the key instruments of power. In Slovakia Dubcek lost his power base once he moved from Bratislava to Prague.

---

[29] Mencl and Ourednik, in Remington, pp. 20 and 25. According to the report of the commission set up by the central committee in April 1968, "Over the years the system established in the early 1950s changed its forms and its personnel, but its basic features—concentration of power in the hands of a small group with strong trends towards one-man rule—remained until 1968" (Pelikan, *The Czechoslovak Political Trials*, p. 248).

In the central committee as a whole, committed supporters of Dubcek clearly were less than a majority, and perhaps not more than a third.[30] In the presidium, conservatives predominated, even after the April plenum strengthened the Dubcek faction. Furthermore, in the central Party secretariat, at the very heart of the system, Dubcek could rely on only two of the nine secretaries. The second-rank secretary, Drahomir Kolder, the only secretary besides Dubcek to sit in the presidium, was to prove his disloyalty in August 1968, when he offered his services to the invading armies.

Dubcek made no immediate effort to purge the Party and build up his own machine within it, partly because he disavowed such tactics, but also because he lacked an adequate base on which to build. Consequently, when he argued the need to create a new relationship between the Party and society, his personal interest coincided with his personal conviction. Only by winning support in the Party at large and in the nation could Dubcek acquire the personal authority by which to rule. But to base authority on popular opinion meant to be dependent on it and implied a need not to antagonize it. Since Dubcek also could not afford to antagonize the Soviet leaders, who believed socialism in Czechoslovakia was endangered by Dubcek's reliance on public opinion, he found himself increasingly in a dilemma.

The Prague Spring at first evolved slowly. Dubcek did little in January except begin the consultations that were to lead by April to the central committee's adoption of the Action Program.

[30] A rough breakdown of the central committee during the Prague Spring (January–August 1968) is one-third pro-Dubcek, one-third conservative, and one-third uncommitted. An attempt at a more refined estimate was made by the newspaper of the youth organization. Of the 110 full members, it estimated the number of conservatives to be in the range between 30 and 51, and supporters of Dubcek at about equal strength, while 30 members were judged to be uncommitted (*Smena*, May 22, 1968; cited by Jancar, p. 164). Subsequently, plans were made to effect a radical change in the central committee: only one-quarter of the existing membership reportedly was to be on the electoral list that was to be submitted to the Fourteenth Party Congress (Golan, *Reform Rule in Czechoslovakia*, p. 234n).

Initially the presidium met only every second week, according to Dubcek, in the belief "that, contrary to the past, it should not deal with details." [31] By March, however, it was meeting much more frequently. By then, also, Party control over the mass media had been greatly reduced, and relatively open debate, including dissent, had become the accepted practice. When General Jan Sejna, Novotny's aggressive supporter in the defense ministry, fled to the United States to avoid being indicted for personal misdeeds, the press began demanding Novotny's resignation as president. According to Tigrid, "Novotny pretended to be deaf to the clamour; for a long time he was assisted in his reluctance to abandon the post by the 1960 Constitution, which contained no provision for removing the President. The public therefore had to wait until Novotny resigned—which he only did under extreme pressure. . . . The operation was a tricky one [involving a threatened] vote of no confidence by the National Assembly if he did not [resign]." [32] Once he had resigned (March 22), groups of youths began forcefully advocating their own candidates to succeed him—men like Cestmir Cisar, a secretary of the central committee, and Josef Smrkovsky, chairman of the national assembly, who were unacceptable to Moscow. (After the Soviet invasion of August 1968, both men were purged.) Instead, the post went to Ludvik Svoboda, an old general whom the nation and Moscow were both willing to accept.

As the inhibitions created by fifteen years of conditioning began to break down, currents of public opinion moved increasingly toward radical criticism of the entire order that Novotny had established. Moscow, observing the consequences of freedom of debate, could not always be sure whether the views expressed in the public media were shared by Dubcek or whether he was unable or unwilling to prevent their expression. For Bolsheviks, in the final analysis, it hardly mattered: liberalism with respect to

[31] Dubcek speech to the central committee, April 1, 1968; in Ello, p. 52. Of course, Dubcek may have deliberately by-passed the basically conservative presidium during the gestation period of the Action Program.

[32] "Czechoslovakia," *Survey*, pp. 154–155.

a deviation is little better than the deviation itself. Moscow began to call insistently for the reimposition of tight control over the mass media, for repressive measures against the "enemies of socialism," and for a purge of reformist members of the Czechoslovak leadership. Dubcek, who had been carried along by the movement of opinion, was now committed to effecting sweeping reforms to achieve socialist democracy. The Action Program which incorporated these reforms aimed at an amalgam of humanism and Western-style freedoms with the continued hegemony of the Communist Party and a foreign policy based on allegiance to the USSR. It was to be carried out under a new leadership to be chosen at the forthcoming Fourteenth Party Congress. Dubcek was unwilling to give in to the Soviet demands, since he believed the Action Program was feasible, and he was convinced that the expressed Soviet fears of counterrevolution in Czechoslovakia were groundless.

Just when the Soviet leaders decided Dubcek's succession to Novotny had been a mistake is not known, but they implicitly acknowledged their error in mid-July, in a joint letter from five ruling parties to the Czechoslovak central committee:

You know that the fraternal parties showed understanding for the decisions of the C.C.P. [Czechoslovak Communist Party] Central Committee's January plenary session [when Dubcek took Novotny's Party office]; they assumed that your party, keeping a firm hold on the levers of power, would direct the whole process in the interests of socialism without allowing anticommunist reactionaries to exploit it for their own purposes. . . . We have repeatedly spoken about all these questions at our meetings, and we received assurances from you that you were aware of all the dangers and were fully resolved to repulse them.

Unfortunately, events moved along a different channel. The forces of reaction, taking advantage of the weakening of party leadership in the country . . . unleashed a campaign against the C.C.P. and its honest and devoted cadres.[33]

[33] Letter of July 15, 1968, in *Pravda*, July 18, 1968; quoted from *Current Digest of the Soviet Press*, August 7, 1968, pp. 4–6.

Despite this public expression of a lack of confidence in Dubcek, Moscow had not yet given up, but was still hoping to compel him to alter his political course. At the same time, Moscow almost certainly had begun thinking about ways to remove him if it became necessary. Dubcek had proved to be a bad first secretary from the Soviet point of view on two counts: he was unwilling to take the required measures against revisionists, and his popularity in the Party and among the people made it difficult for others to do so against his will.

Pressure on the Czechoslovak leadership was being intensified. The letter from the five parties to the Czechoslovak central committee made veiled threats to intervene with force if necessary, threats underscored by extensive military preparations undertaken earlier. Two weeks after the letter was written, the Soviet Party politburo and the Czechoslovak Party presidium met on Czechoslovak territory, at Cierna, close to the Soviet border. This confrontation probably was chiefly intended by Moscow to provide a basis for collective judgment as to whether Dubcek could be induced to meet Soviet demands and, if not, whether an alternative leadership could be formed from his colleagues. The Soviet politburo must have been discouraged. Dubcek stood firm, on the whole, and he seemed to have almost solid support from his colleagues. The Soviet leaders seemed to temporize, at Cierna and perhaps for a short time afterward, hoping a decision to intervene with military force would prove unnecessary, either because Dubcek would alter his course and tighten Party control of the country or because his opponents would be suddenly strengthened. Neither occurred, and it was decided to intervene.[34]

The timing of an invasion was limited by circumstances to the interval between August 18 and 28: it could not occur between August 9 and 17, when Tito, Ulbricht, and Ceausescu, in rapid succession, would be visiting Czechoslovakia; and it was best that it come before the scheduled meeting of the central com-

[34] See the account by Richard Lowenthal, "The Sparrow in the Cage," *Problems of Communism*, November–December, 1968, pp. 2–28.

mittee on August 29 to approve final arrangements for the congress. Once the congress convened (September 9), many of the conservatives on whom the USSR still relied were certain to lose their remaining positions of power. The timing of the invasion would be limited even further if it was designed to occur while the presidium was having its regular meeting on August 20. Moscow apparently relied on a core of leaders in the presidium, including Drahomir Kolder, Vasil Bilak, and Alois Indra, to persuade the presidium to reverse its course as a result of the invasion, placing Dubcek in a minority and forcing him to acquiesce to the invasion and occupation of the country or resign his office. If this was the Soviet plan, it was based on a gross miscalculation. When the presidium, while still in session shortly before midnight on August 20, learned of the invasion, a majority passed a resolution criticizing it.

Dubcek, remarkably, expected the invasion authorities to deal with him as first secretary: "I thought that someone would come to me on behalf of the allied troops and that we should accordingly convene a Presidium Meeting to decide on further action." [35] Actually, once Dubcek failed to approve the invasion, the Soviet leaders had no further reason to let him remain in office. A few hours after the invasion began, Dubcek was arrested, and the following day he was publicly blamed by the USSR for the need to invade Czechoslovakia:

A demarcation of forces within the Presidium of the C.C.P. Central Committee became evident in the course of the meeting in Cierna-on-Tisou. While a minority of Presidium members, headed by A. Dubcek, took overtly the right-wing opportunist stands, the majority adopted a principled line and affirmed the necessity of waging a resolute struggle against . . . connivance with the reactionaries. However, right-wing revisionist elements among the leadership of the Communist Party and the government of Czechoslovakia thwarted fulfillment of the understanding [on the need for tightened party control] reached in Cierna-on-Tisou and Bratislava [where several Communist parties

[35] Speech to the central committee, September 26, 1969; in Shawcross, p. 292. According to Shawcross, the text was smuggled out of Czechoslovakia in December 1969.

met subsequently]. . . . As a result of their perfidious, treacherous actions, a real threat arose to the socialist gains of Czechoslovakia. . . . In this situation it was necessary to act.[36]

A terrible fate was in store for Dubcek, who like Imre Nagy was accused of jeopardizing the foundations of socialism. The physical brutality to which he was subjected (along with Cernik and others abducted to Moscow) was perhaps in part a consequence of the Soviet leaders' vindictive anger against the men who had failed to justify Moscow's confidence in them.

The Soviet leaders probably counted on the presidium's approval of the invasion; when they failed to get it, they had to find another basis for rule. That the USSR did not aim at a restoration of Novotny was made clear at the outset by Soviet statements voicing approval of the January plenum. Once a leader has been discredited, as Rakosi was in October 1956 and Novotny in August 1968, Moscow generally has had the good sense not to attempt a restoration. Instead, the USSR was counting on several key opponents of Dubcek's post-January policies, including Kolder, the second-rank secretary, who apparently was intended to replace Dubcek. The Soviet ambassador, Stepan Chervonenko, tried to induce President Svoboda to invest Alois Indra with governmental power, thereby maintaining the regime's continuity, but Svoboda refused to replace the legitimate government of Cernik, although Cernik was now in Soviet custody. Plans to set up a new "revolutionary" authority, as was done in Hungary in November 1956, were undermined by the Party's success in convening the Fourteenth Congress on the second day of the occupation, with almost 80 percent of the elected delegates present. Of course, the decisive obstacle to the various Soviet plans was the overwhelming popular opposition to the occupation. Any government established in these circumstances, whatever the authority it invoked to legitimate itself, would be a quisling government without popular support, hence of limited value to the occupying powers.

In this impasse, President Svoboda proposed going to Moscow

[36] *Pravda* editorial, August 22, 1968; in Remington, p. 322.

to discuss the situation. The shape of the negotiations that grew
out of his visit was not anticipated by either side. Before leaving
Prague, Svoboda announced that he would return the same day
(August 23); in fact, the talks lasted four days. The Soviet leaders expected to negotiate with Svoboda on the basis of the *fait
accompli* of having Dubcek and Cernik in Soviet custody; instead, Svoboda refused to negotiate without their participation.
In the intense bargaining that followed, Soviet military control of
Czechoslovakia proved decisive. Dubcek and Cernik were freed
and allowed to remain in office—a humiliating reversal for the
Soviet leaders—but they now held office at the sufferance of the
occupying power. Their hope of continuing the Prague Spring
was strong, but it proved to be illusory.

Having now come to terms with the invasion while retaining
a measure of the people's support and allegiance, Dubcek was
able to win their acquiescence in the "temporary" occupation and
the measures that flowed from it. From the Soviet point of view
leaving Dubcek temporarily in office had an advantage: in the
very process of assisting "normalization" Dubcek would discredit
himself, until a point finally would be reached when the Soviet
authorities could demand Dubcek's removal without having to
fear a strong public reaction.

While he could no longer base his position in the leadership
on the people's positive support, Dubcek was able briefly to capitalize on his usefulness to the Russians to strengthen his personal
position and that of the liberals associated with him. At the August plenum of the central committee held upon his return from
Moscow, eighty delegates from the nullified Fourteenth Congress
were added to the central committee and an enlarged presidium
was elected in which Dubcek had a strong majority. But the decisive fact about Czechoslovak politics now was the presence of
the Soviet army, which made its weight increasingly felt. Finally,
in late March, anti-Soviet demonstrations in Prague following the
Czechoslovak ice-hockey victory over the USSR provided the excuse the Russians needed; on April 17, Dubcek resigned as first

secretary. Previously, on April 11, Husak had delivered a speech criticizing the Party's weak leadership of the past year and calling for decisive leadership. According to Golan, "Husak's speech bore all the signs of a deal between him and the conservatives to replace Dubcek's leadership, a deal if not engineered at least supported by the Soviets." [37] Perhaps it was partly for this reason that Dubcek opposed Husak's nomination, at the central committee meeting on April 17, to replace him and proposed Cernik instead.[38]

Within the framework of Czechoslovak political realities, Husak was a logical choice to succeed Dubcek. While politically active in the Prague Spring as deputy head of the government, he was not closely associated with Dubcek, so he was not a target of Dubcek's enemies. Unlike several candidates for the post (notably Kolder, Bilak, and Indra), Husak had not compromised himself in the August days by offering himself to the occupying powers. Finally, unlike Lubomir Strougal, who had been Novotny's minister of the interior until 1965, Husak was in no way implicated in the repressions and failures of Novotny's rule. Despite his previous close association wiith Novotny, Strougal was Husak's strongest rival for the post of first secretary. As head of the Czech Bureau, created to carry out Party work in the Czech lands after the occupation, Strougal was second only to Dubcek in the Party and ranked ahead of Husak, the leader of the Slovak Party committee; nevertheless, Strougal was passed over in favor of Husak.

Beginning in 1963, when Novotny was unable, for whatever reason, to put a protégé at the head of the Slovak Party, that party has been used repeatedly as a political base for struggle against the Czechoslovak Party's leader in Prague. Dubcek so used it in the long struggle against Novotny from 1963 to 1967. Bilak used it on behalf of the conservative opposition to Dubcek

[37] *Reform Rule in Czechoslovakia*, p. 300.
[38] Moravus, "Shawcross's Dubcek—A Different Dubcek," *Survey*, No. 4 (1971), 213. Moravus is the pen name of one of Dubcek's former advisers.

from January to August 1968, when, compromised by his close association with the invaders, he was replaced by Husak. Husak immediately purged the Slovak central committee, fashioning a political weapon for his seven-month fight against the gravely weakened Dubcek, climaxed by victory in April 1969.

While the designating of Husak as Czechoslovak first secretary reflected the balance of forces in the Party presidium, Moscow unquestionably was consulted and probably helped him get the post. Even before the invasion, it should be noted, Dubcek had acknowledged Moscow's right to a voice in deciding who would sit in the Party leadership.[39] Now, with an occupation force of several hundred thousand, Moscow certainly had a veto, at least, on the choice of a first secretary. The USSR required a leader on whom it could rely and who also had a measure of popular support. On both grounds Husak was acceptable. Moreover, in the years ahead Moscow was free to play on the ambitions of Husak's opponents as a means of protecting Soviet interests. Strougal, in particular, although he was passed over for the post of first secretary in April 1969, continued to play a key role in national politics. On June 3, 1969, the Party presidium assigned

[39] Dubcek is sensitive about this question, but he alludes to it in his speech to the closed meeting of the central committee on September 26, 1969: "We did present a report to our Soviet comrades on . . . those problems of cadres to which we intended to give urgent attention during our pre-Congress Plenary Session. The session was to take place on the 29th [of August], the date was chosen after the Bratislava meeting. . . . We also discussed the internal question of cadres. Now, in the interests of the international movement, I would have never brought this matter into the open but for the present tendency to disclose things in such a manner. It stands to reason that I did not discuss this before a wider forum. If some people now want to censure me for not having submitted this matter for implementation through Party organs immediately after the Cierna meeting, they should think again and realize what would have happened at the time" (Shawcross, p. 289). What this means in plain words is that the Czechoslovak leaders had agreed to Soviet demands on personnel appointments ("cadres") and were going to implement the agreement by action at the highest level but did not dare speak of this to lower Party organs.

Strougal the task of deputizing for the Party first secretary, thereby formalizing his position as the second-rank secretary and putting him in line to succeed Husak if his performance in office proved unsatisfactory. Some months later, however, on January 29, 1970, Strougal had to give up his powerful position in the Party apparatus when he was transferred to the post of head of the government. On this occasion no one was designated to deputize for Husak, and subsequently the Czech Bureau itself was abolished. The steady build-up of Husak's authority continued at the Fourteenth Party Congress, in May 1971, when he was given the elevated title of general secretary. In consolidating his position, however, Husak was limited by his evident incapacity to make radical changes in the composition of the top Party bodies.

Dubcek remained in the presidium, an isolated and in fact powerless figure. This was only the third time in the history of the Communist states of Eastern Europe that a former Party first secretary retained membership in the top party body; the previous instances were those of Ochab in Poland and Chervenkov in Bulgaria, after the two men vacated their posts in 1956.[40] The effect was different in the two earlier cases. Ochab, who had never consolidated his position as first secretary, posed no threat to Gomulka. On the other hand, Chervenkov, who had exercised autocratic rule for a half-dozen years, was for a long time able to prevent the stabilization of Zhivkov's power because of his great personal influence in the Party and state bureaucracies. Although Dubcek lacked such influence, he remained a symbol of the Prague Spring for many Party members and ordinary people. This posed certain problems, to which Dubcek subsequently called attention: "After that I was not entrusted with any Party or other official work. I was even officially excluded from . . . Party meetings and other organized events. At first I thought that the intention was to keep me as a former First Secretary in the

[40] Later, Ulbricht became a fourth.

background. This I considered both right and quite natural: frankly I understood." [41] Only later did Dubcek come to realize that he was being eased out of the leadership altogether and made a scapegoat for the "excesses" of the Prague Spring. His former colleagues were taking no chances.

The mismanaged succession in Czechoslovakia in 1968 was probably the greatest avoidable Soviet failure since Stalin excommunicated Yugoslavia in 1948. The costs of the failure in Czechoslovakia are not easy to assess, even at this writing, six years after the Soviet invasion. The costs have doubtless been less than appeared likely in the immediate aftermath of the invasion, but substantially greater than a superficial judgment might now suggest. To the deepened hostility of the Czechoslovak peoples toward the USSR and the setback to the leftist movement in Western Europe, one probably must add Communist China's reappraisal of its foreign policy that led toward rapprochement with the United States.

The invasion was justified by the "threat . . . to the socialist gains of Czechoslovakia"; Peking had good reason to suppose that Moscow saw in Mao's Cultural Revolution an even greater threat to the socialist gains of China. The benefits derived from the invasion are even harder to assess. Certainly the action helped to stabilize the Soviet position in Eastern Europe. If the congress had met, it would have provided Dubcek the means for consolidating his leadership and giving effect to his program. What the results would have been in the long run cannot be known, although almost certainly the costs of any subsequent Soviet military intervention would have been greater.

The clearest lessons to be learned by the Soviet leaders from the Novotny succession are that they cannot stand aside when the successor is designated and that they must exert their full powers to ensure that the man chosen has ability, can win a measure of support from his own people, and will be loyal to

[41] Speech to the central committee, September 26, 1969; in Shawcross, p. 296.

Moscow on all decisive questions. It is also clear that their failure during the Prague Spring to maintain a resolute attitude toward the Czechoslovak leaders led them into deep trouble, but the lesson to be drawn from this experience is not the need to be resolute but, rather, the need for a united leadership in Moscow —a lesson that was learned long ago but is very difficult to act upon.

8

Poland's Riotous
Succession (1970)

"I ask for a frank answer from the First Secretary of the
Central Committee of the PUWP [Polish United Workers
Party]. Is it necessary to shed blood to change the Central
Committee and the government? Is it not possible to con-
sider a fixed term of office in order to avoid a repetition of
1956 and 1970?"—Question directed to Edward Gierek,
January 24, 1971, at a meeting of striking workers at a ship-
yard in Szczecin.[1]

The invasion of Czechoslovakia in 1968 not only stabilized the
Soviet position in Eastern Europe, but it also strengthened the
Soviet commitment to the existing leadership in the area and
slowed the movement of the area's politics. Nevertheless, two
years later the accumulated grievances resulting from Gomulka's

[1] Quoted in *Problems of Communism*, September–October 1972, p. 4.
This chapter, in addition to primary sources, draws upon the following:
Nicholas Bethell, *Gomulka* (Middlesex, Eng.: Penguin, 1972); Jacob
Bielasiak, "The Gomulka Succession," seminar paper (Cornell University,
1972); Adam Bromke, "Beyond the Gomulka Era," *Foreign Affairs*, April
1971; reports of Michael Costello written for Radio Free Europe Research;
Michael Gamarnikow, "A New Economic Approach," *Problems of Com-
munism*, September–October, 1972; A. Ross Johnson, "Poland: End of an
Era?" *Problems of Communism*, January–February 1970, and "Polish Per-
spectives, Past and Present," July–August, 1971; Richard F. Staar, "New
Course in Communist-Ruled Poland?" *Current History*, May 1971; and news
articles in the *New York Times* and the *Neue Zürcher Zeitung*.

long rule led Polish workers to demonstrate violently against his policies, thus making him vulnerable to his opponents in the leadership. Weakened physically as well as politically, Gomulka was forced from power.

The circumstances in which Gomulka came to the leadership in 1956 had left their mark throughout the period of his rule. Like Kadar in Hungary, he previously had been expelled from the Party; when Gomulka returned to it, he was placed at the head of the Party apparatus. Unlike Kadar, Gomulka never wholly made himself its master. Although he had headed the Party apparatus after the war, he did not in 1956 possess a strong personal political machine within the Party, and he did not set about to create one. He relied instead upon a small number of personal partisans and undertook to stand above the existing factions, balancing them against each other to maintain an equilibrium. He sought to control the factions, not to dominate them, and as a result factional activity in the Polish Party was more open and persistent, and reached deeper into the middle levels, than in any other Party of the Soviet bloc.

Although Gomulka was brought to power in 1956 on a wave of popular support and with the active help of intellectuals and factory workers, he did not retain the support of either for long. He gradually lost the support of the intellectuals—first by rejecting their demands for greater freedom, later by taking repressive measures against them; he lost the support of the workers by failing to satisfy their material demands and nationalist sentiments. The peasants at first actively supported Gomulka because he permitted them to withdraw from collective farms and to cultivate their own lands and allowed the Church a measure of autonomy; later they took these concessions for granted. If there was relative political stability in the early and middle sixties, it was based in good part on popular inertia and lethargy. That Gomulka's rule could last fourteen years was owing to the narrowness of his horizons. He did not seek to transform Polish society in order to bring it to socialism, nor did he attempt to reform the regime so that it could win popular support. Like Novotny in Czechoslovakia, Gomulka made little effort to resolve the country's fundamental problems or to anticipate new social problems before they became acute. In Party affairs also, he was no Bolshevik seeking to root out dangers before they could grow, but for the most part he dealt with them only when he had to, thus allowing factional tendencies to flourish. If his cautious methods of ruling permitted political and economic problems to accumulate and deepen, the methods had the virtue, at least, of husbanding his political capital: it was fourteen years before he had expended it.

During the first half of his rule, Gomulka's primacy was unchallenged and he stood above the political struggle. The dominant issues and the factions which articulated them stemmed from the crisis of October 1956. Liberals of the Pulawska faction, who wanted to reform the system to win popular support for the regime as a more stable basis for Party rule, confronted conservatives of the Natolin faction, who believed that such efforts necessarily endangered the Party's rule. By 1964 the liberals largely had met defeat in the top leadership, although a number found places at the middle level. The conservatives were split into supporters of Gomulka, some of whom had top positions (for example, Eugeniusz Szyr and Kazimierz Witaszewski), and opponents, who criticized Gomulka's alleged revisionism and lack of principle, but with little effect.

In the last half of Gomulka's rule his authority came under serious attack. The earlier issues persisted, but liberals were on the defensive and suffered defeat. Later, economic difficulties led to criticism of Gomulka's management of the economy, which increasingly became the dominant issue, and Gomulka's belated efforts to cope with it finally led him to disaster. Gomulka's defeat of the liberals in the mid-sixties did not lead to a further consolidation of his rule, but to an intensification of factionalism which at times eroded his authority, and which Gomulka could control only by tactical maneuvers and a further concentration of power within the narrow circle of his own group. The two major factions that emerged at this time were to survive Gomulka's rule and confront each other during his succession. The Partisan faction consisted of veterans of the Communist underground during the German occupation, and was headed by Mieczyslaw Moczar, minister of the interior. The second major faction, headed by Edward Gierek, was based on the provincial Party apparatus, particularly in upper Silesia, but also included younger, technically trained administrators.

Moczar's faction is perhaps unique in the history of Communist states. Factions generally originate close to the summit of power, usually in the shadow of a personal ruler and with the aim of influencing his actions. Moczar, however, was not even in the politburo when his faction took shape in the early sixties, so one of its key aims was to win places for itself in the policy-making bodies. Although it engaged in factional struggle within the Party, it also had important populist features, since it was based on mass organizations, particularly the organization of veterans of the wartime guerrilla struggle and the auxiliary workers' militia. The chief power base of the faction was in the political police, which Moczar administered as minister of the interior until 1968, and for which he retained some responsibility at least until the spring of 1971. Moczar, in his struggle against the Gomulka leadership, which controlled the politburo and the secretariat, could depend on a capacity to mobilize the nationalist, anti-intellectual sentiments of broad groups of the Polish people; the support, in any confrontation, of the veterans' organization and the volunteer militia; and the assistance of security forces, which could be used to spy on the top leaders and, in the event a coup was attempted, to constrain them physically.

Deploying these varied forces against the Gomulka leadership, the Moczar faction had a large impact on Polish politics, although it did not achieve its presumed aim of replacing Gomulka with Moczar. The persistence of its struggle and the extent of its successes, despite its lack until 1968 of representation in the politburo, are remarkable. The Partisans failed in a bid for politburo representation at the Fourth Party Congress in 1964, but they continued to strengthen their forces. Their opportunity came in the aftermath of the Arab-Israeli war of June 1967, when the worldwide Communist line favoring the Arab countries met resistance within the Polish Party. Later, encouraged by developments in the Prague Spring of 1968, Polish students began to demonstrate for educational reform and greater personal freedom.

The Moczar faction now seized its opportunity. It took the lead in attacking Jewish leaders among the students and extended the attack to encompass the few remaining Jews in official posts. The faction's ability to publicize its anti-Jewish and anti-intellectual sentiments showed how much Gomulka's control of the press had been weakened. Since these sentiments met with a favorable response from important segments of public opinion, Gomulka was unwilling to set himself against them, but instead began maneuvering to prevent the Jewish issue from further weakening his position. After remaining silent for a time, he finally spoke out, encouraging Jews to emigrate and supporting a purge of pro-Israel officials, while offering a measure of support to Jews who were willing to conform to Communist discipline. His object was not so much to protect the liberals and remaining Jews in positions of authority as to take personal control of the campaign against them. In this Gomulka succeeded.

While the Partisans achieved their aim of forcing a purge of their enemies, they were unable to replace them with their own supporters. When a new central committee was elected in November 1968, over a third of the full members were dropped; eliminated were almost all Jews, former Socialists, and liberalizers ("revisionists"). Nevertheless, the Partisans failed to increase significantly their own strength in the committee. Instead, there was an influx of nonofficials, so-called worker-activists (15 of the 91 full members) and a sharp increase in the representation of the provincial Party *apparat* (from 14 to 21), largely at the expense of the government (whose representation was reduced from 30 ministers to 18). The changed composition of the central committee reflected a marked shift in the center of political gravity from the government to the Party apparatus, a shift that was to be carried even further by the post-Gomulka leadership.

Moczar did manage to secure a place for himself in the politburo (though only as a candidate member) and in the secretariat, where he was given responsibility for Party supervision over the security forces. But he had to resign as minister of interior, and was unable to secure the post for one of his own supporters. Ultimately, then, Moczar forced his way close to the center of power, but he lost administrative control over the security forces; he forced Jews and revisionists from office, but the issue of their participation in public affairs consequently lost much of its potency for use in future campaigns. Moreover, the new central committee chosen at the climax of Moczar's unsuccessful campaign appeared hostile to his faction, a factor of crucial importance in the Gomulka succession that lay ahead. The result of the confrontation between Moczar and Gomulka in 1968 was a clear victory for Gomulka that preserved his dominant position in the Party for the next two years. At the same time, the newly elected officials in the central committee were not personally committed to Gomulka and could not be relied upon to defend him.

The other major faction, headed by Gierek, was perhaps not as well organized as Moczar's, but it was more attuned to the regime's problems of modernization and economic development and it had an important place in the institutions of rule. But it also, like the Partisans, lacked strong representation at the center of power, where Gomulka was dominant. Gierek himself was an influential member of the politburo, but he was not currently a member of the secretariat. Furthermore, he was unable to participate fully in the politburo's work, since his main job was as first secretary in the Silesian industrial center of Katowice. His national reputation was based on his success in directing the province's industry, and in winning resources from the central leadership for its development. Even after the defeat of Moczar, in 1968, Gierek's influence in policy-making and in the central administration was not enhanced. He remained in Katowice—an indication that his role in the 1968 battles, while important, was not crucial and did not require Gomulka to reward him. Key responsibility for planning the major economic reform initiated after the Fifth Congress (November 1968), which preoccupied the Party during the next two years, was given to an opponent of Gierek, Boleslaw Jaszczuk. Gierek remained outside the secretariat, although one of his chief supporters was added to it (Jan Szydlak), along with a possible supporter of Moczar (Stefan Olszowski).

The balance of forces after the Fifth Congress persisted until the crisis of December 1970. Although Moczar had demonstrated that he could compel Gomulka to adopt policies he previously had resisted, he had little to show for his half-dozen years of struggle for power except his own belated promotion to membership in the secretariat and candidate membership in the politburo. Nevertheless, Moczar retained a degree of influence in the security forces and in the military, and he was a potential rallying center for advocates of hard-line policies, who disapproved of Gomulka's evasion of difficult decisions and his half measures. Gierek retained a limited influence in the politburo and, indirectly, in the secretariat, and considerable potential strength in provincial Party organizations, where a number of former subordinates from the Katowice Party organization held important posts. Although Gomulka's personal rule had been brought in question in 1968 by his need to adopt policies forced upon him by a rival for the leadership, he continued to dominate the central bodies that made policy and appointed personnel. By eliminating liberalizers from positions of influence, Gomulka removed a potential danger from the Right, and by withstanding

Moczar's challenge at the Fifth Congress, he won a respite on the Left. True, his repressive measures had made opponents of the writers and students; far more important, the workers were increasingly disaffected because poor management of the economy had led to slowed industrial growth and hardly any growth of real income. As a result, Gomulka's remaining political credit with the people was running low.

That Gomulka governed as an autocrat in his last years was later asserted separately by both the politburo and the central committee, and they offered persuasive evidence. The February 1971 report of the politburo that came to power after Gomulka's ouster asserts, "The [former] Politburo and CC [central committee] of our party bear, as a whole—though in varying degree —the moral and political responsibility for that fact that they failed to prevent the gradual growth of the despotic methods of governing used by the first secretary." [2] The politburo accounts for this failure (and tends to excuse it) by the sense of futility felt by central committee members and their fears of laying themselves open to charges of factionalism in any struggle to restrain Gomulka's exercise of power. An effective struggle would of course have required covert meetings to organize and plan a strategy, and such activities are not only prohibited by the Party statute, but in practice are subject to severe sanctions by the ruler whose power they seek to limit. While it would be easy to dismiss the politburo's assertions about Gomulka's autocracy as attempts to evade responsibility for the debacle of December 1970, the politburo provides unusual and telling detail in specifying the ways in which Gomulka exercised autocratic power over

---

[2] Special issue of *Nowe Drogi* (Warsaw; no date) presenting materials from the central committee's plenary session of February 6–7, 1971; trans. in Radio Free Europe Research (hereafter abbreviated RFE), *Polish Press Survey,* July 14, 1971, No. 2313, p. 20. Almost a year later, in reporting on its work between the two congresses of the Party (1968 to 1971), the central committee acknowledged its failure "to prevent autocracy" (*Trybuna Ludu* [Warsaw], December 5, 1971; trans. in RFE, *Poland,* No. 10, March 14, 1972).

the politburo and the central committee. Since the account is also an authoritative statement about the exercise of personal dictatorship in Communist regimes, it warrants quotation at length:

The Politburo, which still met regularly [i.e., weekly] toward the end of the 1950s was doing so less and less often during the last five years. In the last few years, the Politburo used to meet only a few times annually, and there were practically no meetings of the CC secretariat. The possibilities for discussion and an exchange of views at the meetings of these political bodies became practically nonexistent. The whole range of subjects discussed by the Politburo became increasingly more dependent on the interests and concepts of the first secretary of the CC. The majority of the decisions of the CC secretariat were passed by negotiation and under conditions where the opinion of the first secretary made their passing a foregone conclusion. The CC plenum was made to discuss problems which had been presented in an unprepared manner, often badly selected and formulated, too concerned with technical matters, and removed from the sphere of politics. As a rule, the meetings of the CC were attended by a large number of economic and state activists, often numerically superior to that of the total number of the members and alternate members of the CC.

Within the Politburo, there grew up a small core of people, favored by the first secretary, which became known as the select leadership: it brooked no criticism nor any overtures coming from outside. This unofficial body kept tight rein over the Politburo and the CC. Comrade Zenon Kliszko molded the cadre policy and, to a great extent, exerted control over the sphere of ideological activities, while Comrade Boleslaw Jaszczuk, to all practical purposes, held in his hands complete control over the entire economic policy. These two comrades, having unusual possibilities of influencing the views and decisions of the first secretary of the CC, were actively supporting—or even suggesting themselves—various wrong concepts, and suppressing any kind of criticism of these concepts. The possibilities for discussion or a comparison of views diminished with every year and, as a result, the supposed unanimity of the decisions reached by the Politburo and the CC was increasingly becoming an empty and illusory formality.

The leadership's contacts with the party gradually became nothing but an empty gesture, reserved for galas and ceremonial occasions.

The more that the first secretary cut himself off from the *aktif* [the broad circle of leading figures in the Party], the more he lost touch with reality, while, at the same time, he was gradually concentrating in his hands more and more autocratic power.[3]

Infrequent, poorly prepared meetings of the politburo, plenums of the central committee too big for serious deliberations, the small circle of confidants who are delegated large powers over appointments and the economy, the increasing isolation of the arbitrary autocrat—these are characteristic features of the last stages of tarnished personal rule in a Communist regime.

Moczar, in his speech to the CC plenum in February 1971, further characterized Gomulka's increasing isolation:

[Gomulka was] undoubtedly an autocrat. There was no place in his entourage for people who were disobedient. That was what Comrade Wieslaw [Gomulka's wartime pseudonym] simply could not tolerate; he would get rid of them, and at the same time, he would never accept the idea that one simply cannot rule the party in such manner, that one should listen to the opinions of others. On how many occasions, in various circumstances, have there been discussions on this subject among the comrades who were very offended—in fact, very offended—by Comrade Wieslaw's ways. I mean here, of course, private conversations. . . .

As a result of such carryings-on by his flatterers, Wieslaw simply shut himself away in his private office, and gradually cut himself off from all his contact with people, contacts which once—as I remember—were necessary to him, at least to a certain point.

He became even less accessible, and in turn, people began to avoid him, simply not wanting to meet him on account of his occasionally sharp manner.[4]

Although Moczar may have exaggerated in order to saddle Gomulka with the entire blame for the collapse of the Party's policies in December 1970, the picture he draws has verisimilitude.

The increased powers acquired by an autocrat do not necessarily enable him to rule more effectively. The central organs

[3] *Nowe Drogi*, special issue; RFE, *Polish Press Survey*, No. 2313, pp. 17–18.

[4] *Ibid.*, No. 2314, p. 3.

under Gomulka, like those under Novotny in 1967, increasingly
were cut off from lower-level organizations, thereby weakening
central control. Since the Party and state bureaucracies failed to
understand or disagreed with the decisions emanating from the
center, they implemented them halfheartedly and only partially.
Moreover, the politburo intervened excessively in the economic
work of the government, undermining its authority, while the
central Party apparatus, by its excessive interference, hampered
operations of the economic ministries and enterprises. When,
toward the end of his tenure, Gomulka exercised his power to
make major decisions, he was handicapped by gaps in the administrative control required to implement them properly.

In the two years of rule that remained to Gomulka after he
defeated Moczar at the Fifth Congress, he belatedly addressed
himself to the crisis of economic stagnation and to the diplomatic
opportunities opened up by West Germany's new policy toward
Eastern Europe. In fact, he became preoccupied with them. Perhaps he was pushed into a re-examination of Poland's policy
toward the Federal Republic of Germany by the USSR, which
was itself engaged in a reassessment of its own policy; it is also
possible that he was impelled to sponsor measures of economic
reform by young technically trained officials who saw the dangers
of continued economic drifting. Whatever the sources of these
policy innovations, it seems clear that Gomulka's main rivals,
Moczar and Gierek, neither originated them nor pressed him to
adopt them. (On the contrary, Gierek expressed reservations
about some of the new measures, particularly changes in the
wage-incentive system.) It was Gomulka who decided what had
to be done, and once his mind was made up, he had little difficulty in getting the necessary decisions adopted.

Gomulka had the power to make important decisions; he
lacked the means to make that power secure. In 1969, Gomulka
no longer possessed the moral authority and prestige needed to
withstand the failure of his new policies. He lacked popular support, and a significant part of the *apparat* questioned his leader-

ship. Moreover, his personal control of the security forces was in doubt. Since his rival, Moczar, with long experience in the ministry of internal affairs, was currently the secretary responsible for supervising that ministry, Gomulka could not be certain that he would be protected against a political conspiracy. This was a most unusual situation for a Communist leader. If Gomulka downgraded the threat of a conspiracy, his confidence may have been based on the mutual antagonism of his rivals and on the fact that such conspiracies had not succeeded in the Communist states of Eastern Europe. True, in 1964, Khrushchev had been ousted from power in the USSR by a conspiracy;[5] but plotters outside the Soviet Union faced an added obstacle: they could never be sure, even if their coup succeeded, that Moscow would let it stand. In this sense, the security of Gomulka's power ultimately depended on action by Moscow—which may help to explain why, in so many matters, Moscow could rely on Gomulka's support.

The deliberations on economic reform that claimed much of Gomulka's attention in 1969 and 1970 led him to adopt measures contrived by a small circle of economists and administrators. Aimed at rectifying major defects in the price structure and in the monetary system, these measures required important sacrifices from the workers, but they were promulgated shortly before Christmas (December 13, 1970) without regard for the effect on workers' morale. Their announcement led immediately to demonstrations by dock workers in Gdansk, which soon became violent and spread to other port cities. They were quickly met with brutal force by the auxiliary militia and, with less bru-

[5] The parallel between the Khrushchev and the Gomulka ousters is instructive. In both, two hostile factions joined to achieve a common aim, the conspiratorial removal of the leader. The armed forces and the political police were favorable or neutral, and their responsible officials were rewarded by the coup leaders. While planning for the Soviet coup probably began well before the event, the Polish coup was conceived shortly before its execution. In the succession that followed in each country, the hostile factions resumed their struggle.

tality, by the armed forces. According to the official figures, forty-five persons were killed, over a thousand injured, and almost three thousand arrested. Just as at Poznan fifteen years earlier, violent suppression of the workers brought the legitimacy of the leadership into question.

In particular, the suppression gave rise to three sensitive questions: Granted that the measures incensed the workers, was not the leadership responsible for the bad economic situation that alone could justify them? Were the reforms really necessary, and even if they were, did not the leaders blunder in announcing them during the Christmas season? Having provoked the demonstrations, should the leadership have responded with force, and, in any case, was not the force excessive? The thrust of these questions required the leadership either to stigmatize as enemies of socialism the thousands of workers who had demonstrated, and thus to infuriate the entire nation, or to acknowledge its own culpability for this violent encounter of the proletariat with its own dictatorship. In the search for answers to these questions, Gomulka's political interests diverged sharply from those of his rivals, Moczar and Gierek, while theirs for the moment converged. Both saw the crisis as an unexpected opportunity to strike against Gomulka.[6]

According to the politburo's report on the December events, rendered to the February 1971 plenum of the central committee by the men who ousted Gomulka, he dangerously mishandled the demonstrations from their inception. He responded in the autocratic manner to which he had become accustomed, without consulting the politburo. Gomulka characterized the demonstrations as counterrevolutionary and refused to recognize their source in the workers' valid grievances. His only reply to the demonstrations, almost from the beginning, was to oppose them with brute force. According to the politburo report, his attempt

[6] Though Gomulka was then sixty-six years old, he gave no sign of retiring from power. Gierek was fifty-eight on January 6, 1971; Moczar, a year younger.

to resolve the conflict by using force could only lead to much
bloodshed and to the opening of a chasm between the Party and
the nation.[7] To prevent such consequences, key members of the
politburo decided to change the country's political leadership.

The politburo was not summoned by Gomulka to discuss the
disturbances until Saturday, December 19, when they were in
their sixth day. Before the meeting convened, Gomulka became
ill and was hospitalized, so he could not attend. Chaired instead
by Jozef Cyrankiewicz, the head of government, the meeting
decided to turn sharply away from the course Gomulka had
been following.[8] "Having made an assessment of the situation on
the coast and throughout the country, the politburo decided to
summon a plenum of the Central Committee on the following
day, December 20, with a view to undertaking indispensable
political and personal [personnel?] steps"—namely, the removal
of Gomulka and the establishment of a new ruling group. This
was the decisive moment in the political crisis, but unfortunately
it remains shrouded in mystery.

Did Gomulka summon the politburo in order to demand its
approval of his handling of the crisis and of the further measures
required by the spread of strikes, or was he compelled to call the
meeting by rising opposition within the leadership? Was action
against Gomulka made possible only by his illness, or had the
plot been set in motion previously, thus perhaps contributing,
along with the demonstrations, to the breakdown in Gomulka's
health? According to the politburo report, the decision to remove

[7] *Nowe Drogi*, special issue; RFE, *Polish Press Survey*, No. 2313, pp. 2–8.
The politburo's version of the December events is presented at length
below.

[8] That Gomulka's absence may have made a difference is suggested by
a subsequent remark of Cyrankiewicz characterizing previous politburo
meetings at which Gomulka was present: "It was not possible to present
one's views . . . at the meetings of the Politburo, for it only aroused the
egotistic sensitivity of Comrade Gomulka and assailed his sense of authority" (statement at plenum of central committee, February 6–7, 1971, *Nowe
Drogi*, special undated issue; trans. in *Problems of Communism*, September–October, 1972, p. 5).

Gomulka was prompted, not by his illness, but by "the most urgent political necessity . . . to amend the current political errors, and to bring the political crisis to a stop." [9] Gomulka's illness only provided his opponents with an opportunity to act against him for reasons that had nothing to do with his health. Even so, to capitalize on this conjunction of circumstances so favorable to their enterprise, Gomulka's opponents had to enter into a conspiracy. Gomulka had shown himself unwilling to enter into talks with the demonstrators and determined to stay in power. This is evident from the government's early characterization of the demonstrators as enemies of socialism, and by its contention that the announcement of the price changes before Christmas was a "collective" decision. The politburo report itself seems to hint at the need for a conspiracy when it speaks of Gomulka's removal as a matter of "the most urgent political necessity." Whether or not the conspiracy depended for its success on Gomulka's illness, once he was hospitalized, Gomulka's capacity to resist the conspiracy was at an end.

Although key details of the conspiracy are shrouded in mystery, its broad outlines can perhaps be reconstructed. It probably took shape between December 14 and 19. Before the fourteenth, an agreement between Gierek and Moczar on a collaboration to unseat Gomulka would have been unlikely, since the prospects of a coup were dubious until the demonstrations had discredited Gomulka's rule. By the nineteenth, when the politburo met, the conspiracy almost certainly was under way; otherwise, it seems doubtful that a decision to oust Gomulka could have been imposed on a body that was still packed with Gomulka's supporters.

During those six days when the conspiracy took shape and was executed, the army command did nothing to oppose it, and may have given it active support, for on the day following Gomulka's removal, the minister of defense, Wojciech Jaruzelski, became the first Polish professional soldier to be chosen a candidate member of the politburo. The minister of the interior, Kazimierz

[9] *Nowe Drogi*, special issue; RFE, *Polish Press Survey*, No. 2313, p. 8.

Switala, probably did not actively oppose the coup either, for the post-Gomulka leadership kept him in office for a time despite the workers' hatred of him for his role in the violent suppression of the demonstrations in Gdansk. The decisive figure in preventing the security forces from protecting Gomulka's political power probably was Moczar himself, for he was the secretary charged with Party supervision over the political police.

By such connivance Gomulka was prevented from learning of the conspiracy in time to act against it. Moczar's reward was to be promotion to full membership in the politburo. Gierek, since he replaced Gomulka as first secretary, clearly was a central figure in the plot, and he may well have been its creator and organizer. At this time, however, he still lacked a place in the central secretariat, so key roles may have been played by his supporters in that body, principally Jan Szydlak. The politburo report refers to healthy elements in "the central party aktif" that played a positive role in the December crisis—presumably Gierek's supporters, but perhaps the Moczar faction as well.[10]

When the politburo finally met on Saturday, December 19, it did not act immediately to replace Gomulka with Gierek, but did so only after long debate. An account of this debate (though a self-serving one) appeared in a "statement" of Ryszard Strzelecki, a close supporter of Gomulka, to the central committee. He denied that the summoning of the central committee was a matter of controversy in the politburo. (This was rebutted by several leaders, who claimed that Strzelecki and others had opposed con-

---

[10] "However, fortunately for the party, these painful shortcomings in the methods of management [of the central Party links] were not a universal phenomenon. In spite of waning statutory possibilities for a political discussion, there remained, however, inside the central party aktif, comparatively great sincerity and freedom in exchanging views, and there emerged critical opinions and true assessments of reality. In such a situation, this had a positive influence and contributed to the fact that the CC was capable of standing up to the December crisis, of making a change in leadership in keeping with the statutory norms, and of appointing a new ruling collective capable of leading the country and the nation out of a difficult situation" (*ibid.*, p. 20).

vening the central committee as long as possible; indeed, when the central committee met on the day after this politburo session, it removed Strzelecki from the politburo.) Strzelecki did acknowledge that the politburo had argued about the *manner* of "Comrade Gomulka's withdrawal from the position of first secretary."

It really took quite some time for us to arrive at a decision. There was no question of Gomulka's continuing as first secretary. It was out of the question for this situation to continue for reasons of his state of health, as well as because of his methods of work, which could no longer be tolerated. Many comrades were of this opinion, and I was among them.

There was also no doubt about electing Comrade Gierek to take over the position of first secretary. The controversy which made the discussion so long concerned the way in which to inform Comrade Gomulka of the plenum's decisions. This was a delicate and tricky problem, because, according to medical opinion, he had suffered a cerebral hemorrhage and there was danger that a massive hemorrhage might follow. Therefore, it was imperative to pass on to him that decision of the plenum in the most delicate manner possible, and, at the same time, to obtain from him his resignation without endangering his health.

After an admittedly long, controversial discussion, in which I took active part, we decided that Comrade Cyrankiewicz and Comrade Kliszko should undertake this mission. At the beginning, it was also suggested that Comrade Gierek accompany them, but he declined, quite wisely, to approach Comrade Gomulka in this matter. We accepted his decision as fitting, and left it at that.

The two mentioned comrades talked to Comrade Gomulka and obtained from him his oral resignation from the position of CC first secretary. Thus this very difficult—in my opinion—matter for the party, as well as for a leader of many years' standing, was solved in a decent manner, which was also reflected in the official communique.

This was the only matter which aroused any controversy during the discussions at that session.[11]

[11] Statement of Ryszard Strzelecki to eighth plenum of central committee, February 1971, *Nowe Drogi;* trans. in RFE, *Polish Press Survey,* August 31, 1971, No. 2315, p. 3.

Moscow presumably was told of the coup only after it had succeeded. Gierek now had little reason to fear a Kremlin veto, however, since the violent reaction to Gomulka's economic policies no doubt had discredited him in Moscow, as it had in Poland.

Gomulka's removal, then, unlike Novotny's in Czechoslovakia, was not the culmination of an open struggle waged by rivals in the leadership. Since Gomulka controlled the politburo and the central committee, political action in those organs would not have been sufficient, even after the riots occurred. To remove Gomulka, two elements were necessary: the workers' violent demonstrations and his rivals' conspiracy. Either alone would probably not have sufficed. The demonstrators could discredit Gomulka, but they lacked the means to remove him; only his own colleagues (or Moscow) could do that, and probably only by conspiratorial means. On the other hand, the military and the security forces presumably would have discharged their obligation to protect Gomulka against a conspiracy if he had not previously been discredited by the demonstrators.

The workers, having proved their determination to assert their demands even in the face of violence, acquired a voice in the politics of the leadership which they continued to make heard for some weeks after the ouster of Gomulka. They demanded and obtained the ouster of men whom they considered especially responsible for the conditions leading to the uprising: of Stanislaw Kociolek from the secretariat, Ignacy Loga-Sowinski from the post of head of the trade unions, and Kazimierz Switala from the ministry of the interior, as well as various provincial leaders who had particularly offended them. Moreover, by continuing to agitate and strike, they finally secured the remission of Gomulka's price reforms. After a time, workers' demands ceased to play an independent role in Poland's higher politics, but perhaps chiefly because their immediate material demands were effectively being met.

Gomulka and four of his partisans were dropped from the politburo at the December meeting of the central committee, while seven of its twelve members—a bare majority—retained membership. Since one of the seven, Loga-Sowinsky, a long-standing Gomulka associate, was dropped from the politburo two months later, his retention in December may have reflected an unwillingness to remove half of the politburo at one stroke, thereby violating the fiction of politburo continuity.[12] An alternative explanation that has been given is that Loga-Sowinsky deserted Gomulka in a crucial vote on his continuation in office and was rewarded by being allowed to stay on, while the four politburo members who remained loyal to Gomulka were purged along with himself. However, in the rush of events following the riots and Gomulka's illness it seems unlikely that Gomulka's fate was decided by a simple majority vote in the politburo.

In the aftermath of Gomulka's defeat at the December plenum of the central committee, his rule was attacked as autocratic and neglectful of the people's material welfare; the attack was in conformity with the Communist tradition of condemning former rulers. Gomulka, unlike Khrushchev, did not even have the dubious satisfaction of being overthrown by the man he had chosen to succeed him. Needing all the power he could muster after 1968 to protect his position, Gomulka doubtless could not have afforded to make arrangements for his succession, but there is no reason to suppose that he intended either Moczar or Gierek to be his heir. Moreover, Gomulka's program for the country, based on the new economic reform, was rejected by those who followed him. Having wholly used up his political capital in fourteen years of rule, Gomulka had nothing left with which to influence what came after him.

While Gomulka ruled, his partisans held all the most powerful positions, and his two factional opponents were even kept from

[12] A similar delicacy was shown in the USSR after the purge of Khrushchev's opponents, the so-called "anti-Party group": five of the eleven members in the politburo were purged in June 1957; a sixth was purged a year later.

the second echelon of power. Moczar still had not been appointed a full member of the politburo, or Gierek a member of the secretariat. Both appointments were made in the course of the division of spoils immediately after Gomulka's ouster. Five new members were added to the politburo: three partisans of Gierek (Jan Szydlak, Edward Babiuch, and Piotr Jaroszewicz) and one or two from the Moczar faction (Moczar himself and possibly Stefan Olszowski). The Gierek faction added two new members to the secretariat (Gierek himself and Babiuch, the new cadres secretary), providing three (Jan Szydlak was the third). The Moczar faction, however, which already had Moczar and perhaps Olszowski in the secretariat, added no new members. The distribution of posts between the two factions favored Gierek, although some balance was maintained between them in the top organs.

What could not be balanced, and what gave Gierek a critical advantage, was his appointment as first secretary. The removal of Gomulka and his closest followers from the secretariat had opened the way to the top office for the leaders of the two rival factions. Why Gierek, though his experience in the central secretariat was limited and had ended six years previously, got the post instead of Moczar, who was already present in the secretariat, is not wholly clear.[13] Gierek's strength in the provincial Party apparatus was a crucial factor. Moscow's preference, whether known or guessed, may have added weight to Gierek's claim to the office, since Soviet economic assistance was obviously going to be required

---

[13] In this (if in little else) Gierek resembled Alexander Dubcek, who also came to his Party's top post from an important local Party organization (Slovakia) but lacking long and intensive experience as a secretary of the central committee. Of the previous twenty-one years, Gierek had spent eighteen in Katowice and only three in Warsaw, where he worked on the staff of the central Party apparatus from 1954 to 1957. During the next thirteen years his residence was in Katowice, where he worked full time as the provincial first secretary. While he retained the title of secretary of the central committee from 1957 to 1964 and probably attended meetings of the secretariat, it seems doubtful that he was able to use the office to build up a base of power. In any case, he was not a member of the secretariat from 1964 to December 1970, when he returned as its first secretary.

by the new leadership. If the choice of Gierek was the result of bargaining, Moczar may have acquiesced in Gierek's assumption of the post, in the hope that an inability to deal with the intractable problems created by the riots would soon discredit him. If Gierek played the leading role in the coup, as seems likely, this may have been the decisive factor.

Gierek's strategy once in office was the classic one: to use the powers of the first secretary to dominate the secretariat, extend his control over the other key institutions, and thus secure the succession. In order to maneuver freely in dealing with the country's severe economic and social problems—including continuing strikes and a weakened national morale—Gierek had reason to move quickly against Moczar if this could be done without endangering the leadership's stability. Key objectives were to deprive Moczar of responsibility for military and security affairs and to eliminate him from the secretariat. Moczar's strategy was necessarily limited by his past experience. Probably it continued to be based on his influence over the security forces, his capacity to win powerful hard-liners to his cause, and his continued appeal to nationalist elements in the population. His immediate aim was to prevent Gierek from consolidating his power and thus to keep the succession open.

The struggle between the two rivals was brief and intense, perhaps because of their ages (Gierek was fifty-eight, Moczar fifty-seven), which made them men in a hurry. Evidence bearing on control of the security forces emerged quickly, though it was ambiguous. The interior minister, Kazimierz Switala, was replaced on January 23, allegedly at his request, because of "ill health," but at least partly because of the repeated demands of workers in Gdansk, who held him responsible for the December 14 order to fire on them. Whatever the reason for the move, it obviously had important implications for the security forces, and hence for the succession struggle.

The new minister, Franciszek Szlachcic, was a career police

official. He had served in that capacity in Gierek's territory in Silesia before coming to Warsaw in 1967 to serve in the ministry of interior under Moczar, to whose faction he reputedly belonged. Although Moczar may have been responsible for his 1971 promotion, Szlachcic confronted a problem of divided loyalties, as appeared from an unusual announcement of the responsibilities of members of the Party secretariat: "Edward Gierek: Responsible for the entire program and head of the Central Control Commission. Major General Mieczyslaw Moczar: Army, security services, administration and health." [14] In the circumstances of the struggle between the two men, Szlachcic had to decide whether to be loyal to the man who was directly responsible for the security services or to the man who headed the entire program.

The two factions appeared to be at a stalemate in late January, when the expected meeting of the central committee was postponed, and in early February, when it finally took place. Loga-Sowinski and Kociolek were then dropped from the politburo, partly, at least, because of an extrinsic factor—the demands of the workers. Since no one was elected to replace them, the politburo was left with only ten members, instead of the customary twelve. In the interval between the February and April meetings of the central committee the struggle reached its height. Press criticism at that time of those who failed to approve of Gierek's election as first secretary may have been directed against the Moczar faction. This criticism is most apparent in an article by a key journalist, Ryszard Wojna, who asserted that the election of Edward Gierek as first secretary and the consequent changes in the style of government "were received by the nation with almost unanimous approval. The word 'almost' applies to all those who, as a result of the changes, felt themselves endangered in their positions and in their manner of exercising authority. . . . The opponents of the general renewal in our republic are ready, through their

[14] Statement by Jerzy Solecki, a Party spokesman, at a news conference; reported in *New York Times*, February 9, 1971.

actions, to bring about a reaffirmation of the false thesis that society should be ruled over rather than ruled with." [15]

Subsequently, after Moczar's defeat, the central committee's report on the Party's work between the fifth and sixth congresses (1968 to 1971) also alluded to the factional struggle that was waged following the December crisis:

The time of overcoming the crisis, the first months of 1971, proved that in addition to the overwhelming majority of party members devoted to its cause and behavior in accordance with the principles of democratic centralism there were also people in the party who did not know how, and did not want, to commit themselves in difficult situations in favor of correct issues and principles, to the party's decisions, and did not subordinate themselves to party discipline, yielding instead to demagogy.[16]

While it is not known what forms of indiscipline and demagogy the Moczar faction engaged in, punitive sanctions were taken against it soon after the February plenum, thereby exposing the weakness of Moczar's position.

A close associate of Moczar in the defense ministry, General Grzegorz Korczynski, resigned his post in the defense ministry on March 12, allegedly because of "failing health," but probably because of his responsibility for the brutal actions of troops under his command in the December fighting. At the end of March, Moczar failed to be appointed a member of the Polish delegation to the Soviet Party congress. Although he greeted the Polish delegation on its return from the Soviet Party congress on April 9, he then disappeared from public view for seven weeks. On April 16, the plenum of the central committee elected a new secretary, Stanislaw Kania, who began to perform some of the functions for which Moczar had been responsible. Shortly afterward, news reports began to appear in the Western press of a

---

[15] The article appeared in *Zycie Warszawy*, of which Wojna was then deputy editor, on February 19, 1971 (in RFE, *Poland*, No. 7, March 3, 1971).

[16] *Ibid.*, No. 10, March 14, 1972.

heart attack suffered by Moczar. He reappeared suddenly on May 27 in the company of Gierek, with the aim, apparently, of demonstrating the leadership's unity, but his rapid political decline continued. After several weeks Moczar was appointed to an honorific state office that has repeatedly been assigned to disgraced Party leaders. When the central committee met a few days later, he was released from his post as secretary. Thus in six months Gierek had succeeded in expelling his chief factional rival from his main base of power. Subsequently, at the Party congress in December 1971, he ousted Moczar from the politburo.

How did Gierek accomplish all this? Why did Moczar fail to wage a more effective struggle? We know what happened, but too little of why it happened. Did Moscow play an important role in Moczar's defeat by actively opposing him? (His precipitate decline began after the Polish delegation, headed by Gierek, returned from the Soviet Party congress on April 9.) Was Moczar's rumored illness a real factor in his defeat? (He did not appear in public from April 9 to May 27.) Was Gierek simply far more astute and politically experienced than Moczar? (While Gierek was handicapped by relative inexperience in the secretariat, Moczar had had no experience in the Party *apparat* before 1968, when, at the age of fifty-four, he became a Party secretary; till then his career had been basically that of a police official with a penchant for demagogy.) Moscow, Moczar's health, Gierek's astuteness and knowledge of the workings of the Party *apparat,* Gierek's success in ending the strikes—probably all these were involved, though as yet we cannot assign them weights or reconstruct their interaction. The Polish leaders, like the Soviet leaders in the Khrushchev succession, effectively screened information about the details of the struggle over the Gomulka succession. As a result, our knowledge of developments in the top Polish leadership is far greater for 1956 and 1968 than for December 1970 and the first half of 1971.

By defeating Moczar, Gierek took a large step toward consolidating his position. He capped the victory by purging from the security apparatus about two hundred officials,[17] thereby avoiding Gomulka's error of permitting an opponent to influence the work of the institution he relied on to safeguard his own power.

Although Gierek had succeeded, by the summer of 1971, in reducing the power of his strongest rival, he had not yet resolved the succession. For this he needed a central committee that would allow him to reconstitute both the politburo, which had fewer members than usual and included potential rivals like Moczar and Cyrankiewicz, and the secretariat, which had rising young figures like Olszowski and Josef Tejchma (a politburo member since 1968), who did not owe their places to Gierek and had already developed followings of their own. Gierek scheduled a Party congress to meet just one year after he had come into office, although the Party statute did not require a congress to be held before the summer of 1972. He used the period of preparation to carry forward the rebuilding of the shattered Party, replacing twelve of the nineteen provincial first secretaries with his own partisans. As a result, when the congress assembled in December 1971, its machinery was responsive to Gierek's wishes.

The central committee approved by this congress differed radically from the one chosen only three years previously. Almost half the members elected in 1968 were demoted, leaving the survivors heavily outnumbered by newly elected members (49 to 66).[18] Approximately three-fourths of the candidates were new to the central committee. Moreover, the men approved by the central committee for inclusion in its leading organs constituted a new leadership, largely chosen by Gierek. Of the twenty top leaders (members and candidates of the politburo, secretaries and "members of the secretariat"), thirteen entered this select circle of leaders only after Gomulka's ouster; three entered it in 1968

[17] Adam Bromke, "Poland under Gierek," *Problems of Communism,* September–October, 1972, p. 3.

[18] Less than one-fourth of the 1971 central committee had been full members in 1964.

(Wladyslaw Kruczek, Stefan Olszowski, and Jan Szydlak); three others in 1964 (Mieczyslaw Jagielski, Piotr Jaroszewicz, and Jozef Tejchma); only Gierek had occupied such a post before 1964. Moreover, four of the six men who were already in this small circle of leaders when Gierek became first secretary have since been promoted to full membership in the politburo. Thus, while Gierek has not chosen all the members of this core leadership, he has chosen most of them, and all but two appear to owe important promotions to him. If a small dark cloud still remained on Gierek's horizon, it may have been owing to the presence in the secretariat of Tejchma and Olszowski, men whom Gomulka had raised to high office. If so, it was dispelled after the elections for the *Sejm* (the Polish legislature) in March 1972, when Gierek transferred the two men into the government, where great ambitions, if they harbored them, posed less danger. In little more than a year after the fall of Gomulka, Gierek had resolved the crisis of succession and established his own personal rule.

While the 1970 workers' demonstrations enabled Gierek to come to power without having to wait for a prolonged erosion of Gomulka's position, they also complicated the problem of governing afterward. Similarities between the events of October 1956 and those of December 1970 should not be allowed to obscure the crucial differences: the popular upsurge in October 1956, though it stemmed from deep disaffection, was positively directed to restoring Gomulka to power; the demonstrations of December 1970 were directed against the government's measures and aimed to bring Gomulka down. Gierek seized upon the occasion to take power; it was by no means thrust upon him by trusting workers. Gomulka came to power holding the confidence of the workers and with a relatively free hand to deal with the country's ills; Gierek was met with deep skepticism, for the workers' dismal experience with Gomulka left them with little faith in his heirs. Because they had little faith, however, the people also had modest hopes. Knowing the outcome of the Prague Spring, the Polish nation seemed content, at least for the time being, to bank its hopes on Gierek's good intentions and reputation for getting things done.

Since Gierek rejected the notion that the workers' demonstrations aimed at counterrevolution and since he acknowledged the justice of their declared grievances, he was obliged to seek immediate remedies for them. Yet for almost two months strikes continued, although the violence abated, while Gierek resisted the demand to rescind Gomulka's price increases. Finally, intimidated by the spreading strikes and assisted by a Soviet loan, Gierek gave way on the issue. Gradually, from a series of *ad hoc* concessions to the workers there emerged a basic change in priorities: Gomulka's orthodox policy favoring the preferential growth of heavy industry was replaced by a policy of increasing consumption in proportion to the growth of the economy. Besides raising the income of low-paid and skilled workers, the government made large concessions to the predominant private sector in agriculture. Aided by two good harvests in 1971 and 1972 (after the two poor ones that had contributed to Gomulka's downfall), the country succeeded in sharply increasing meat production and ending the food shortages that had helped spark the December 1970 demonstrations. By the end of 1972, Gierek had substantially reduced disaffection among the workers, particularly in the coastal areas where the 1970 disturbances began.

Those disturbances were only an acute manifestation of basic social and economic problems that beset Poland. Would the new Gierek leadership be able to contribute to their solution? Fundamental changes were required, including a radical reform of economic management to increase efficiency, new forms of worker participation to improve incentives and labor productivity, and a measure of liberalization in the control of literature to win back active support from Poland's intellectuals. Of these, only the first was a matter of concern to the Gierek administration. After committing himself to a systematic reform of economic management and the avoidance of Gomulka's sporadic tampering with the economy, however, Gierek came to realize the economic and political complexities involved and seemed to let the problem fade from view. Since his rule was narrowly based on the secretariat and the Party apparatus, it was not likely to produce fundamental changes in the character of the regime, nor was there reason to believe that Gierek was personally committed to make such changes. Having resolved the crisis of succession and attained personal rule, he apparently aimed at achieving another "small stabilization," like Gomulka's of 1956, but on a new and more durable basis.

The outcome of the 1970 disturbances revealed once more that means were available to the peoples of Communist states to change their rulers, though the methods had serious limitations. They were costly and dangerous, uncertain in their consequences, and better suited to remove an unsatisfactory ruler than to install an acceptable one. By their strikes and demonstrations, the Polish workers, without active support from any other major social group, did effect an immediate change in the Polish leadership and, by continuing pressures over a number of weeks, a subsequent change in the government's economic policies—changes that were as sweeping as those brought about by electoral politics in democratic countries. Yet it is questionable that they would have succeeded if there had not been, inside the Communist Party, an alternative leadership ready to oust the entrenched but discredited incumbent administration. To date there have been only two successes comparable to that of the Polish workers in achieving their *political* objectives in 1970: [19] in Budapest in October 1956, when students and young workers succeeded in their aims of forcing Erno Gero from power and of bringing Imre

[19] The workers in Communist states have had more success in using strikes and demonstrations to get redress of their *economic* grievances: in Pilsen, Czechoslovakia (May 1953); in East Berlin (June 1953); in Poznan, Poland (June 1956); and of course in the Baltic ports of Poland in December 1970.

Nagy into the leadership (Nagy of course shortly afterward was arrested); and the Polish workers' demonstrations in Poznan and Warsaw (in June and October 1956) which induced Ochab to resign in favor of Gomulka.

Strikes and demonstrations are hardly a satisfactory substitute for elections as far as workers are concerned, and the cost in blood and wealth may yet make Communist leaders ponder the question asked of Edward Gierek by a workers' delegate: Was it "necessary to shed blood to change the Central Committee and the government?" [20]

[20] *Problems of Communism,* September–October, 1972, p. 4.

9

East Germany's Imposed Succession (1971)

Six months after Gomulka's ouster in December 1970, Ulbricht gave up power in Berlin.[1] No clear connection between the two events is discernible, and the circumstances surrounding them were basically different. Gomulka resigned as first secretary only after his position had been gravely weakened by the violent demonstrations of Polish workers; Ulbricht, on the other hand, left office when his position, to all appearances, was strong, so that a plausible (though false) case could be made at the time that he had resigned willingly. Moreover, Ulbricht, having at his disposal great power that he believed secure, had long since selected an heir presumptive, Erich Honecker, who in fact succeeded him as first secretary; Gomulka's power, on the other hand, had been too vulnerable for him to attempt such a selection, and Gierek, the man who eventually succeeded him, was a recognized rival.

[1] In addition to primary sources, this chapter draws upon the following: David Childs, *East Germany* (New York: Praeger, 1969); Welles Hangen, *The Muted Revolution* (New York: Knopf, 1966); Heinz Lippmann, *Honecker and the New Politics of Europe;* Heinz Lippmann, "The Limits of Reform Communism," *Problems of Communism*, May–June, 1970; Peter Ludz, "The SED Leadership in Transition," *ibid.;* Peter Ludz, "Continuity and Change since Ulbricht," *Problems of Communism*, March–April, 1972; Peter Ludz, *The Changing Party Elite in East Germany* (Cambridge, Mass.: MIT Press, 1972); and Jean Edward Smith, *Germany beyond the Wall* (Boston: Little, Brown, 1969).

Ulbricht's position had become strong and secure only in the late fifties, after he had recovered from the de-Stalinization campaign. He saw the need to win Khrushchev's favor, particularly after Khrushchev achieved personal rule in June 1957 by purging "the anti-Party group." Aiming to prove himself a model Khrushchevite, Ulbricht now assiduously emulated Khrushchev's reforms, while carefully shaping them to fit East Germany's circumstances. He even belatedly carried out a limited program of de-Stalinization along the lines previously advocated by Khrushchev and the East German opposition, although he did so only after the erection of the Berlin wall in August 1961 made him sure that he could control the consequences of de-Stalinization. After Khrushchev was removed, Ulbricht adapted East German policy to the style of the new Soviet leadership, although without giving up any of his own power. By reaching an accommodation with Moscow, Ulbricht deprived potential rivals of the hope of outside assistance. This enabled him to deter serious challenges to his position from 1958, when he defeated the Schirdewan-Wollweber faction, until 1971.[2]

Ulbricht's Succession Arrangements

Ulbricht's certainty that his great power was secure led him to go farther than any other Communist leader of Eastern Europe in arranging for a successor. Moreover, his confidence in those arrangements was so great that a decade later, when he left office, they were still in effect. His succession arrangements are a textbook example of how to prepare an orderly succession. He early chose the candidate who was to succeed him, groomed him for the position of heir presumptive, and finally, once his own power was consolidated, delegated important powers to him. (This model procedure, it will be recalled, suffers from a basic flaw: the danger it poses to the power of the ruler.)

[2] Schirdewan was the Party's second secretary; Wollweber headed the political police. See Chapter 4, above, for a discussion of the opposition to Ulbricht stemming from the Twentieth Congress of the Soviet Communist Party.

The heir presumptive, Erich Honecker, was twenty years younger than his mentor. Honecker had not been in exile with Ulbricht in the USSR, but came to his attention only after the war. The son of a Communist and already a professional Party worker while still in his teens, Honecker worked in the underground after the Nazis came to power, was arrested, and spent ten years in prison. Although he had proved his loyalty to the Communist movement, he had a necessarily limited experience of the world when Ulbricht chose him in 1945, over several others, to head the youth organization. Honecker worked effectively in this crucial post and in 1950 was elevated to the politburo as a candidate member. He was so close to Ulbricht politically that Ulbricht's opponents in the politburo, fearing to challenge the leader directly because of Moscow's support, began instead to attack his protégé.

Until this point Honecker's career clearly depended on the support of his patron. Ulbricht's position was weakened, however, after Stalin's death and the outbreak of workers' demonstrations in Berlin. At a meeting of the politburo Honecker's loyalty to his patron was put to the test. At this critical juncture, according to Honecker's former deputy (Heinz Lippmann, now a journalist in the West), Honecker confided to him his uncertainty about whether he should continue to back Ulbricht:

"They're all attacking Walter. He'll probably be defeated. But the worst thing is that I don't know what I should do myself." He sounded weary and depressed; I had never heard him talk like that before. He was in no hurry to go back into the meeting—almost as if he hoped to avoid having to make a decision.[3]

In the end, he stuck by Ulbricht and thus benefited when the Soviet army suppressed the demonstrations and Moscow decided to give Ulbricht its full support.

Two years later, at age forty-three, Honecker was sent to the elite Higher Party School in Moscow for advanced training, in-

[3] Lippmann, *Honecker and the New Politics of Europe*, p. 158; quoted previously in Chapter 4, above.

cluding the study of Marxist-Leninist doctrine, a subject in which
Honecker previously had shown little interest and, according to
his former deputy, was deficient. One of his classmates there was
Alexander Dubcek, who was ten years younger than Honecker
but already at a comparable stage of his career. Both men were
being groomed for top posts in their respective parties, and at
the same time their qualifications for high office doubtless were
being tested by the Soviet leaders.

Honecker returned from Moscow in the fall of 1956, before
completing the two-year course. His new post was Party secretary
for security affairs, which involved supervising the new East
German army as well as the ministry of state security. Honecker's
position was particularly sensitive, since the ministry's head, Ernst
Wollweber, was a key figure in a faction then actively opposed to
Ulbricht. Honecker played a key role in this factional struggle,
which lasted until 1958 and culminated in the defeat of the group,
led by Karl Schirdewan, and its ouster from the politburo.

If previously Ulbricht had favored Honecker for the succession
only provisionally, after he had proved himself in the Schirdewan
affair Ulbricht proceeded to carry his succession arrangements
forward.

[Honecker's] loyal service to Ulbricht was rewarded. In addition to
security, he was given charge of the division Schirdewan had headed:
the division of leading party organizations and SED cadre policy. This
made him the most powerful man in the SED leadership after Ulbricht. . . . From the first he had been careful not to allow any
Politburo member but himself to control the party organizations, the
cadres, and the armed services simultaneously.[4]

To those engaged in East Germany's higher politics it was clear
that Honecker was now the heir presumptive. Subsequently there
were other signs. In 1963 and 1967, for example, after Ulbricht's
presentation of the reports of the central committee to the sixth
and seventh congresses, Honecker gave the reports that were
second in importance: in 1963 on the new Party statute, and in

[4] *Ibid.,* p. 181.

1967 on Party organization. Since reporting on these subjects is normally the prerogative of the second secretary, who is responsible for the Party's organizational work, the view that Honecker was indeed the heir presumptive was strengthened. Rumors to that effect circulated in the West and were given wide credence.

Ulbricht was sixty-five in 1958, which helps to account for his willingness at that time to designate an heir presumptive. Honecker was experienced in Party work and in the leadership of mass organizations, but not in the work of the government. The succession arrangements that Ulbricht made in mid-1958 were maintained thereafter. They were on several counts remarkable. As Ulbricht's first and only heir presumptive, Honecker was assigned a share of the ruler's power that probably was unmatched in any Communist state. Nevertheless, Ulbricht apparently did not set up elaborate machinery to fix its limits. Honecker remained Ulbricht's heir presumptive for over a decade—until Ulbricht resigned from power in 1971—a tenure that has rarely been exceeded in any Communist state.[5]

What accounts for Ulbricht's unusual confidence in Honecker? His loyalty to the movement had of course been demonstrated during a decade of imprisonment under the Nazis, and his personal loyalty to Ulbricht during the acute crisis of June 1953 and the more extended political crisis of 1956 to 1958. Honecker had shown his competence to deal with difficult situations on a number of occasions, not least when he supervised the secret preparations for the erection of the Berlin wall, which caught the Western governments by surprise. Honecker's expressed views on policy questions were close to Ulbricht's and doubtless reflected his strong influence. Neither man was attracted by the liberal trends that periodically emerged in the Party, but both were favorably disposed toward economic reforms that promised increased efficiency. They were resolute in carrying out repressive

[5] Liu Shao-ch'i's tenure as heir to Mao Tse-tung ended in disgrace in 1966, but it apparently had started even before the beginning of the Chinese People's Republic.

measures they believed necessary, like the rapid collectivization of agriculture in 1960, but they were committed to improving the life of the people when this posed no threat to political stability. Granted that Ulbricht's aim was to ensure the continuation of his policies after his departure, it is understandable why he chose Honecker to succeed him and why, with that end in view, he kept him for so long as heir presumptive.

Yet, despite the political closeness of the two men, Ulbricht's succession arrangements clearly involved certain risks. First, there was a danger that Honecker might arrogate to himself even greater power than Ulbricht had delegated to him or wanted him to have. Ulbricht's method of dealing with this problem contrasts with that of Khrushchev. Khrushchev circumscribed the power of the heir presumptive by opposing to him a number of rivals, particularly an archrival, or counterheir.[6] At the same time, Khrushchev tried to prepare the heir presumptive and even, in some measure, the counterheir for the exercise of rule. The Soviet heir presumptive in the late fifties and early sixties, Frol Kozlov, whose entire career had been in the Party apparatus, was assigned to the post of deputy chairman in the council of ministers for several years, presumably in order to broaden his political experience. Leonid Brezhnev, who during these years was the counterheir, was removed from the Party apparatus for a time to serve as head of state. Ulbricht, on the other hand, since he did not balance Honecker's *power* with that of strong rivals, evidently employed other means to safeguard his own position: he severely limited Honecker's *preparation for rule*. Throughout his quarter-century of association with Ulbricht, Honecker was given almost no experience of economic administration or of foreign affairs, except in dealing with other Communist states.[7] Similarly, he had

[6] Gheorghiu-Dej in Romania acted similarly: having established Ceausescu as the heir presumptive, he conferred on Draghici the powers of a counterheir.

[7] Here Honecker's experience was extensive. He was a member of the German Democratic Republic's delegations to important meetings of the Communist movement.

almost no experience in the council of ministers or in the council of state. Ulbricht limited Honecker's political experience to the spheres of mass organizational work (with youth and the Party) and of the key levers of power (cadre selection and the supervision of defense and state security agencies). The result, as was presumably Ulbricht's intention, was to lessen Honecker's qualifications for rule, so that others were less likely to see in him an immediate alternative to Ulbricht's own rule and so that Honecker was less tempted to reach out for the leadership prematurely.

Ulbricht not only kept Honecker from direct involvement in economic administration; he also developed a circle of leaders for consultation about, and for administration and supervision of, the economy who were not drawn from the youth organization or the Party apparatus, the breeding ground of Honecker's protégés. These men were well educated and were familiar with modern technology and control techniques. While the chief reason for their promotion to the politburo by Ulbricht doubtless was to take advantage of their special skills and training, it may also have served the purpose of further limiting Honecker's influence in an important area of policy.

Besides granting Honecker great appointive powers, Ulbricht granted him a long tenure as heir presumptive. Consequently, rising young Party officials and ambitious professional leaders saw the need to accommodate themselves to Honecker's future power, making it a factor in careerist calculations. How this affected their relations with Ulbricht is not known, but once Ulbricht was removed, the long period of anticipation probably made it easier for them to accept Honecker as the new Party leader. Similarly, the Soviet leaders' long acquaintance with Honecker (beginning with his residence in Moscow in the mid-fifties) and their long habituation to the notion that he would in time succeed to a ruler's position doubtless made it easier for them to hasten the time of the transfer of power once they saw an advantage in doing so. Considering the stake that so many groups acquired in Honecker's succession, one wonders whether Ulbricht, though he initiated his

arrangements for the succession willingly, may have found with
the passage of time that if he had reason to change them, he
would find it difficult to do so.

Another danger to which Ulbricht's succession arrangements
gave rise was that Honecker might use his position to supplant
Ulbricht by means of a *coup d'état*. Actually, Ulbricht had little to
fear from an independent move by Honecker to seize power. In
no state of the Soviet bloc could a dissident group reasonably
carry out a coup against the existing leadership without having
grounds for belief that the Soviet Union would tolerate its action
and accept the outcome. This was pre-eminently true in East
Germany, where twenty divisions of the Soviet army were stationed to protect Soviet interests. To act against Ulbricht,
Honecker would need virtually explicit Soviet approval. This may
have led Ulbricht to underestimate the threat posed by Honecker
to his own rule, because Moscow seemed unlikely to give its
approval to such a change in leadership. Ulbricht was to learn,
however, that once Moscow found itself at odds with him on a
key issue of policy—particularly one that affected the Soviet
security position in central Europe, such as the terms of a settlement with West Germany—his long established arrangements for
the succession would become a crucial point of vulnerability.

The Transfer of Power

When Ulbricht resigned as first secretary on May 3, 1971, in
favor of Erich Honecker, it was uncertain whether the resignation
was the consummation of his arrangements for an orderly succession or whether he suddenly had been forced from power. At first,
there was a general tendency to assume that the retirement was
voluntary. Ulbricht was almost seventy-eight years old and signs
of aging had been evident in recent months.[8] He had been to the

---

[8] According to Wolfgang Leonhard, it was obvious that Ulbricht had
aged: "One of the last speeches he couldn't read to the end, and he sometimes forgot what he was actually speaking about" ("Ulbricht and His
Successor," *East Europe*, October 1971, p. 19). As recently as his seventy-
fifth birthday, in 1968, Ulbricht had struck observers as robust and vigorous.

USSR for five weeks after February 8, 1971, where he spent his annual vacation. Despite indications that Ulbricht suffered from the defects of his years, evidence soon emerged that he had in fact resigned against his will. For example, the Ulbricht cult expired when he was removed, and his role in creating the East German regime failed to receive due recognition. While overtly he was treated with respect, there were undertones of criticism. Important elements of the general policy which Ulbricht had been preparing for adoption at the forthcoming SED congress were sharply modified, and when the congress met, Ulbricht failed to make an appearance. Finally, four-power negotiations of the occupying powers in West Berlin (the United States, the USSR, France and Britain) suddenly began to make rapid progress shortly after Ulbricht resigned, as though an obstruction had been removed.

The decision to replace Ulbricht seems to have been made during the first twelve days of April 1971, when Ulbricht, Honecker, and other top East German leaders were in Moscow for the Twenty-fourth Party Congress. The delegation arrived on March 29, and Ulbricht, as the representative of the SED, spoke to the congress the following day. The coming change in the leadership may have been signaled by a striking change in the rank-order listing of members of the delegation. It did not directly involve Ulbricht, whose name did not appear, because he failed to participate with the others in the usual political tourism. In *Pravda's* listing of April 3, Honecker's name followed that of Willi Stoph, the chairman of the council of ministers, in accordance with established protocol: the head of government precedes the second secretary of the central committee but follows the first secretary. The order of the two names was reversed, however, on the following day, a change that would have been warranted only if Honecker now occupied the post of first secretary.[9]

When Brezhnev met with the German Democratic Republic

---

[9] Formally, of course, Honecker could not yet have been the first secretary, since only the SED central committee could elect him to the post. In any case, a final decision may not yet have been made.

(GDR) delegation on April 12, it was the third time Ulbricht met with Brezhnev in two months. It is interesting to speculate on Brezhnev's aims and impressions at the two previous meetings (February 8 and March 14).[10] Did he try to influence Ulbricht to soften his position on the terms of a settlement on West Berlin? Did he begin the effort to persuade him of the need to hand over the reins to a younger man? What was his personal judgment about the damage wrought by age to Ulbricht's faculties? Did Ulbricht fight desperately to stay in power, risking the anathema that Communist historiography visits on all who defy the ruling powers; or, recognizing his declining powers and suddenly weary of it all, did he consent numbly and give way? To agree would have been wholly out of character. Since he still had great ambitions for himself and for his regime—ambitions that were jeopardized by his retirement—it seems clear that Ulbricht resigned involuntarily. But how much force still remained at that time in what had once been an overpowering will can only be conjectured. According to one East German source, "He went down fighting, trying to the very last to assert his old authority." [11] Ulbricht himself, in his speech announcing his resignation, observed, "To be frank, my decision has not been easy for me." [12] Perhaps Ulbricht's own recognition of his waning powers was a consideration in his agreement to retire, but if so, there is no reason to suppose that it had much weight in comparison to the external pressures that were brought to bear.

By its very nature, the decision to force Ulbricht's retirement from the post of first secretary was one in which the East German

[10] The Soviet announcement that Brezhnev and Ulbricht had met was curiously worded: "During the talk the unity of views and positions of the central committees of the CPSU and SED on the questions discussed was once more confirmed" (*Pravda,* March 15, 1971). Did Ulbricht's *personal* views no longer need to be taken into account?

[11] *New York Times,* June 22, 1971, p. 2.

[12] Statement to central committee, May 3, 1971; trans. in British Broadcasting Corporation, *Summary of World Broadcasts;* Part II: "Eastern Europe," EE 3675, B4, p. 5, May 5, 1971 (hereafter abbreviated BBC, *Summary*).

people took no part. There is a contradiction between the cult of the leader, which implies that the people's fate depends upon the great talents of the Party's first secretary, and the fact that no attempt is made to provide a constitutional pretense that the people participate in choosing him. Actually, by 1971 the people of East Germany had come to *accept* Ulbricht, if not to esteem him, whereas Honecker was little known.

One of Moscow's aims in removing Ulbricht was to increase its own leverage on the East German leadership—a goal that would not be served by simply replacing Ulbricht with another personal ruler. Moscow needed stability in East Berlin, but preferably a stability based on collective rule, in which Honecker's dominant position, acquired through Soviet assistance, would be balanced by the power of others. A key figure in the new structure as it emerged was Paul Verner, a member of the delegation that was in Moscow when the agreement was reached to replace Ulbricht. Subsequently, after the decision was announced, Verner received Honecker's former position as the second-rank secretary responsible for cadres and security affairs.

Although Verner and Honecker have a simliar background—imprisonment in Nazi camps, work in the youth organization, and membership in the secretariat of the central committee—Verner's record appears to make him more a rival than a simple partner of the new first secretary. As long as Verner retains supervisory responsibility for the regime's coercive forces, Honecker's capacity to aggrandize personal power would seem to have relatively fixed, if broad, limits. In the past, men in comparable positions to Verner's—Zaisser, Wollweber, and Honecker himself—sooner or later found themselves in opposition to the first secretary. Honecker and Verner, together with Willi Stoph, who remained for a time the head of the government, made up a loose triad within the larger collective of the politburo, and this situation probably provided Moscow with the leverage it required.

The fact that all three men—Honecker, Verner, and Stoph—

were in Moscow in April during the Soviet Party congress and
benefited from Ulbricht's replacement suggests that the three
played a role, perhaps jointly, in the maneuvering that forced
him out. Other East German Party leaders may also have been
consulted before the delegation set off for Moscow, although extensive consultations would have alerted Ulbricht to his danger.
If he had learned what was afoot and succeeded in confining the
engagement to the SED, Ulbricht probably would have won a
new victory to set alongside those of 1953 and 1957. Instead, the
small conspiratorial group from his own circle wisely transferred
the battlefield to the Kremlin. The decision to retire Ulbricht from
his position as first secretary, like the earlier decisions to retire
Chervenkov, Rakosi, Gero, Nagy, and Dubcek, almost certainly
was made by a few Russians sitting in Moscow.

Ulbricht's absence from East Germany during seven of the
nine weeks preceding the decision to replace him doubtless made
it easier to carry it out.[13] In the last analysis, attempts to resist
Moscow would have been doomed because of East Germany's
importance to the USSR. If Czechoslovakia was invaded to protect the USSR's communications with East Germany, surely the
large Soviet forces already present in East Germany would have
been used without hesitation to preserve the Soviet position in
East Germany itself. Moreover, serious resistance to Moscow
could only have been based on nationalist feelings in East Germany. To invoke them in a hopeless cause would have made a
shambles of Ulbricht's life work.

In passing, it might be observed that the power to replace the
first secretary—which Moscow has exercised in Bulgaria (1956),
Hungary (1956) and Czechoslovakia (1969), but not in Romania
or Poland (or Yugoslavia or Albania)—has always been available

---

[13] Gero similarly had been out of Hungary for many weeks preceding the
1956 uprising, and this clearly limited his capacity to resist the Soviet decision to remove him. He was as much out of touch with the Party apparatus as with popular sentiment.

to Moscow with respect to East Germany. If it had not been exercised previously it was not because Moscow lacked the means, but because it feared the costs. However dissatisfied Moscow had been at times with Ulbricht, it had been unwilling to unseat him because of concern that the resulting divisions in the leadership might be difficult to overcome, and that these in turn might encourage disaffected groups in the society to create disturbances. By 1971 these concerns had become less weighty: the Berlin wall had made it easier to control popular disaffection; Honecker had emerged as a reliable and dependent leader; Ulbricht's age made it unlikely that he could continue much longer in any event, and his obstruction of Soviet foreign policy gave Moscow a strong incentive to replace him without waiting for the need to arise.

Once Moscow had decided to remove Ulbricht, his fate was sealed. Even so, negotiations apparently were conducted to secure his acquiescence, and the agreement that was reached involved elements of compromise. Ulbricht resigned as first secretary, thus giving up personal rule, but he was allowed to remain as head of state and also became Party chairman. Ulbricht's post, chairman of the *Communist Party* of a state, must be distinguished from Mao Tse-tung's, chairman of the central committee of the Communist Party of a state. As chairman of the whole Party, Ulbricht had the higher-sounding title, but it was largely honorific, as the central committee indicated when it announced on May 3 that it had elected him "Chairman of the SED in honor of his services." Ulbricht's post was not an office of the central committee; the position conferred no authority to act on the committee's behalf and added nothing to what power remained to Ulbricht.

By accepting these terms, presumably worked out in general form while the protagonists were still in Moscow, Ulbricht assumed an obligation to support in public the fiction of a wholly voluntary transfer of power. Usually, when a Communist ruler is forced from power, the formal transfer of authority is not the occasion for elaborate public ceremony; in this instance, the words of both principals, Ulbricht and Honecker, were reported at some length, presumably in an effort to make the fiction credible.

Ulbricht, on the whole, publicly carried out his part of the bargain during the next two months until, in the last hours before the June convocation of the Party congress, the compromise agreement somehow broke down. From the beginning, however, Ulbricht gave some indication of his true feelings. In his resignation speech, he emphasized his reluctance to give up the post: "To be frank, my decision has not been easy for me, having been in this office for two decades." It was made with mature consideration after thorough discussion in the politburo, because "the years are demanding their due." Then, in accordance with his long-standing intention, although surely not at a time or in circumstances of his own choosing, Ulbricht nominated his heir presumptive to succeed him.

I therefore consider that the time has come to deliver this office into younger hands, and I propose that Comrade Erich Honecker be elected First Secretary of the SED Central Committee. . . . I am firmly convinced that our Central Committee and our Politburo will lead the Party, even after approving my proposal at today's session, as firmly and unitedly as until now. The election and the activities of Comrade Erich Honecker as First Secretary . . . will guarantee this. This is the unanimous opinion of the Politburo, and this is also my firm conviction.[14]

Despite this expression of confidence, Ulbricht's review of Honecker's record is largely descriptive of his offices and proven loyalty but is strangely deficient in praise of Honecker's qualities and *accomplishments:*

The Central Committee and the entire Party knows and values Comrade Erich Honecker, who since his earliest youth has fought in the ranks of the revolutionary German workers' movement, who as a leading official has helped to organize the anti-fascist resistance struggle. As we all know, Comrade Erich Honecker has undergone a hard training in the political class struggle against fascism by spending 10

14 BBC, *Summary,* B4, p. 5.

years in the prisons and concentration camps of fascist Germany. Since the unification Congress he had been a member of the Party Executive and of the Central Committee and for over 20 years without interruption he has been a member of the Politburo.

Ulbricht took the occasion to anticipate a criticism of his personal mode of rule, a criticism that had already been made privately, no doubt, and would shortly be made publicly: "Dear Comrades of the Central Committee, on this occasion, I should like to say a few words about the situation in the Party leadership. I think it is no exaggeration to say that during the decades of my activities it has been possible to create a firm, solidly united and truly collective Party leadership. This is true both of the Central Committee and the Politburo." [15] Actually, it was true of neither, as Honecker was to make emphatically clear six weeks later at the Party congress, when he strongly criticized violations of the principle of collective leadership.[16]

On the occasion of Ulbricht's resignation speech, however, Honecker said nothing on the subject. In accepting the post of first secretary, Honecker expressed special thanks to Ulbricht, "under whose leadership I have worked in the Politburo for over two decades." Honecker had worked even more closely with Ulbricht in the Party secretariat, and this remained the organ on which, as first secretary, he had to rely in any attempt to succeed to Ulbricht's full power. In his brief acceptance speech, Honecker went out of his way to elevate the authority of the secretariat, making it the equal, perhaps even the superior, of the politburo: "We can build on the tested collective spirits of all executive bodies of the Party, from the primary organizations to the Central Committee, its Politburo and Secretariat." [17] While understandable in terms of Honecker's political strategy—the classic strategy of a first secretary—this assertion of the secretariat's authority, coming at the very moment of Honecker's accession to office, demonstrated unsual boldness and self-confidence. To some ex-

15 *Ibid.*, B, p. 5.   16 See below, pp. 208–209.
17 BBC, *Summary*, B, p. 7.

tent, this confidence was borne out when the Party congress met the following month: staff members of the secretariat were favored in promotions to the central committee, while three of the four promotions to the politburo went to secretaries.

Ulbricht says he resigned because of his age. Age is a disability that ordinarily does not appear suddenly, yet Ulbricht's retirement required the plenum to alter radically the agenda for the June meeting of the Party congress. It was to be expected that Honecker, as the new first secretary, rather than Ulbricht, would give the major report to the congress; but besides changing the speaker, the plenum also changed the nature of his report, thereby changing the theme and character of the congress. The ideological emphasis of the report Ulbricht was scheduled to give, "The Fully Developed Social System of Socialism in the 1970's," was absent from the speech Honecker actually gave, which was the usual "accountability report" of the central committee on its activities since the preceding congress. The other reports originally scheduled also stressed ideology and were similarly replaced by the customary reports, one on Party affairs and one on the forthcoming economic plan. The change in theme reflected not only the technical and nonideological orientation of the new leadership but also its disagreement with the tendency of Ulbricht's ideological innovations.

Ulbricht for some time had been emphasizing the special character of the East German road to socialism. Because Germany, unlike Russia, was already "a highly developed industrial country" when it undertook the transition to socialism, it had to take "a different course" from that of the USSR.[18] He therefore offered East Germany as a model for the developed countries of Western Europe. Moreover, Ulbricht claimed that "in the course of shaping the developed social system of socialism, certain

[18] Speech by Ulbricht on the hundredth anniversary of Lenin's birthday, *Neues Deutschland*, April 18, 1970; trans. in Foreign Broadcast Information Service (hereafter abbreviated FBIS), *Eastern Europe*, No. 85 (May 1, 1970), Supplement 10, pp. 59ff.

elements of the transition to communism already are being created." [19] While such claims reflected favorably on Ulbricht's record of accomplishment as the long-time ruler of the East German state, they imposed upon his heirs goals and constraints on policy that they evidently did not welcome. Furthermore, these claims were a source of annoyance to the Russians. The claims were little in evidence when the Eighth Congress met in June, and Honecker made a point of retreating from Ulbricht's ideological pronouncements:

Certainly, some time will elapse and much remains to be done before we can say that socialism has been completed in the GDR. This requires a higher level of productive forces, socialist social relations, and socialist consciousness of the people. Each 5-year plan period and party congress brings us nearer and nearer to this goal. At the eighth party congress, too, we can report significant progress.[20]

The implication was that no special stage had been reached in East Germany's progress toward socialism and communism; hence there had been no valid reason for the congress' original agenda—with its strong ideological overtones—which the central committee had adopted in January at Ulbricht's prompting.

By the time the congress met on Tuesday, June 15, 1971, Ulbricht's relations with the new leadership had obviously worsened. On the preceding day, Ulbricht had continued to perform his role of the retiring Party leader engaged in easing the transfer of power to younger hands. He appeared at the airport for several hours, seemingly vigorous and in good health, to greet foreign delegations arriving for the congress. When the congress convened, however, it was told that Ulbricht was ill and would not appear to deliver his scheduled opening address. This was the first item on the new agenda that had been adopted for the congress by the central committee when Ulbricht resigned. Such

[19] Ulbricht's report to central committee, *Neues Deutschland,* January 30, 1971; in FBIS, *Eastern Europe,* February 5, 1971.

[20] Report of central committee, *Neues Deutschland,* June 16, 1971; in FBIS, *Eastern Europe,* No. 122 (June 24, 1971), Supplement 43, p. 22.

an address was advantageous for the new leadership, since it accorded with the image of orderly succession; but Ulbricht may have understood that his remarks on this portentous occasion would provide an opportunity to express strong personal views in a kind of political testament. Whatever the previous understanding about Ulbricht's opening address, his failure to deliver it was due not to illness but to pique. It was a deliberate rebuff to the leadership, which responded by disseminating a damaging account of Ulbricht's resignation, one that contradicted the official version. This account, including an explanation of why Ulbricht failed to attend the congress, was given to the *New York Times* in a Washington-type "backgrounder" that permitted the use of the information, but without personal attribution.[21]

"Authoritative sources" told David Binder, the resident *Times* correspondent in Berlin, that on the morning of June 15, shortly before the congress was to open, Ulbricht's wife, Lotte, went to the house next door, where Honecker lived, and said to his wife, Margot (herself a leading Party official): "My husband is ill and will not attend the party congress." The top leaders supposed he was only "sick with rage," but after an embarrassed silence of a couple of days they issued a medical bulletin stating that Ulbricht was confined to bed after experiencing "an acute circulatory disturbance." After returning from the airport reception the day before the congress opened, according to Binder's account, Ulbricht had been given the text of the speech he was to deliver at the congress, written by an assistant to Honecker. He apparently found it unacceptable. At the same time, he was given the text of Honecker's report to the congress. He doubtless saw there the long passage which criticized him, under a thin veil of anonymity, for various sins: disregard of the collective, lack of receptiveness to criticism, and the belief that he was infallible. Honecker also alludes to measures that had been taken to correct Ulbricht's errors and to discipline him, thus proving that Ulbricht was not, as he supposed, "entirely out of reach." This remarkable passage warrants quotation at length:

21 *New York Times,* June 22, 1971.

It came to light that the tasks posed by the seventh party congress [1967] required even broader development of internal party democracy. The party insured that the Leninist norms of party life were *not only acknowledged in words but also observed by all.* . . . Collectivity is an indispensable precondition for a realistic tackling of problems, *especially new and complex ones.* Subjectivism, obstinacy, window-dressing, and *disregard of the collective can be combatted* most effectively through the collective action of all leaderships. Such tendencies, *wherever they appear, must be combatted* without compromise. Criticism and self-criticism . . . contribute to the . . . wisdom of the collective and of every individual comrade. . . . But we must admit frankly here that *there are some comrades who have forgotten* how to appreciate the value of criticism and self-criticism. *They consider themselves wiser* than the collective; they do not like constructive contradiction; *they think they are infallible and entirely out of reach.* Such an attitude *must be corrected* through the strength of the collective so as to prevent serious harm to the future development of the respective section. Firm party discipline, as well as *receptiveness to criticism* and open discussion prior to the adoption of resolutions, are part of internal party democracy. . . . This discipline is *the same for all.*[22]

Rather than subject himself in person to such criticism, Ulbricht decided not to be present when it was delivered. As a result, "his" opening address to the congress was *read* for him, just as it had been *written* for him; Ulbricht provided only his name. It is a bland and innocuous speech, unobjectionable in itself, but hardly a fitting farewell from the man who had served Communism his whole life and who had founded and sustained the East German regime for a quarter of a century.

Why did Honecker engage in this extremely sharp criticism of Ulbricht—though without mentioning his name—thereby putting in question the myth of a smooth transfer of power? Once Ulbricht had ended his struggle to retain power and had cooperated in the first phase of its transfer, the myth probably had lost some of its usefulness. Honecker's colleagues doubtless wanted from him a public commitment that he, unlike his predecessor, would subordinate himself to the collective. Ho-

[22] Report of central committee, FBIS, *Eastern Europe*, No. 122 (June 24, 1971), Supplement 43, pp. 50–52; my italics.

necker himself had reason to demonstrate that he stood on his own two feet and was no longer his patron's creature. Besides these political reasons there were probably personal ones that added a strong emotional tinge to action that basically was politically motivated. Honecker owed his political career to Ulbricht; as is well known, such obligations generally do not give rise to simple gratitude but, rather, to mixed emotions, including resentment. Moreover, during the quarter of a century in which Honecker lived in Ulbricht's shadow, any conflict of wills that arose required of Honecker that he give way. Long repressed feelings of ambivalence and hostility doubtless gained expression when Honecker participated in securing Ulbricht's removal, and may even have encouraged him to take the initiative, which entailed serious political risks. Once he succeeded in ousting his mentor, Honecker's feelings of guilt probably required him to justify what he had done by pointing to deficiencies in Ulbricht's political character. Such feelings presumably contributed to the intensity of expression with which Honecker castigated Ulbricht's violations of the principles of collective leadership—an intensity that is in marked contrast to the usual flatness of Honecker's speech. No doubt such complex psychological motives were also involved in Khrushchev's attack on Stalin and in Ceausescu's criticisms of Gheorghiu-Dej, and are factors in the general tendency of Communist leaders to criticize the strong rulers who preceded them.

In the account leaked to the *New York Times,* for which Honecker presumably also bears responsibility, several reasons are given for the unseating of Ulbricht: "First, his attempt to conduct a policy on West Germany that was independent of the Russians; second, his establishment in the last four years of "a personal apparatus above the apparatus of the Central Committee," and third, his insistence on a great leap forward, in the Chinese Communist pattern, skipping the phases prescribed by the Soviet leaders."[23] The initial charge is a reference to Ul-

[23] *New York Times,* June 22, 1971.

bricht's efforts to start a dialogue with the Social Democratic Party in West Germany, both when it was an opposition party and, later, when it was the dominant party in the coalition government. Neither attempt, it appears, was fully coordinated with current Soviet foreign policy. The second charge seems to refer to changes Ulbricht introduced in obscure recesses of the political machinery where the powers of his personal office were articulated with those of the central committee secretariat. Such changes, since they downgraded the central committee's apparatus, in which Honecker had entrenched himself, posed a special threat to Honecker. The third charge is probably based on Ulbricht's boastful contention that in building "a developed social system of socialism" East Germany had succeeded in creating certain elements of the transition to Communism, the highest stage of human society. While the leak to the *New York Times* was manifestly designed to discredit Ulbricht, independent evidence (presented below) exists for at least the first and third charges.

East Germany after Ulbricht

Once Ulbricht resigned, the stalemate that had persisted for some time in the four-power negotiations on Berlin suddenly was broken. The progress that followed culminated in August 1971 in an agreement that was later ratified. While Ulbricht's terms for settling outstanding issues with West Germany, particularly about West Berlin, had made it difficult to reach an agreement, Honecker's publicly expressed position was hardly less intransigent. As far as the negotiations were concerned, the advantage to Moscow of having effected the change in leadership was not so much that Honecker's views were closer to its own, but that he was less able than Ulbricht to make difficulties over them. Ulbricht's entrenched position in the government he had directed for a quarter of a century had made him difficult to control, whereas Honecker, to consolidate his position, necessarily depended on Soviet support. Presumably the agreement by which Moscow unseated Ulbricht required Honecker to subordinate East Germany's interests, as he perceived them, in the terms of a settlement to the overriding Soviet objective of ensuring that there actually was a settlement, with less advantageous terms if necessary.

Even after he became first secretary, Honecker's publicly expressed position on the negotiations (as in his major speech to the Eighth Party Congress in June 1971) retreated little from the one he had taken previously. But he now went to unusual lengths to emphasize East Germany's close relations with the USSR and their identical views on all questions. Moreover, Honecker acknowledged that West Berlin had a special political status, and he wished for a successful conclusion of the four-power talks on West Berlin, on which the overall agreements between West Germany and Poland and between West Germany and the USSR depended.

Berlin was one issue on which Ulbricht apparently had been more unyielding than Honecker, perhaps because Ulbricht still harbored hopes for the ultimate unification of Germany. As recently as 1968 he had introduced into the state constitution the phrase "socialist state of the German nation." Honecker, on the other hand, speaks of "the so-called unity of the German nation." He has repeatedly stressed that the building of socialism in East Germany leads to its increasing divergence from West Germany, to a deepening of the line of demarcation between the two states "in all spheres of social life." [24]

When the congress was first scheduled in January, it was not intended, of course, to come so soon after Honecker was appointed first secretary, but it enabled him to move early to consolidate his position. [25] Honecker's capacity to initiate changes at

[24] Report of the central committee, FBIS, *Eastern Europe*, No. 122 (June 24, 1971), Supplement 43, p. 17.

[25] The fact that the congress could be held on schedule under circumstances radically different from those originally intended and at a time of uncertainty regarding the succession indicates how completely such bodies are controlled by the powers that be, and how limited is the scope for in-

the congress, however, was limited. A purge of Ulbricht's most loyal collaborators was ruled out, since it would have been difficult to replace them without disturbing the balance in the new collective leadership. Moreover, a purge once begun could endanger all the top leaders. Consequently, only one-ninth of the full members in the old central committee were demoted (15 of 131), and only one-seventh in the new central committee were elected for the first time (19 of 135). Nevertheless, of the 15 who were dropped, most were officials in economic management, while of the 19 who were promoted "almost all," according to Peter Ludz, were Party officials.[26] Thus Honecker did succeed in increasing the representation of the Party apparatus—his chief base of power—in the central committee, though only within narrow limits. Heinz Lippmann, Honecker's biographer and former deputy, has reported that more than 50 full members of the central committee are former associates of Honecker (in the youth organization or elsewhere), and has estimated that "well over half" of the central committee are supporters of Honecker. Estimates of this kind, which are based on data about members' careers, necessarily are of uncertain reliability. At best they indicate certain potentialities which might figure in Honecker's calculations if he tried to create an effective organizational basis for personal rule.[27]

As is usual in a Communist succession, the new first secretary found it difficult to pack the politburo with his own supporters. Nevertheless, the central committee elected in June did choose two new full members (out of sixteen): Werner Lamberz and

---

fluence that can be exerted from below. It should be noted, however, that the proceedings were not televised or radio-broadcast live, as had been done at the Seventh Congress in 1967, possibly because the new leadership was uncertain of the delegates' reactions to recent developments (*New Leader*, July 12, 1971, p. 4).

[26] "Continuity and Change since Ulbricht," *Problems of Communism*, March–April, 1972, p. 66.

[27] Lippmann is also of this opinion ("The Limits of Reform Communism," *Problems of Communism*, May–June, 1972, pp. 225–228).

Werner Krolikowski, both young *apparachiks* and, seemingly, supporters of Honecker. In addition, the minister of state security, Erich Mielke, who had worked closely with Honecker in that post since 1957, was elevated to the politburo as a candidate member. On the whole, Honecker's capacity to influence new appointments to the top Party bodies at the time of the congress was impressive, but they were too few to give him decisive control over the making of policy.

Honecker had greater freedom to effect changes within the Party apparatus. Of the fifteen provincial first secretaries, six were replaced in the first months of Honecker's tenure as first secretary; at least four of the new men had previously been his close associates: Konrad Naumann (East Berlin); Horst Schumann (Leipzig); Werner Felfe (Halle), and Hans-Joachim Hertwig (Frankfurt). His hold on the central committee staff, which had been substantial even under Ulbricht, was strengthened. The key departments formerly supervised by him— leading Party organizations, cadres, and security affairs—continued to be headed by men he had appointed, and close associates of earlier times headed the departments concerned with mass organizations.[28]

At the time of the congress, Honecker still had no important state or government office. The way in which this deficiency was remedied provided a measure of Honecker's capacity to acquire new positions of authority. When the *Volkskammer* (parliament) met on June 24, shortly after the congress, Honecker was given the less important of Ulbricht's two state posts, that of chairman of the national defense council. While the effective powers of the defense council are unclear, constitutionally it is subordinate to both the council of ministers and the council of state. Ulbricht remained chairman of the council of state, although "official sources" had predicted in June 1971 that, after the parliamentary elections, he would be replaced.[29] The failure to oust him may have been due to the efforts of Honecker's opponents.

[28] *Ibid.*, pp. 226ff.   [29] *New York Times,* June 25, 1971.

If Ulbricht had been replaced as head of state, Honecker might have sought to assume the post himself or, alternatively, to transfer Stoph into it, thereby creating a vacancy at the head of the government which Honecker could try to fill with one of his own partisans. Ulbricht's continued presence in the leadership, though expedient for preserving the political balance, probably was a source of embarrassment to his former lieutenants, who for so long had been obliged to practice the rites of his cult. Ulbricht's capacity to use his office as a base of power or influence was limited, however, by the removal of his long-time associate, Otto Gotsche, from the post of council secretary.

While Ulbricht continued as head of state with greatly diminished authority, Willi Stoph, as head of the government, increased his already considerable authority over the state bureaucracy and the economy. This was partly because the so-called technocrats, men like Gunter Mittag and Werner Jarnowinsky, though they remained in the party Secretariat, lost some of their authority over the economy to the council of ministers, and to Stoph as its chairman. Honecker's relationship to Stoph in this period resembled Brezhnev's to Alexei Kosygin, in that both heads of government had important spheres of responsibility, particularly in industrial administration, that were not fully controlled by the first secretary. Honecker's problem was more severe than Brezhnev's, for he had less experience in industrial administration, and the man Honecker had to deal with, Willi Stoph, unlike Kosygin, had extensive experience in security and Party affairs.

Even if the personal rivalry between Honecker and Stoph was not acute, the situation in which they found themselves created tension between them. Stoph's position at the head of the government, together with Paul Verner's as secretary for cadres and security affairs, limited Honecker's capacity to arrogate personal power. The three men did not constitute a ruling triumvirate, since Honecker's power considerably outweighed Stoph's and Verner's, and even the three together lacked decisive power.

Nevertheless, to strengthen his position within the collective leadership, Honecker would have to replace Stoph and Verner by men more amenable to his influence.

Honecker made an early move against Stoph in May 1971 by appointing Horst Sindermann, a rising Party official, as Stoph's first deputy chairman. This had the effect of limiting Stoph's scope for independent action and providing a suitable candidate for his office when the time came to remove Stoph. Honecker's opportunity came two years later when Ulbricht died, and Stoph was "elevated" to Ulbricht's former office of head of the state council, whose importance had declined after its incumbent lost the top Party post. Stoph, having acquired this eminent, but not very powerful, position, had to give up the post of government head. His replacement, as expected, was Horst Sindermann, who apparently owed his appointment to Honecker and could exercise the powers of his new office less freely than Stoph had. Both appointments were approved by the People's Chamber after Sindermann and Stoph had been nominated to the new posts by Honecker. During the proceedings, which were televised, Stoph appeared drawn and grim. Earlier in the year, he had disappeared from public view for extended periods, the official reason being that he needed rest cures because of bad health.[30]

Honecker's ability to reduce Stoph's power indicated how powerful he had become within the collective leadership. The durability of that mode of rule in East Germany was problematic. Continued rule by a collective leadership depended on a number of factors, including the capacities and ambitions of Honecker and his rivals for leadership; the performance of the economy in maintaining growth and in satisfying the people's demands for consumer goods; the effect on the East German people of increased contacts with West Germany; and, finally, what might be decisive, Soviet estimates of whether it was preferable to deal with a collective leadership, like the present one, or with Honecker as a personal ruler.

[30] *New York Times,* October 4, 1971.

Why was the transfer of Ulbricht's power to the collective leadership achieved without disruption and in a relatively orderly fashion? The chief reason is the USSR's special position of hegemony in East Germany, a position that the USSR *requires* because of East Germany's pre-eminent strategic and economic importance, and which it *guarantees* by the presence of twenty Soviet army divisions. The SED has known considerable factional struggle in the quarter century of its existence, but the powerful Soviet presence has helped to prevent it from getting out of hand. Ulbricht's political mastery doubtless contributed importantly to the reduced turbulence of East German politics, particularly after 1958, when he established unchallenged personal rule; but the USSR and its twenty divisions have also been great stabilizers, most notably in the fifties and again in the seventies.

Nationalism has at various times galvanized domestic politics in most of the Communist states of Eastern Europe, giving rise to deep factional splits and serious political conflicts, but it has not yet done so in the German Democratic Republic, where *East German* nationalism is probably too weak to have a major effect and *German* nationalism has seemed too dangerous to be unleashed. Since the leadership's hold on the republic's people remained questionable (hence Honecker's preoccupation with the "demarcation" [*Abgrenzung*] of the two states in Germany and his extreme hostility to social democracy) and since, after May 1971, East Germany also lacked an established personal ruler, it had to rely heavily on Soviet support. This dependence was an added source of Moscow's power to exert leverage on East German politics, which it used to smooth the transfer of Ulbricht's power.

A second key factor limiting conflict in the top leadership was its own recognition of the dangers it faced. East Germany is the only Communist state that must compete with a democratic state whose people are of the same nation. Despite the regime's economic successes and its gains in winning international acceptance, it remains vulnerable to popular disaffection arising from the lag between its living standards and West Germany's and from the continuing division of Germany. Because of their concern about popular disaffection, the East German leaders have good reason to maintain a common front; to that end, they, like the leaders in other Communist states, have demonstrated a capacity to limit their mutual political conflict.[31]

Another reason for East Germany's ability to limit the struggle for succession is the substantial power attached to the office of the first secretary. Just as Ulbricht's personal power waned rapidly once he was removed from the post, so did Honecker's expand from the moment he occupied it, though to a point far short of that previously exercised by Ulbricht. As this study repeatedly has had occasion to stress, the powers accessible to the head of the Secretariat, while they do not guarantee personal rule, give an important measure of stability to the system which it otherwise would lack.

Finally, Ulbricht's long-standing succession arrangements, ironically, helped to ease the transfer of his power and to stabilize the political situation afterwards. Honecker's tacit designation as heir presumptive made it easier for others to accept him as the leading figure in the post-Ulbricht collective leadership. Moreover, having long since been responsible for personnel appointments, Honecker had placed many former associates in key positions and thus acquired some claim on their allegiance, at least in the short run. This enabled him to exercise considerable power in the party apparatus, and to exert influence in the other institutions as well. At the crucial moment of succession, Honecker's exposed position as heir presumptive might have led rival candidates to combine against him, but the danger was in some measure reduced by their need to form a combination against Ulbricht in order to remove him.

[31] The limits to struggle among the leaders set by their common ends have on occasion broken down. This has happened for two distinct reasons: (1) some of the leaders have associated themselves with popular demands; (2) some of the leaders have associated themselves with demands made by the Soviet leadership.

Ulbricht, like Khrushchev earlier, presumably had mixed feelings about the outcome of his succession arrangements. Each man could derive satisfaction from the fact that his Party office was transferred in orderly fashion to the heir he intended, although the transfer was neither at a time nor in circumstances of his own choosing. (A good design for an orderly transfer of power in Communist states, it would appear, is for the ruler to commit himself to a set of succession arrangements, and for the heir presumptive to use the advantageous position he has thereby acquired to oust the ruler.) Once Ulbricht and Khrushchev were removed, not only did their personal cults cease to exist, thus exposing their factitious character, but both men were also subjected to implicit criticism, even ridicule. On the whole, Ulbricht certainly fared much the better of the two. Although Ulbricht, when he resigned, was eight years older than Khrushchev had been in 1964, he was allowed to remain as head of the council of state and was also awarded the honorific post of chairman of the SED. His eightieth birthday, on June 30, 1973, it is true, received little notice, but when he died a month later (August 1) of a stroke, he at least was given an honorable burial—an act of homage which Khrushchev's colleagues denied him. Each man could complain that his successor had modified or discarded ideological innovations, institutions, and policies that he had originated. Perhaps the saddest consequence for each was the discovery that he was dispensable.

PART III

SUCCESSION ARRANGEMENTS OUTSIDE THE SOVIET BLOC

10

Tito's Succession Arrangements

The succession arrangements so far discussed have followed a single basic pattern: the personal ruler concentrates an unusual amount of power in the hands of one of his deputies, a strongly entrenched figure in the central Party apparatus, whom he intends to succeed him. This method, which Stalin first employed, with extreme caution, in the USSR, has subsequently been widely used in other states of the Soviet bloc. Even outside the bloc, the initial succession arrangements of Tito and Mao Tse-tung were also based on this model. After a time, however, both men abrogated the arrangements they had made previously.[1] They abandoned the idea of a single heir presumptive, and began to experiment instead with arrangements based on a balancing principle, in which factional groups, generations, geographic regions and institutions were set against each other in order to make it difficult, even in the succession, for any single individual or group to become dominant.

Tito's personal domination of the Communist regime in Yugoslavia from its inception until the present has been unmatched in

---

[1] De Gaulle, on the other hand, was unable to alter his arrangements for the succession: though he deprived Pompidou of his status as heir presumptive, he was unable to prevent him from succeeding to the presidency.

any Communist state.[2] As a result, the question of succession has strongly colored Yugoslav politics almost from the beginning. Only in Yugoslavia and China has the question been discussed publicly and explicitly, together with the arrangements made to anticipate it.

Josip Broz Tito, though close to the top in the Yugoslav Communist Party, managed to survive Stalin's massive purge of the Communist parties of Eastern Europe (1937–1939) and to emerge as the new general secretary. He was given the task of co-opting a new leadership, drawn of necessity from native, inexperienced Yugoslavs, to replace the Moscow-based, Comintern-trained leaders whom, ironically, Stalin had destroyed in his efforts to ensure the reliability of the Yugoslav Communist Party. Stalin thus enabled Tito to create a new party, which passed out of Stalin's control in 1941 when the Germans invaded Yugoslavia. It was eventually dominated by one man, a remarkable leader whom Stalin did not really understand when he chose him to lead the Party and whom he later grossly misjudged. Because

[2] This chapter, in addition to primary sources, draws upon the following: Phyllis Auty, *Tito* (New York: McGraw-Hill, 1970); R. V. Burks, *The National Problem and the Future of Yugoslavia* (Santa Monica, Calif.: Rand Corporation, 1971); Milorad M. Drashkovitch, "Succession and the Charismatic Leader in Yugoslavia," *International Affairs* (New York), No. 1 (1964), 54–66; George Hoffman and Fred Warner Neal, *Yugoslavia and the New Communism* (New York: Twentieth Century Fund, 1962); Paul Lendvai, *Eagles in Cobwebs;* Viktor Meier, "Yugoslav Communism," in William Griffith, ed., *Communism in Europe,* Vol. I; Fred Warner Neal, *Titoism in Action* (Los Angeles: University of California Press, 1958); Paul Shoup, *Communism and the Yugoslav National Question* (New York: Columbia University Press, 1968); Paul Shoup, "The National Question in Yugoslavia," *Problems of Communism,* January–February 1972; Josip Broz Tito, *Selected Speeches and Articles* (Zagreb, Yugoslavia: Naprijed, 1963); Wayne S. Vucinich, ed., *Contemporary Yugoslavia* (Los Angeles: University of California Press, 1969); M. George Zaninovich, *The Development of Social Yugoslavia* (Baltimore: Johns Hopkins Press, 1968); and Gary Wolfe, "The Tito Succession after Rankovic," research paper (Cornell University, 1970), and Stephen Sestanovich, "Tito's Succession Arrangements," research paper (Cornell University, 1972).

Tito's successes in leading the Party to power are in marked contrast with the Party's abysmal failures till then, Tito has no peers or rivals in the Yugoslav Communist movement.

The Communist Party won its sovereign role in Yugoslav politics by its leadership of the partisan war against the German occupation and by its effective struggle against rival, narrowly based ethnic movements during the war years. It not only captured Yugoslav nationalism, as the Chinese Communist Party captured Chinese nationalism, but in a measure it helped create a new national sentiment which till then had largely been attached to the component nations of the Yugoslav state: Serbian, Croatian, Slovenian, and so forth. Yugoslavia was created only in 1919, and Serbian hegemony was the chief integrative principle between the two world wars. The German occupation deepened national animosities, resulting in the killing of many thousands of Serbs at the hands of the Ustashi—Croatian nationalists—and in extensive reprisals against the Croats. The Communist Party, as the only effective national organization, provided the hard core of leadership to the partisan resistance forces and won broad support during the war. In order to broaden the social basis of opposition to the Germans the Communist Party was, however, kept submerged during the war years while the "national front" became the embodiment of Yugoslav nationalism. Consequently, it was Tito personally, the symbol of national resistance to the Germans, rather than the Communist Party, that came to stand for the Yugoslav state.

After the war, the Communist Party helped to unify the country by its tight internal discipline and centralized administration. The struggle against Stalin and the Cominform after 1948 provided a new ground for allegiance to the Yugoslav state. Again Tito, even more than the Party, embodied the national resistance to the country's external enemies. To this day, popular attachment to Yugoslavia may be weaker than ethnic loyalties, and since much of the *national* sentiment is linked to Tito personally, his passing is likely to produce a deep crisis, not only in the Communist Party (since 1952 called the League of Communists), but also in the state itself.

The core of the Yugoslav leadership took form early in the resistance, consisting of Tito and three close followers: Edvard Kardelj, Aleksandar Rankovic, and Milovan Djilas. Tito, the senior figure, was called by the others *stari* (the old man), and was actually about twenty years older than the others in his circle.[3] In a sense, the succession problem first arose in Yugoslavia, as in China, during the war period, when Mao and Tito, still in their early fifties, were special targets of the occupation authorities.

After the Cominform expelled Yugoslavia, in 1948, the question of succession was posed once more, this time in an acute form, since a key Soviet objective was the replacement of Tito. He was several times invited to the Soviet Union for consultations, but refused to go; subsequently, Dimitrov, Gottwald, and Bierut died or became mortally ill while on visits to the USSR. Moscow's candidate to succeed Tito if it was successful in removing him was Andrija Hebrang, a top figure in the Party since the thirties. Hebrang had several times clashed with Tito. He was expelled from the politburo in 1946, although he retained important economic posts. At the outset of the dispute with Moscow, Hebrang had been arrested.

Tito's intended heir at this time is not known; it is doubtful, in any case, that any other single leader could have led the Party in its opposition to Stalin. Moscow concentrated its attacks on Tito, Kardelj, Rankovic, and Djilas, as the chief figures in the leadership. If Tito had been eliminated, the three others might initially have constituted a triumvirate, although of doubtful durability.

[3] Moshe Pijade, a fourth key member of Tito's personal circle, was Tito's contemporary and one-time mentor. He was less powerful than the others and ineligible as a candidate for the succession by reason of his age, ethnic origin (Jewish), and the fact that he was more an ideologist than an administrator or Party organizer.

Fortunately for the country, such a triumvirate was never put to the test.

Djilas and Rankovic were Tito's key deputies in the Party during these years; Rankovic specialized in organization and internal security (he was also head of the political police), Djilas in propaganda. Kardelj, the third senior deputy, concentrated on foreign affairs and supervision of the government bureaucracy. Some Western observers believed that Djilas was Tito's particular favorite among his lieutenants and was meant to succeed him.[4] Djilas' increasingly open criticism of the Communist bureaucracy's role and privileges, however, finally provoked Tito to take action against him. Djilas was expelled from all his posts in early 1954, leaving Kardelj and Rankovic to confront each other. The two men embodied opposing political views: Kardelj was a strong advocate of reforms aimed at decentralization and reduced state control and was wary of close relations with the USSR; Rankovic, a Serbian centralist and long-time security official, tended to be conservative, favoring the preservation of the established institutions, and welcomed closer relations with the USSR.

Tito seemed deliberately to maintain a balance between Kardelj and Rankovic, at least during the middle fifties. In the difficult months of 1957, when attempts were being made to define Yugoslavia's relationship to the Communist camp, Tito was careful on two occasions (in June and in November) to send both Kardelj and Rankovic to Moscow to conduct negotiations. Similarly, after Tito purged Djilas, he replaced him as secretary with Kardelj, who was charged with supervising Party work as Tito's deputy alongside Rankovic. Though not manifestly hostile to each other, the two men were led by this arrangement and by their divergent policy orientations to vie with each other to in-

[4] The evidence—chiefly Djilas' prominent role at the Sixth Party Congress (1952) and his state office of vice president—seems insufficient to warrant this judgment.

fluence Tito. Rankovic and Kardelj may also have believed it necessary to maneuver for position in the event of an early succession, although Tito, in his mid-sixties, was certainly robust and active.

Despite his vigor, Tito, like Mao at that time in China, seemed to withdraw further from the day-to-day administration of affairs. Both men evidently enjoyed the exercise of power on the grand scale: not making the political machine run, but fixing it when it was not running properly and anticipating things that might go wrong with it. Both enjoyed political activity and were concerned about the well-being of those subject to their power. They would not willingly give up power, but neither would they spend all their waking hours working at politics. Their solution was a mode of rule, which seemed to satisfy the personal needs of both men, that may be termed *interventionism*. Each tended to let political affairs take an independent course until he became dissatisfied with their tendency and interfered to change the direction of events. They not only arbitrated disagreements among their lieutenants, but also intervened to change the political structures through which their lieutenants governed. The two aging rulers had already proved themselves before history, had suffered long years for a transcendent cause, and perhaps now felt entitled to concentrate on the public action of greatest interest to themselves. For Mao, the activity was moving among the people so that he learned what was in their minds and could determine what was needed to alter the state of their consciousness. Tito, on the other hand, liked to move in the world of diplomacy, to have personal encounters with great statesmen. Tito's interventions inside Yugoslavia, at least until the seventies, were designed to preserve and improve the existing system: he dealt with perturbations by initiating necessary reforms, overcame friction and resistance by limited purges, and balanced opposing forces to prevent excessive shifts to left or right. On the other hand, Mao's interventions aimed at recovering revolutionary momentum by stimulating the masses to attack the powers and privileges of the official class. Besides concentrating on their special public concerns, both men felt entitled in their later years to indulge their *private* inclinations. Mao's private pleasures were not conspicuous, although they apparently included reading the Chinese classics. Tito, inclined to the enjoyment of luxury and easy living, at least after the immediate postwar years, made no effort to hide the fact that he was living the good life.

Because Tito had withdrawn a considerable distance from day-to-day affairs by the early sixties, it is all the more surprising that he failed to protect his position by continuing to maintain a balance between Rankovic and Kardelj. Instead, he allowed Rankovic to accumulate disproportionate power. Rankovic began with a significant advantage because of his long-standing connection with the political police (the UDBA). Rankovic had created that organization during the war of resistance against the Germans and the accompanying civil war, had used it to destroy the regime's domestic opponents after the war, and in 1948 had turned this powerful weapon against Cominform agents who sought to undermine Tito's rule. In fighting these numerous perils the UDBA waxed strong. Its single master for a quarter of a century was Aleksandar Rankovic. (The fear inspired by the head of the political police can of course be a source of weakness as well as of strength.) Rankovic was also the organization secretary in the late fifties, and in January 1963 he was appointed head of the new organizational-political secretariat of the central committee. Rankovic used information obtained from intelligence activities and the prerogatives derived from his responsibility for cadre appointments to fashion a powerful machine. His chief territorial base was Serbia, and since Serbs dominated the political police, Rankovic's accumulation of power was feared by many because it threatened to impose on Yugoslavia a new form of Serbian hegemony. Rankovic's success in shifting the balance that had existed previously between himself and Kardelj probably was made easier by the weakness of his opponent. Though he is highly intelligent, Kardelj seems to lack

Rankovic's forceful character and driving ambition. More surprising than the easy victory Rankovic achieved in the competition for power is the fact that Tito crowned his success by constitutional and political measures that clearly established Rankovic as his heir presumptive.

Rankovic was formally established as Tito's successor in the
spring of 1963. There is evidence that initially this honor may
have been intended for Kardelj. The preliminary draft of the constitution (authored mainly by Kardelj) designated the chairman
of the federal assembly (Kardelj was the incumbent) to perform
the duties of the president if he was absent or disabled. However, the constitution that was adopted created a new office, that
of vice president of the republic, who was authorized to deputize
for the president; shortly afterward Rankovic was elected to this
post. Nothing is known of why the switch was made. Rankovic's
tenure as heir presumptive was narrowly limited by the provision
that the vice president could serve only one term. Constitutionally, therefore, he could remain in the line of succession to the
head of state only until 1967. The practical significance of this
limitation may not have been great, since constitutional provi-
sions are hardly sacred in Communist states. Moreover, the state
presidency was not necessarily the true medium of succession to
rule. For example, after his term as vice president ended in 1967,
Rankovic's status as heir presumptive could have been renewed
by making him Tito's sole deputy in the Party. What mattered
was Tito's *intention,* and Tito had made it clear for all to see, including Rankovic, that his position as heir presumptive was pro-
visional. The pressure on Rankovic to conform to Tito's expectations during this four-year tenure of office was severe, yet before
his term was up Rankovic's efforts to consolidate his position had
provoked Tito into purging him from the leadership. The curse
of ambition that sometimes lies upon the heir presumptive—
which later brought down Lin Piao—now claimed Rankovic as
its victim. Of course, the eminent position can also confer bless-

ings, such as Ceausescu and Honecker were able to enjoy, but these eluded Rankovic.

The precise circumstances that led Tito to intervene against Rankovic in June 1966 emerged suddenly, but his dissatisfaction with the political situation had been growing for some time. Resistance within the leadership to the Party's policies and to Tito's commands had been apparent for several years and on at least one occasion, in February 1962, had led to Tito's forceful intervention. Yet such resistance continued and was considerably heightened after the enactment in 1965 of economic reforms. Tito spoke of the need to intervene to the central committee plenum that met in July 1966 to consider the Rankovic affair: "And now it has become clear . . . why we have not been able to carry out the decisions which we adopted at Plenums and Congresses, especially at the Eighth Congress [1964]. There followed some sort of stagnation, somehow things failed to run. The decisions were excellent, the people espoused them, rejoiced over them, our working people were happy. . . . Yet, things failed to run." [5] The inefficiencies and friction encountered in the working of the political system, though perceived and recognized as important, had not been looked into.

In rule based on interventionism timing is crucial. However, the signals communicating the need for intervention often fail to reach the intensity required to compel an inattentive or reluctant ruler to take the action required. Tito later acknowledged that he had been tardy in intervening against Rankovic and the political police: "Approaching an outstanding problem such as the one now being considered by this Plenum, it was not easy to take the decision to tackle it, for one could not say with certainty how this would be reflected on our internal life and develop-

[5] Tito's opening speech, July 1966 plenum of the central committee, *Yugoslav Facts and Views* (New York: Yugoslav Information Center), July 14, 1966, p. 2. See also the *New York Times*, July 3, 1966, for an account of the plenum.

ment. . . . [I am] sorry that I did not take action before, for it is I who am responsible for this, as Secretary General." [6]

It is significant that Tito finally intervened only when his own personal and political domain was invaded. "Eavesdropping on conversations in the homes and offices of leading state and party officials" was one of the chief charges made against Rankovic and the political police at the plenum. Tito was outraged that the political police was turned against "comrades, communists, leaders": "We too are to blame for this . . . , we bear part of the guilt for not having noticed earlier what was actually being done, irrespective of the fact that we trusted our comrades. It took a rather long time for this to hit us like an axe between the eyes." [7] The "axe between the eyes" was the discovery of mechanical listening devices in Tito's own home. Only then did he decide to take action, and he did so at once.

Tito's relations with Rankovic had been characterized by ups and downs before the blowup occurred, as Tito revealed in February 1966 to his old and close associate Svetozar Vukmanovic-Tempo: "Tito told me that relations between him and Rankovic were not good. I was not surprised because I knew that Tito was not satisfied with the work of the organization section of the Central Committee headed by Rankovic." [8] The problem was smoothed over, but not resolved, at the central committee plenum in March, and later that month Rankovic represented Yugoslavia at the Soviet Party Congress. Early in June, however, Tito once again called in Vukmanovic-Tempo:

As soon as I entered Tito's office on Uzicka Street, Tito said: "Somebody is eavesdropping on me!" I was completely shocked and at first I did not know what to say. After having recovered from the initial shock, I asked: "But who would eavesdrop on you?" Tito answered: "Marko [Rankovic] and Ceca [Svetislav Stefanovic]." I reacted spontaneously: "I do not believe this!" Tito however said: "I

[6] Tito's closing address, *Yugoslav Facts and Views*, p. 39.

[7] *Ibid.*, p. 40.

[8] "Memoirs of Svetozar Vukmanovic-Tempo," *Politika* (Belgrade), Nos. 19–21; trans. in RFE, *Yugoslavia*, March 25, 1971, p. 5.

have formed a technical commission which has established that my office has been bugged! Even my bedroom! Concealed microphones had been installed everywhere. . . ! By the way, the bugging devices have also been installed in your house!" [9]

On June 16, Tito convened the executive committee (analogous to the politburo in other Communist states) of the Party central committee and attacked Rankovic for eavesdropping on the top Yugoslav leaders. Rankovic denied the charge but resigned his posts. After a second meeting of the executive committee on June 22, a full report was provided members of the central committee. They assembled on Brioni Island July 1 to discuss the Rankovic affair.

That Tito's succession arrangements were a central question at the plenum is evident even from the edited report that was published. Tito himself only *alluded* to Rankovic's machinations to assure the succession: "What is involved here is a factionist struggle of a group, the struggle for power." [10] Other leaders, however, spoke directly of Rankovic's designs on the succession. One major leader in particular discussed the succession problem at length.

Mijatovic then said that there are grounds for the assertion, when we take various events in recent times, that these stories, intrigues, gossip and conjecture about who will succeed Comrade Tito, were known to Rankovic and that they did not disturb him. "As a political man he must have known the consequences of this, that the bureaucrat and those around him, when they observed this, would get wings and would proceed to cultivate and warm up the idea; the more so when they had a feeling that they had his blessing. And we know how it was in Russia in Lenin's time concerning preparations for his successor. I wonder whether we haven't forgotten some of these things, perhaps become somewhat enraptured over the victory of 1948 against Stalinist bureaucracy and despotism, and in those victories which are great in our social development. Have we not underestimated the phenomenon of bureaucracy?" [The speaker seems

[9] *Ibid.*, p. 5. Mao later allegedly also complained that his conversations had been bugged by his heir presumptive, Lin Piao.

[10] *Yugoslav Facts and Views*, July 14, 1966, p. 3.

here to intimate that Rankovic was a potential Stalin who might have corrupted Tito's revolution as Stalin corrupted Lenin's.]

Referring to the market mentality, the speculation about succession, he said that it was stupid and absurd. "The bureaucrat thinks when he sits in the seat of the President of the Republic that he has immediately obtained the same value as his predecessor. We can say today that the entire League of Communists will answer for all this with confidence in Comrade Tito and in our Central Committee, and that this matter [the succession] will relatively peacefully and much easier and more quickly be settled than some think." [11]

The speakers' boldness on this occasion in discussing Rankovic's ambition to succeed Tito and even the Tito succession problem generally (however unwarranted Mijatovic's confidence in an orderly transfer of power) suggests that even then discussion of the problem was not taboo in the Yugoslav leaders' private deliberations. The reason for publishing remarks made on this occasion presumably was to inform the interested public unobtrusively of what Rankovic was really aiming at.

One official with responsibility for personnel appointments who had worked closely with Rankovic in this capacity since 1962 said that cadre affairs did not go well, "particularly after the adoption of the Constitution"—that is, after Rankovic became vice president of the republic and heir presumptive. "I became more and more convinced that something had vanished from Comrade Marko [Rankovic], some character which had adorned him, and that something else had formed"—presumably an ambition to make his succession to Tito materialize.[12]

Rankovic's response to such allegations was to deny that he had been involved in any moves to improve his prospects for the succession:

I regret, Comrades, this speculation concerning succession, etc. I had no part in this and I think you know that I could not have had. First, because I am in question and I can do only what I have been doing. . . . Incidentally, about myself, I have always thought, and I still do,

[11] Speech of Cvijetin Mijatovic to July 1966 plenum, *ibid.*, p. 23.
[12] Speech of Velimer Stojnic, *ibid.*, p. 35.

that I can only carry out, to a certain extent, perhaps interpret policies and positions, because I am not able to participate in the construction of some policies, except on certain questions, that I am not able to participate on a broad scale in creating policy on certain social questions.[13]

By denying that he possesses the qualifications needed to participate in certain kinds of policy-making (presumably economic policy in particular), Rankovic in effect denied that he is qualified to succeed Tito. But his defense is disingenuous: since he is not qualified to succeed Tito, he could not have connived to do so. His modesty at this juncture does not square well with the fact that he had taken considerable risks to consolidate his position as Tito's heir. Tito revealed his own judgment of the man in a short speech he gave to partisan veterans: "[Old revolutionaries] at a certain period of their lives sometimes become untrue to themselves. It is difficult to assess why such a thing happens. It is not such a simple thing as some people think. I think that the conditions in which a man lives and works can sometimes lead to his betraying himself and embarking upon a road which he should not even contemplate." [14] Presumably the *road* upon which Rankovic had embarked was expected to assure him the succession, and the *conditions* in which he lived and worked involved his possession of great power over the political police and the Serbian Party organization.

Tito's initial error, which he acknowledged, was to permit Rankovic to direct the political police for two decades without supervision. This mistake did not have grave consequences for the regime, however, until Rankovic was given a central place in Tito's succession arrangements. Like Ulbricht, Tito allowed his heir presumptive to accumulate too much power; in both cases it was power that combined control over the political police with responsibility for cadre appointments. But since he was sovereign

13 Speech of Aleksandar Rankovic, *ibid.*, p. 32.
14 Toast by Tito, July 6, 1966, FBIS, *USSR and East Europe*, July 8, 1966, sect. nn, p. 3.

in Yugoslavia, Tito could rectify his error. Ulbricht was not sovereign in East Germany, and his mistake proved fatal to his political career when Moscow intervened on behalf of Erich Honecker, his overly powerful heir and successor. Tito survived his faulty succession arrangements, but they cost him a good deal, and he did not repeat his error.

Though he had been burned in his previous efforts to prepare the succession, Tito did not seek to evade his responsibility. On the contrary, he began to speak openly of the problem and of the need to cope with it.

> We must now bear in mind what we shall leave behind. We know what we should leave behind: a strong socialist country with social relations based on equality and democratic principles, particularly on equality among our nationalities, should be left when we go. We must, of course, pay great attention to this problem, and must assume the responsibility in this respect. . . . Various kinds of friction which appear from time to time, owing more to localist than to nationalist causes, must now be correctly solved by us.[15]

Tito's underestimation of the force of nationalism was to be a source of fresh difficulties in the years ahead.

If Tito had designated a new heir presumptive at this point, no doubt it would have been Edvard Kardelj, the most experienced of Tito's deputies, still in his middle fifties. By then, however, it must have been apparent that he was far better qualified by ability and temperament to be the ruler's deputy than to be the ruler.[16] Kardelj remained the second-rank figure. He was "Tito's first comrade-in-arms" and Yugoslavia's second citizen," and he continued to perform key assignments for Tito, but did not occupy a central position at the regime's key levers of control. Tito ceased to rely on a powerful deputy to act on his behalf while he still governed and to prepare to rule after his departure.

---

[15] *Ibid.*, pp. 2–3.

[16] This may also have been true of Georgi Malenkov and Vyachaslav Molotov, and conceivably may yet prove to be true of Chou En-lai.

Instead, Tito altered his mode of rule and departed from the pattern hitherto followed in all Communist succession arrangements by abandoning its central feature, an heir presumptive.

The Rankovic affair brought about fundamental changes in the structure of politics at the summit and altered the framework in which the succession problem could be resolved. The "personal union" of executive offices in the Party and the state was discouraged by the 1969 Party statute, making it difficult for an heir presumptive or any other would-be successor to win commanding positions in the regime's two main branches. The principle of rotation in office, introduced initially as a limited measure to combat bureaucracy and the formation of a privileged governing class, was extended after the Rankovic affair until it applied to everyone except Tito. The separation and balancing of personal powers, rather than their concentration in an heir presumptive, became the basis for Tito's new succession arrangements.

In the summer of 1970, Tito expressed dissatisfaction with the existing succession arrangements and called for supplementary measures to establish a parallel collective leadership in the state. His speech was delivered without a written text (this is characteristic of Tito) and broadcast live. These circumstances may help to account for the unusual frankness with which Tito spoke of widespread speculation on the problem of his succession, as well as of his own deep concern about it:

Much has been written abroad about Yugoslavia disintegrating when I go. In Yugoslavia, too, there have been many and various conjectures about who will take my place. I believe that there would be a very grave crisis. This is my view, perhaps I am not right, but I think that, if I went, this question of who would then take my place and have these—how shall I put it—competences and these rights which I now have—although even under the Constitution my rights are being infringed . . . We must do everything to ensure that our socialist community of Yugoslavia remains strong regardless of whether it is me or somebody else. We must create an organ which will be an authoritative body and which will have full responsibility. . . . In a word, there should be a collective president in Yugoslavia; that is, the members of this Praesidium should bear full responsibility for what is happening.[17]

Tito's expressed fear of a grave succession crisis implied dissatisfaction with the existing arrangements and a belief, presumably, that the new state presidium would make an orderly succession feasible. As Tito made clear, he envisioned a shift of authority from the Party organs (the Party presidium and its executive bureau) and the government (the federal executive council) to the new state presidium, or presidency (both terms were used). The presidium was a superorgan with vast powers designed to give stability to the political system.[18] The new state

---

[17] Speech to Zagreb (Croatia) Political Aktiv ("representatives of economic and sociopolitical life"), September 24, 1970; in BBC, *Summary*, EE 3490, C2, p. 3.

[18] Tito justified the new organ as follows:

> At the Ninth Congress I proposed [the formation of] a Bureau, the Executive Bureau, which nevertheless has co-operated much better despite the fact that it is not exactly a happy combination. We, the Bureau, are not really very happily composed, nevertheless this Bureau has in the main performed in a united way all the tasks with which it is charged. It has worked at full steam. It holds weekly meetings, and so on. I am not saying that frequent meetings are the best thing, or that a piling up of papers on the table is the best thing. I think that perhaps in this connection the work of the Bureau will also have to be improved in the future, because when that forum at the top is formed—the Presidency—this will be a factor which will be, it is understood, in the full sense of the word a socialist factor, the Presidency; but the League of Communists and the leadership of the League of Communists will be freed from those everyday matters in which they are now engaged.
>
> And you see, the League of Communists and its Bureau and its Praesidium concern themselves with everything that happens in our country, whether in the economy or anywhere else, and . . . people now say that a dualism has already set in in the relations between the Assembly and the leadership of the League of Communists. But this will not then be necessary, because the most prominent people of the League of Communists will be up there, and the leadership of the League, the Praesidium, as it will remain, and the Executive Bureau, and so on, will be able to devote themselves

organ was also to acquire some of the power Tito himself exercised as president of the republic. For this reason, he argued, the initiative for the new measure had to come visibly from him. Otherwise, "someone might think that, if this should now proceed without me, the intention was to remove me. Not so." [19]

The outcome of Tito's initiative, after many months of discussion and bargaining, was a constitutional monstrosity, a new twenty-three-man presidium of the republic that operated alongside Tito's office, president of the republic. Once more, as in the period from 1963 to 1966, the vice president was to deputize when necessary for the president, but he clearly was not an heir presumptive: his powers as deputy were limited, and his period of eligibility to serve as deputy was limited to his one-year tenure as vice president. Complications arose in dealing with such questions as the relationship of the new collective state presidium to the government (the federal executive council) and to the president of the republic, which took ten months to iron out. Finally, on July 29, 1971, the legislature (federal assembly) re-elected Tito to a five-year term as president of the republic, in accordance with the new system. In his acceptance speech Tito explained why he had rejected proposals that he be re-elected president for life and stated his aim in taking office under the new system: "My wish is to stay in this position, in this function,

---

to a greater extent to the problem of education, not only of Communists, and will rather become what is truly required of them: that is, the socialist directing factor of our socialist social development. They will become this to a full extent.

We now concern ourselves with everything. So let the [state] Praesidium deal with that, that is, the decisions of the Assembly which will be passed and its own decisions, because I think that the Praesidium will have to have certain rights to pass certain decisions which will not have to be prolonged through the whole process in the Assembly, for discussion there, and what have you. The Praesidium should be able to take such decisions. And thus [the Executive] will be much better than it is today, and the responsibility will be passed to more people and not just to a small group of people. [*Ibid.*, pp. 4–5]

[19] *Ibid.*, p. 5.

as long as I am certain that I am able to discharge it, or only for a year or so, to help the new highest leading body, that is, the presidency of the Socialist Federal Republic of Yugoslavia, to function completely normally." [20] As it turned out, the powers conferred upon the new state presidency were much fewer than Tito had originally proposed in September 1970, and it was doubtful whether in Tito's absence its normal functioning would provide effective rule.

The result of Tito's continuous reorganizations following the Rankovic affair was a multiplicity of policy-making collective organs: the Party presidium, its executive bureau, the state presidency, and the federal executive committee (i.e., the government). Composed of representatives whose political ties were to the republic or territory from which they were drawn according to a principle of parity, this collection of collectives, with ill-defined jurisdictional boundaries and without the authority of established bodies that have already proved their worth, did not inspire confidence. If they had been allowed to establish their own procedures and to work out accommodations with each other, the organs might have provided the stable framework for the succession that was Tito's goal. Instead, as we shall see, a series of political, social, and economic crises provoked Tito's intermittent interventions, which often bypassed the collective organs, revealing their powerlessness—at least as long as Tito still lived and ruled.

The new system of collective leadership in the Party and in the state, particularly its reliance on the rotation principle, did accomplish some important objectives. As a result of the system, Tito's generation of revolutionary leaders, men born in the 1890's and in the first decade of this century, passed from power while he still lived and ruled. They were replaced in the chief

[20] Speech to federal assembly, July 29, 1971; *ibid.*, EE 3749, C, p. 5. An alternative rendering of this passage has him remain in the post for "a few more years" (*New York Times*, July 30, 1971).

central organs—the Party presidium, the state presidency, and the federal executive council—for the most part by able, educated men born in the second and third decades of this century. These men acquired experience in responsible posts, and, though of diverse nationalities, they also learned to work together, to bargain with each other, and to reach workable agreements on issues that were not too divisive.

But many crucial divisive issues remained. As Tito tried to arrange an orderly transfer of power to a collective leadership that could cope with the country's grave problems, those problems kept erupting, in defiance of Tito's own efforts to deal with them. Having countered Rankovic's efforts to establish Serbian hegemony in 1966, Tito now found himself moving too far in the opposite direction, encouraging republican autonomy. In the spring of 1971 it was already apparent that the Croatian Party leaders, in their efforts to win genuine support from the people, had inadvertently stimulated a resurgence of Croatian nationalism which they were having difficulty in controlling. A by-product was a rise in tension between the Serbian and Croatian leaderships. Tito intervened, but only to smooth things out. His pronouncements since the Rankovic affair on such topics as self-management, democracy, and autonomy apparently had undermined the credibility of his threats to act ruthlessly against persistent opposition. In the fall of 1971, when student demonstrations in Croatia began to get out of hand, Tito intervened again, this time decisively, carrying out a massive purge of the Croatian leadership, student organization, press, and so forth.

The difficulties in Croatia stemmed in good measure from resurgent nationalism, but this was only part of the problem. Just as, in 1966, Tito awoke to find that he had lost control of affairs to Rankovic and the organizations the latter controlled, now he became aware that power had slipped into the hands of republican leaders (many of them relatively liberal), of ethnic organizations, and of professionally trained economists and administrators (the latter became known as the "technocratic danger"). To deal with this diffusion of political power, Tito decided, in late 1971, to extend his purge of liberal political leaders.

Until then the political structure Tito had created after 1966 still remained intact. If a period of tranquillity had followed the turbulent phase of 1971 and early 1972, the various collective organs might finally have begun to operate as they were meant to. For various reasons, however, Tito was not willing to permit a period of tranquillity. One reason was his concern for his own power. There is inevitably a paradox in a ruler's efforts to order his succession. To do so he must possess considerable power, but in the act of arranging the succession a measure of this power necessarily passes out of his hands; the problem worsens with the passage of time. Tito (like Mao) had occasion to complain of his loss of power, not only when his succession arrangements had centered on Rankovic, in the early sixties, but also in the post-Rankovic period, when they were based on institutional dispositions. Institutional succession, more than personal succession, requires an ordered set of expectations, so that jurisdictional lines between the supreme organs are clarified and ambitious leaders enabled to make reasonable decisions regarding the offices they ought to seek. These requirements could be met only if Tito did not disturb, by his interventions, the constitutional order that he was trying to create and if he did not revoke the power he had previously delegated to institutions. Tito, however, was unwilling to meet the necessary conditions. He was caught between two worlds: the old world of his personal rule and the new world of collective leadership that he sought to create. To the extent that the new institutional structure began to take shape, Tito's threats to intervene lost their credibility; consequently, in order to exert his will in particular issues that arose he found it necessary to intervene *in fact*, thereby subverting his own succession arrangements.

The problem Tito faced in the aftermath of the Croatian crisis of 1971 was not only one of reasserting his own power, however.

Tito also had lost confidence in the political structure that had evolved under his direction. He had come to believe it was radically defective, inasmuch as the republics had escaped from control by the center.[21] Moreover, Tito had previously underestimated the dangers to Yugoslav socialism of nationalist sentiment in the increasingly independent republics and of the pursuit of money in the increasingly market-oriented economy; by 1971 he had come to believe that the revolution itself was in jeopardy. He decided that his arrangements for the succession had to be directed toward the preservation of the revolution no less than toward the orderly transfer of power.

Tito's concerns in the early seventies had come to resemble some of those which had led Mao, in the mid-sixties, to initiate China's Cultural Revolution. Like Mao, Tito was disturbed by the growth of a powerful bureaucracy whose members had accumulated privileges based on technical competence and who were increasingly motivated by their own personal interest. Mao believed that the chief source of class privilege in China was the Party apparatus, especially its headquarters, the secretariat of the central committee. Tito, on the other hand, believed that the reason for the growth of bureaucracy and privilege in Yugoslavia, just as for the growth of ethnic nationalism, was the excessive decentralization of the Party apparatus that he himself had instituted after the purge of Rankovic, and in particular the devolution of the powers of the central *apparat* to the Party apparatus in the respective republics. Tito's remedy with respect to institutions, therefore, was almost the opposite of Mao's. Mao undertook in

[21] A key report delivered by Stane Dolanc, the secretary of the executive bureau, to the conference of the League of Communists of Yugoslavia in May 1973 states: "We must admit that in the past few years we in the center have, on many occasions, not been in a position to take timely action, or to react more consistently and comprehensively to various events, precisely because relations in the organization were not clear enough and because the principles of democratic centralism [in particular, the principles of centralism] had begun to be seriously violated" (*Yugoslav Facts and Views*, No. 79 [June 18, 1973], p. 31).

1966 to abolish the central secretariat and to purge its chief figures (T'eng Hsiao-p'ing, P'eng Ch'en, and the heir presumptive, Liu Shao-ch'i); Tito, on the other hand, decided to reconstitute the central *apparat* as a key institution of the Yugoslav regime. His object was to re-establish a strong centralized headquarters that would monitor the implementation of the Party's policy and that would have a decisive voice in all important personnel appointments.

Previously, in the system that emerged following the 1966 purge of Rankovic, the component republics had acquired virtual control over personnel policy. One consequence was that the transfer of cadres between the republics was restricted. National feelings no longer were effectively opposed by a powerful central bureaucracy but, instead, were reinforced by the separate bureaucracies in the republics. By moving to centralize control over policy implementation and personnel appointments after the Croatian crisis of 1971, Tito hoped at once to prevent the growth of factional power based on particular republics and to ensure that socialist morality was not undermined by the pursuit of privilege and personal wealth. Appointments were not to be made only on the basis of technical competence and education; greater weight than before was to be given to social origins, ease of communication with the workers, and ideological commitment.

The new political structure that Tito worked to establish before the Tenth Congress (May 1974) embodied major changes that reversed the direction in which his reforms had been moving the political system and significantly altered their character. The state no longer was held to be in the process of withering away; instead, Tito asserted that the state had to be "strengthened' to enable it to suppress the forces of counterrevolution. The League of Communists, which for a long time had been discouraged from exerting direct control in political and economic affairs, was now told to exercise its powers as "the leading force" in Yugoslav society. The League's executive bureau of the presidium, instead of being freed from "everyday matters," as Tito had promised in

September 1970, began to concern itself with them more than before. A new and powerful official, secretary of the presidium's executive bureau, was appointed to head the central Party apparatus, and he became Tito's chief agent in creating the new system.

Having set this new course, Tito convened the Tenth Party Congress on May 27, 1974, two days after his eighty-second birthday, to sanction it. Tito did not commit himself at the congress to a definite set of succession arrangements, but rather showed a determination to retain personal control of affairs. Shortly before, the National Assembly had chosen Tito president of the republic, and the congress itself chose him president of the League of Communists; in both instances no limit was placed on his tenure of office. Though this may well have been Tito's last congress, he did not behave as though it were. He delivered the main report to the congress himself (in an abbreviated version), for example, thus passing over an opportunity to indicate to the Party and the nation whom he meant to inherit his supreme Party office. As far as one could tell from his actions, Tito's plans did not exclude the possibility that the next Party congress, due to meet in 1978, might be asked to elect him president with unlimited tenure once more, at the age of eighty-six.

As the League of Communists emerged from its Tenth Congress, Tito had still to work out a coherent set of succession arrangements that was congruent with the regime's institutions. Tito's apparent intention of restoring a strong central Party *apparat*, headed by the secretary of the executive bureau, if fully realized, would once more provide a mechanism for the transfer of personal power. Indeed, the incumbent secretary, Stane Dolanc, potentially a personal heir, was able and knowledgeable about Party affairs. He ranked high in the leadership, perhaps second after Edvard Kardelj. However, while Kardelj's revolutionary record and personal closeness to Tito had made him for three decades an authoritative figure near the top of the leadership, Dolanc's power and personal prospects depended on his office.

While the principles of short tenure and rotation in office remained in effect, he could not be sure of occupying the post for long.

In a sense, the two men were complementary figures; Kardelj possessed authority and experience, Dolanc power and personal ambition. A duumvirate, with Kardelj at the head of the state and Dolanc at the head of the Party, might have a certain attraction for Tito as a means of arranging his succession. Such an arrangement, however, might give rise to powerful objections: first, Dolanc, like Kardelj, is a Slovene, and the principle of ethnic balance would be violated by their joint rule; second, Tito still seems committed in his succession arrangements to a collective leadership, not a leadership centered on one or two persons. Nevertheless, within that collective, Kardelj and Dolanc are evidently meant to occupy important places.

In assessing the prospects of the Tito succession it is useful to review the record of his previous succession arrangements. He must be credited with boldness, both in concentrating great power in Rankovic's hands initially and in afterward dispersing power widely to the republics. Tito should also be credited with open-mindedness, which helps to account for the repeated shifts in his attitudes, opinions, and policies since 1952. On the whole, however, Tito's judgments about the forces and tendencies in Yugoslav politics must be faulted. It is hard to believe that he himself is content that he has made the various advances and retreats in his dispositions for the succession that have created such turmoil in Yugoslav politics. In fact, a note of exasperation has been increasingly evident in Tito's offhand remarks on the subject of succession.[22] Certainly his miscalculations have contributed to the resurgence of old passions and to renewed conflict between old enemies, thereby preventing achievement of the unity Tito seeks.

---

[22] "I do not have a lot of time. I am pretty sick of constantly being bothered by these individuals, and therefore I now have to do everything. And I can do it" (interview in *Vjesnik* [Zagreb], October 8, 1972; in RFE, *Yugoslavia*, October 10, 1972).

Tito's efforts to foster constitutionalism may give rise in the succession to jurisdictional conflicts between the embryonic institutions he has created, and to heightened instability stemming from uncertainty about where true power lies. Bargaining between the republics, with factional alignments cutting across ethnic lines, may move the country toward a confederation unless Tito's current efforts at recentralization take hold. The number of men who have held high office in the regime is now large as a result of rotation, and they may see no reason, in the period of succession, to defer to others whom they believe to be no abler than themselves. The result could be fragmentation of power and acute conflict, which, if sufficiently prolonged, could lead to the dissolution of Yugoslavia as a state.

In his efforts to avert the evils that may result from the succession, Tito evidently relies heavily on the army, as well as on the central Party apparatus. The army, whose officer class is made up chiefly of Serbs, was introduced as an active factor in Yugoslav politics by Tito himself, when he threatened to use it if necessary during the 1971 Croatian crisis. (Like General Charles de Gaulle in the French crisis of 1968, Tito consulted with the generals to ensure their support before taking strong political action against the dissident elements.) The army's political role was strengthened at the Tenth Congress, when military men were elected to more than 10 percent of the places in the central committee. A resolution of the succession effected by the army or by a revitalized central Party apparatus, or by a combination of the two, might lead to a renewal of the Serbian dominance of the country that existed between the wars. Yugoslavia might get an interval of stability, but in time rule by Serbs probably would give rise to strong opposition from the economically advanced Yugoslav nations, which once more would threaten Yugoslavia's independence or survival.

The circumstances prevailing when succession is initiated can substantially influence the outcome in any regime. The Yugoslav succession seems particularly susceptible to factors that are not intrinsic to the succession process. Economic weather strongly affects the game of politics; the worsening economic situation in Yugoslavia during the last few years—inflation, adverse trade balances, declining growth rates—unquestionably has intensified ethnic rivalries. If the succession occurs during an economic downturn, the crisis may be severe and may continue without resolution for a time, while an upturn may ease the succession crisis considerably. (Even a growing economy, however, may give rise to great battles among those in pursuit of better shares.) Adverse circumstances in the international environment will probably have an opposite effect: stormy conditions that pose threats to Yugoslavia's integrity will tend to enforce unity and stabilize the regime, although extreme adversity, such as a failure to find allies or receive outside assistance, could lead to a collapse of will and a weakening of national unity. Détente between the great powers, by easing external pressures on Yugoslavia, may encourage Yugoslavia's rival nationalities to struggle more intensely against each other. The reciprocal effect of a deep Yugoslav succession crisis on international politics and on what remains of the cold war could be significant, giving rise to great tensions among the great powers, but almost certainly not to war.

The mere passage of time before succession occurs can alter the weight of the contending forces—including Tito's capacity to influence the outcome. Meanwhile Tito, though obsessed (like Mao before the Cultural Revolution) with the question of how much time remains for him to prepare the succession, speaks with confidence of his continuing good health: "There are various stories circulating that I have thrombosis or paralysis. They will have to wait for it a very, very long time. If they heard the beating of my heart, they would be very disappointed, they would dismiss it [the rumor] with a wave of the hand and realize that they will not see it happen." [23]

Aged leaders often do not show their age so long as they rule, but after they retire they may rapidly decline or meet an early

[23] *Vjesnik*, April 19, 1972; in RFE, *Yugoslavia*, May 24, 1972.

death. This was true of Winston Churchill, Konrad Adenauer, Charles de Gaulle, and Walter Ulbricht. On the other hand, General Francisco Franco, Mao Tse-tung, Chiang Kai-shek, and Josip Tito have gone on and on. Indeed, Tito's chances of postponing the succession for a considerable time seem better than his chances of resolving it by his succession arrangements.

II

Mao's Succession
Arrangements

Mao Tse-tung began to make his original succession arrangements, including the tentative choice of an heir presumptive to head the Communist movement in China, in the period before the Communists' conquest of power.[1] At the first Party congress that

[1] This chapter draws upon the following: A. Doak Barnett, *China after Mao* (Princeton: Princeton University Press, 1967); A. Doak Barnett, *Uncertain Passage* (Washington, D.C.: Brookings, 1974); Philip Bridgham, "The Fall of Lin Piao," *China Quarterly*, No. 55 (July–September, 1973); Philip Bridgham, "Mao's Cultural Revolution: Origins and Developments," *China Quarterly*, No. 29 (January–March 1967), 1–35; Philip Bridgham, "Mao's Cultural Revolution in 1967: The Struggle to Seize Power," *China Quarterly*, No. 34 (April–June 1968), 6–37; Philip Bridgham, "Mao's Cultural Revolution: The Struggle to Seize Power," *China Quarterly*, No. 41 (January–March 1970), 1–25; Robert Elegant, *Mao's Great Revolution* (New York: World, 1971); Jack Gray, ed., *Modern China's Search for a Political Form* (New York: Oxford University Press, 1969); James Chieh Hsiung, *Ideology and Practice* (New York: Praeger, 1970); Kai-yu Hsu, *Chou En-lai* (Garden City, N.Y.: Doubleday, 1968); Chun-tu Hsueh, ed., *Revolutionary Leaders of Modern China* (New York: Oxford University Press, 1971), especially Howard Boorman, "Liu Shao-ch'i"; *Issues and Studies* (Taipei); Joint Publications Research Service, Translations on Communist China (Washington, D.C., 1970——), No. 90, *Selections from Chairman Mao*, JPRS 49826 (1970); Stanley Karnow, *Mao and China* (New York: Viking, 1972); John Wilson Lewis, *Leadership in Communist China* (Ithaca, N.Y.: Cornell University Press, 1963); Robert Jay Lifton, *Revolutionary Immortality: Mao Tse-tung and the Chinese Cultural Revolution* (New York: Random House, 1968); André Malraux, *Anti-Memoirs* (New York: Bantam, 1970); David Milton, Nancy Milton, and Franz

250

Mao personally controlled (the seventh, in May 1945), Liu Shao-ch'i's report, on the Party statute, was the second in importance. He also was chosen the senior secretary of the central committee; Mao held the supreme post of central committee chairman. On several occasions, when Mao was away for extended periods engaged in negotiations, Liu deputized for him as acting chairman. This happened in the critical period from August to October 1945, and again in the early months of the new regime (1949–1950). In the decade before 1966, Liu's name came immediately after Mao's in the Party's rank list of the leadership. Previously, from 1945 to 1956, the name of Chu Teh, who is even older than Mao, had come second. By the mid-fifties, when the Party apparatus had become the dominant institution, Chu and others of his generation were more respected than powerful; Liu's power, on the other hand, corresponded to his high rank.[2]

Liu Shao-ch'i's position as Mao's heir presumptive and chief executive officer was an element of a larger scheme for ruling China while Mao lived and for arranging an orderly succession. The two aims were readily linked, because Mao by temperament

---

Schurmann, *People's China* (New York: Vintage, 1974); Ching Ping and Dennis Bloodworth, *Heirs Apparent* (New York: Farrar, Straus & Giroux, 1973); Jeremy Rabkin, "Prospects for the Mao Succession," seminar paper (Cornell University, 1974); Thomas Robinson, ed., *The Cultural Revolution in China* (Los Angeles: University of California Press, 1971); Stuart Schram, *Mao Tse-tung* (Baltimore: Penguin, 1967); Franz Schurmann, *Ideology and Organization in Communist China* (2d ed; Los Angeles: University of California Press, 1968), especially the Supplement; Edgar Snow, *The Long Revolution* (New York: Random House, 1972); Edgar Snow, *Red China Today* (2d ed.; New York: Vintage, 1970); and articles on Mao Tse-tung, Lin Piao, and Chou En-lai in Rodger Swearingen, ed., *Leaders of the Communist World.*

[2] The situation of Vyachaslav Molotov, who ranked second to Joseph Stalin from the early thirties to the early fifties, was more like Chu's than Liu's. Throughout those years Molotov was cut from the Party apparatus, so that his power often was less than that of Stalin's other lieutenants. Moreover, while Molotov was prominent throughout this period, his authority fluctuated markedly; at times (as in 1936 and 1953) his place in the leadership, and even his life, were in jeopardy.

favored the delegation of large powers to subordinates. From the very beginning of the new regime in 1949, Mao's position in it was somewhat erratic. His involvement in affairs was neither constant nor comprehensive. He tended to intervene either piece-meal, if a matter particularly interested him or caught his atten-tion, or on a massive scale. Mao seemed at times to stand out-side the political system on a high eminence where he deliberated on questions of ideology and on the grand strategy of the revolu-tion. His sphere of action came to be known as the "second front." Periodically, however, Mao descended to initiate and closely direct great campaigns designed to advance the revolution or to save it. Among these were collectivization (1955); the Great Leap Forward (1957); and the Cultural Revolution (1966). When he was not engaged in such campaigns, ordinary decision-making—the formulation of specific policies and the overseeing of administration—had little attraction for Mao, and such func-tions were assigned to the Party secretariat and the state coun-cil. This realm came to be known as the "first front." The division of responsibilities between the two fronts originally developed informally. Subsequently, for reasons connected with Mao's health and the problem of his succession, it was formalized by dividing the politburo standing committee for work on the two separate fronts.

The existence of the two fronts was revealed by Mao only after the system had broken down and he had found it necessary, in 1966, to initiate the Cultural Revolution. His account of the two fronts appears in several speeches and reports that were dis-seminated by the Red Guards but not publicized through regular channels.[3] According to Mao, work among the top leaders, since the founding of the regime, had been divided along two fronts; as the two fronts were not united, this had bad consequences, particularly "later," when those working on the first front did

[3] These materials have been translated by the Joint Publications Research Service and distributed by the United States Department of Commerce: *Translations on Communist China*, No. 90, *Selections from Chairman Mao* (referred to hereafter as JPRS).

things improperly and Mao, on the second front, neglected to act; Mao was the author of this defective system; it was devised for reasons of state security and to deal with the problem of succession, whose importance was pointed up after 1953 by the "lessons" of the Stalin succession; the advantage for succession of this division into two fronts was that the top leaders (that is, members of the standing committee of the politburo who worked on the first front) acquired "prestige," thus facilitating an orderly transfer of power when Mao died.[4]

Subsequently, the political character of the succession became far more important to Mao than ensuring an orderly transfer of his power. Instead of seeking to avoid "great convulsions," he came to believe they were necessary: "Revolutionary successors of the proletariat are invariably brought up in great storms." [5]

[4] Since Mao apparently spoke without a text, his remarks are discursive and his meaning at times is obscure. For this reason, and because of their crucial bearing on the question of Mao's succession arrangements in the first two decades of the regime, the relevant passages warrant quotation: "For 17 years, there is one thing which, to my mind, has not been done properly. Originally, for the sake of the State security and in view of the lessons in connection with Stalin of the Soviet Union, we created two fronts. I was in the second front while other comrades were in the first front. Now it appears that this has not done us any good. The result was that we were very scattered. When we entered the city, we could not be concentrated. It looked as though many independent kingdoms were set up. Therefore, the 11th Plenary Session [August 1966] changed this. Then, since I was in the second front, I did not take charge of daily work. Many things were done by others and their prestige was thus cultivated, so that when I met with God, the State would not be thrown into great convulsions. Everybody approved this view of mine. Later, comrades in the first front failed to do some of the things properly, and some of the things which I should have done was [sic] not done by me. Therefore, I am also responsible. The blame cannot be entirely laid at their doorsteps. Why do I say that I am responsible? First, the Standing Committee [of the politburo] was divided into the first and second fronts. It was I who proposed a struggle against the secretariat. . . . For 17 years, the first and second fronts have not been united. Like others, I am also responsible for this" (speech at a central committee work conference, October 25, 1966, *ibid.*, pp. 13–15).

[5] Quoted by Chou En-lai in his report to the Tenth National Congress of the Communist Party of China, delivered August 24, 1973; trans. in *Peking Review*, September 7, 1973, p. 25.

In another speech, in a passage explaining the reasons for the two fronts, Mao says nothing of security considerations (which were important "originally"—that is, in the early years of the regime, when it was weak and vulnerable) but speaks of his "poor" health and of the need to give his intended heirs an opportunity to hold power and win prestige before he died.[6]

My own responsibility is the first and second fronts. Why divide it into the first and second fronts? First because [my] health is poor, and second because of the lesson of the Soviet Union. Malenkov was immature. He had not held power before Stalin's death. Every time he drank to [Stalin's] health he laid it on thick. So I wanted to have their prestige established before I died, but I had not expected that things would turn out the other way. . . . My first and second fronts have gone to the opposite side.[7]

The two-front arrangement resulted in Mao's loss of control over affairs, and even, he says, of influence over subordinates.

Comrade T'ao Chu says that power has fallen to the hands of subordinates. But I deliberately let it fall that way. However, they have now set up independent kingdoms. There were many things about which they did not consult with me, for example, the land problem, the Tientsin speech, the cooperatives of Shansi, negation of investigation and study, and the acclamation of Wang Kuang-mei. [The reference is to public praise accorded the wife of Liu Shao-ch'i.] These things should have been discussed by the Central Committee and decisions taken on them. Teng Hsiao-p'ing never consulted with me. He has never consulted with me about anything since 1949. In 1962 four vice premiers, Li Hsien-nien, T'an Chen-lin, Li Fu-ch'un and Po I-po suddenly went to Nanking to see me. Later they went to Tientsin. I forthwith gave them my approval, and the four went home. But Teng Hsiao-p'ing never came.

He lists, allusively, a whole series of important developments over two decades about which he was not consulted in advance

---

[6] Mao nowhere specifies the nature or causes of his poor health. Edgar Snow reports that when he saw Mao in January 1965, "one of the chairman's doctors informed me that Mao has no organic troubles and suffers from nothing beyond the normal fatigue of his age" (*New Republic*, February 27, 1965).

[7] Speech at a report meeting, October 24, 1966, JPRS, pp. 10–11.

and of which he presumably disapproved.[8] Mao's account is truncated and, although he admits making mistakes, he is not completely candid. His loss of power to subordinates was not altogether deliberate (even though he says, "I deliberately let it fall that way"), and is not wholly accounted for by Mao's poor health and concern about the succession. Failure of the Great Leap, for example, by damaging Mao's prestige, probably led to some reduction in his power.[9] Nevertheless, the picture Mao draws of a ruler who on occasion willingly stands aside from ordinary political affairs and who delegates large powers to the men who are to succeed him rings true and is supported by independent evidence.[10]

Although Mao says that his succession arrangements led to power slipping from his hands, he fails to specify who was meant to succeed to his power. This is hardly surprising, since by then Liu Shao-ch'i had been replaced as heir presumptive. Mao ob-

---

[8] "I was not satisfied with the Wu-ch'ang conference [November, 1958]. I could do nothing about the high targets. I came to Peking to hold a conference. You held one for six days, but I could not hold even a one-day conference. It did not matter that quotas were not fulfilled. Do not grieve over it. After the Tsun-i Conference [power] was concentrated in the Central Committee. But after the 6th plenary session in 1938, none of such things as the South Anhwei incident involving Hsiang Ying, P'eng Te-huai and the New 4th Army, P'eng's big battle of one hundred regiments and his setting up of an independent kingdom, were reported to me in advance. After the 7th Congress [1945], the Central Committee was not given to any one individual. When Hu Tsung-nan attacked Yenan, the Central Committee was split in two. I remained in north Shensi with Chou En-lai and Jen Pi-shih, while Liu Shao-ch'i and Chu Te [were elsewhere]. . . . Things were still comparatively centralized. After our entry into many groups. We were further scattered particularly when the first and second front [sic] were set up. After the finance and economic conference in 1953, you were asked to keep one another and the Central Committee, as well as the localities, informed" (*ibid.*, p. 10).

[9] Mao at one point hints at an involuntary reduction in his authority when he says that he "was not satisfied with the Wu-ch'ang conference." This was the occasion, in November 1958, when Mao's "proposal" that he not stand again for the office of chairman of the republic was "approved."

[10] This evidence is considered below.

serves, however, that Liu Shao-ch'i and Teng Hsiao-p'ing share
with him responsibility "for failing to run the Central Committee
well." [11] Elsewhere he speaks of the lessons of the Soviet Union:
"Malenkov was immature. He had not held power before Stalin's
death. . . . So I wanted to have their prestige established before
I died." [12] In view of Liu's favored position for many years, there
can be no question that he was meant to have the highest place
in the post-Mao leadership.[13] The man who later was called
"China's Khrushchev" originally was conceived of by Mao as
China's Malenkov: Mao's heir presumptive, however, unlike
Stalin's, after acquiring experience and prestige, would succeed
to power at the proper moment and, assisted by colleagues similarly experienced and prestigious, become the ruler.

Liu Shao-ch'i in some ways was an odd choice for the role of
heir presumptive. Colorless and without personal warmth, he
lacked popular appeal and was too close in age to Mao: the difference between them was only five years. Liu Shao-ch'i had
taken little part in the 1934 long march to the northwest, the
great revolutionary event comparable to the seizure of power in
Russia's October revolution, and he had come late to Mao's
guerrilla stronghold in Yenan. Liu had engaged in trade union
affairs in the cities, in organizing the underground in Japanese-
occupied areas, and subsequently, like Stalin, in creating an effective Party apparatus. He was preoccupied with practical
affairs rather than with great ideas—normally a useful trait in a
leader who is to consolidate a newly established regime—but

[11] Speech, October 24, 1966, JPRS, p. 15. Teng-Hsiao-p'ing in 1955 had
replaced Liu as general secretary of the central committee. The post had
been downgraded earlier, at the time of the Tsunyi Conference in 1935,
when Mao won control of the Party from the Comintern protégés who till
then had dominated the central organs by controlling the office of general
secretary. That office once more was downgraded, and subsequently
eliminated, when Mao instituted the Cultural Revolution.

[12] *Ibid.*, p. 10.

[13] Mao told British Field Marshal Bernard Montgomery, among others,
that Liu was to be his successor (*Sunday Times* [London], June 12, 1960).

Mao, as it transpired, did not aim at consolidation. Moreover, Liu apparently was not driven by a great personal ambition to be supreme ruler. These characteristics of the man, although they did not make him an ideal choice to inherit Mao's power, did perhaps make him a good choice to occupy the office of heir presumptive.[14] As the number-two man in the regime, Liu served well for almost two decades, organizing the implementation of Mao's programs and perhaps discouraging more ambitious men from coveting the succession. Mao finally came to realize, however, that Liu's political character not only disqualified him as successor, but even jeopardized the revolution, as Mao conceived it, while he still lived.

The public record, on the whole, bears out Mao's contention that extensive arrangements for the succession contributed to a dispersion of his power. Analysis is complicated, as noted previously, by the fact that the failure of policies Mao had espoused at times also led to reductions in his authority and power.

The campaign in the USSR for collective leadership following Stalin's death manifestly affected China, as it did the other states of the then Communist bloc, though to a lesser degree. After Khrushchev's anti-Stalin speech in February 1956 pointed up the dangers of personal despotism, the Mao cult in China declined sharply in importance, particularly affecting the claims made for "Mao's Thought."[15] Moreover, the effect of downgrading Mao was actually to strengthen Liu's status as his political heir. The central committee's report to the Eighth Congress (September 1956) was given, not by Mao, as in 1945, but by Liu Shao-ch'i.[16]

[14] The ideal vice president in the American system, on the other hand, must be qualified to serve as president, but little is required of him so long as he remains vice president.

[15] In North Korea, Moscow's anti-Stalin campaign encouraged the opposition to criticize Kim Il-sung for his authoritarian rule at a plenum of the central committee in August 1956. The critics were defeated and purged.

[16] Similarly, Malenkov, rather than Stalin, gave the report to the USSR's Party congress in 1952.

It stressed collective leadership and mentioned Mao personally hardly at all; in contrast, Liu's speech to the previous congress (1945) referred to Mao dozens of times. The new Party statute, unlike the previous one, nowhere mentioned "Mao's Thought." It created a new post, honorary chairman of the central committee, but left it vacant, doubtless intending Mao to occupy it in the not distant future—perhaps before the next congress of the Party—as a way station on the road to retirement. Any efforts subsequently made to move Mao from the post of Party chairman to that of honorary chairman did not succeed. Nevertheless, Mao was induced, in November 1958, to withdraw as a candidate for re-election as chairman of the Chinese People's Republic.[17] When the time came, five months later, for Mao to step down from the post,[18] the man chosen to replace him was Liu Shao-ch'i. Liu's elevation to the office of state chairman naturally strengthened the widespread belief that he was meant to succeed Mao.

Decisive power, to be sure, remained with Mao, who was still chairman of the central committee and of the politburo. At meetings of these bodies he dominated the proceedings and was able to exert his will. He could induce them to adopt his programs, no matter how far-reaching. In 1957, for example, Mao was the moving force behind the decision to engage in the Great Leap Forward, an ambitious, ill-conceived attempt to achieve vast economic gains simultaneously in industry and agriculture. Although Mao's Great Leap policies were in deep trouble by the summer of 1959 and came under direct attack at the Lushan plenum of the central committee, Mao succeeded in isolating and defeating P'eng Te-huai, his main critic. The Great Leap program was

[17] More precisely, his "proposal" to this effect was "approved" by the Wu-ch'ang Conference. As noted above, Mao said he "was not satisfied with the Wu-ch'ang conference."

[18] This action seemed to parallel the earlier move toward collective leadership in the Soviet bloc, whereby the personal ruler, who headed both the Party and the government, resigned from one of them. By 1958, however, this trend had been reversed, so that Khrushchev, for example, headed the government as well as the Party.

abandoned, presumably because even Mao then saw that its prospects were poor. Mao once again withdrew from his deep involvement in current programs, while Liu Shao-ch'i and other first-front leaders labored during the next three years to help the country recover from the consequences of the Great Leap and from the series of bad harvests that followed because of poor weather. Mao's tendency to withdraw from ordinary political affairs, particularly in the intervals between his major projects, was now accentuated by physical weakness, caused by advancing age and intermittent poor health. His condition imposed on him extended periods of inactivity, during which he disappeared from public view and apparently was inaccessible to his colleagues.

In 1962, concerned about the extent of the retreat from revolution—about policies that concentrated on economic recovery and that fostered the growth of privilege in society [19]—Mao again intervened, on behalf of radical egalitarian measures. However, except in the Chinese army, the People's Liberation Army (PLA), which under Lin Piao was being transformed into an independent political factor allied with Mao, the revolutionary impulse Mao attempted to impart largely spent itself without sufficiently moving the machinery of rule. Mao faced, not open defiance of his will, but evasive actions to prevent its being fully carried out. No longer could he count upon his policies being implemented.

Mao's fears that the regime's institutions were becoming alienated from the masses, as well as from himself, were reinforced by his growing conviction that Khrushchev was truly a revisionist who had taken "the capitalist road"—that is, who favored policies that had the effect of weakening socialism. Stalin's successor was a usurper who had taken power illegitimately

[19] Malraux quotes Mao as saying in August 1965: "Even today, broad layers of our society are conditioned in such a way that their activity is necessarily oriented towards revisionism. They can only obtain what they want by taking it from the masses" (*Anti-Memoirs*, p. 460).

through a conspiracy and had used that power to attack Stalin and subvert the socialist system. Was there not a danger that the men who would follow Mao, particularly the man he had chosen to be his heir, might similarly usurp power and undermine the revolution? Questions of this kind were expressed openly in mid-1964 in the Party's chief publications. An authoritative article polemicizing against Soviet revisionism asked "whether or not we can successfully prevent the emergence of Khrushchovite revisionism in China. . . . [We must] watch out for *careerists and conspirators like Khrushchov* and prevent such bad elements from usurping the leadership of the Party and government at any level. . . . It is essential to test and know cadres and choose and train successors in the long course of mass struggle." [20]

Such talk of successors, "from our highest organizations down," inevitably calls to mind the highest successor, who at that time was presumed to be Liu Shao-ch'i. In retrospect, the need expressed here to prevent conspirators from usurping leadership,[21] the need to choose cadres tested in mass struggle, anticipates the Great Proletarian Cultural Revolution. When Liu was later subjected to this test he failed and was exposed—in the words of the formula later used to characterize him—as "China's Khrushchev." The epithet implies that if Liu had succeeded Mao he would have betrayed China's revolution just as Khrushchev, after succeeding Stalin, betrayed the Russian revolution.

[20] "On Khrushchev's Phoney Communism and Its Historical Lessons for the World," comment on an open letter of the central committee of the CPSU by the editorial departments of *People's Daily* (Peking) and *Red Flag* (Peking), July 14, 1964; trans. in Barnett, *China after Mao*, pp. 192–194; my italics.

[21] Lin Piao played particularly heavily on this theme of the dangers of usurpation during the Cultural Revolution: "The danger comes from the upper level. When Khrushchev emerged from the Soviet Union, the entire nation changed color" (speech at enlarged meeting of the politburo, October 12, 1966, JPRS, p. 76). Later, in his 1969 report to the Ninth Congress, Lin spoke of how Khrushchev and Brezhnev had "concealed themselves in the Communist Party [and] usurped the leadership of the Party of Lenin and Stalin" (*Peking Review*, April 30, 1969, p. 17).

Whatever Mao's suspicions in mid-1964, he as yet had arrived at no definite conclusions. Until 1965, Mao said later, "we had overconfidence in others. The time our vigilance was aroused was when the 23 Articles were drafted. At the time neither Peking nor the Central Committee could find any means to cope with the problems that arose." [22] This belated awakening in Mao of vigilance with regard to his heir presumptive (and presumably others on the first front) came not long after the unseating of Khrushchev on October 14, 1964. One can only wonder whether the displacement of Khrushchev by his heir presumptive, Leonid Brezhnev, stimulated Mao's fears regarding his own heir.

Mao's mood of uncertainty in early 1965 is reflected in his conversation with Edgar Snow in January. He seems doubtful whether sufficient time was left for him to intervene before he died. At one point, according to Snow, Mao said that "he was getting ready to see God very soon," but shortly afterward he observed that "death just did not seem to want him." [23] In dealing with such incalculables affecting political strategy as one's own death, one's temperament and subjective tendencies doubtless tend to be determining factors, and on fundamental issues affecting the revolution Mao throughout his life had been an activist. Later that year, in an unusually frank interview with André Malraux, Mao seemed to lean toward a new intervention: "If our methods are the right ones—if we tolerate no deviation—China will be restored to greatness. . . . But in this battle . . . we are alone. . . . I am alone with the masses. Waiting." Malraux believed that Mao still hesitated.[24] In the following weeks, however, Mao launched his attack: "In September and October last year [1965], it was asked: if revisionism emerged in the Central Committee, what should the localities do about it? I then felt that in Peking

[22] Speech at central committee work conference, October 25, 1966, JPRS, p. 13. The term "23 Articles" refers to a project of Mao's to improve the Party's style of work.

[23] Edgar Snow, "Interview With Mao," *New Republic*, February 27, 1965.

[24] Malraux, *Anti-Memoirs*, pp. 466–468.

my suggestions could not be put into practice. Why is it that criticism of Wu Han was started not in Peking but in Shanghai? Because Peking had no people to do it." [25] The "criticism of Wu Han," an indirect attack, in the guise of literary criticism, on the entire leadership of the city Party organization in Peking, was a major initiative in Mao's campaign to deprive Liu of the succession. Shortly before this initiative was taken, Lin Piao had published an important ideological work dealing with revolutionary strategy.[26] This carried forward the concerted build-up of Lin to provide Mao with an alternate heir.

The final decision to get rid of Liu Shao-ch'i was apparently made in January 1966.[27] Mao gave Edgar Snow an account, but he did not allow Snow to quote directly.

The showdown came in the debate over what was to become of Mao's program for the cultural revolution. At a decisive meeting Liu Shao-ch'i stubbornly opposed Mao's first and primary point: "to overthrow those persons in authority who are taking the capitalist road, to criticize and repudiate the reactionary bourgeois academic 'authorities' and the ideology of the bourgeoisie and all other exploiting classes, and to transform education, literature and art and all other parts of the superstructure not in correspondence with the socialist economic base. . . ." Liu had to choose between wrecking his own machine, or a test of strength. He remained defiant. And thus on January 25, 1965 [sic] at a decisive meeting, and not before, Mao decided that Liu had to go. So I was told by a very responsible person.[28]

[25] Speech at central committee work conference, October 25, 1966, JPRS, p. 13.

[26] "Long Live the Victory of People's War!" *Jen-min Jih-pao* (Peking), September 3, 1965.

[27] The date in *1965* given by Snow almost certainly is due to an error, presumably Snow's. The question at issue between Liu and Mao, that of overthrowing "persons in authority who are taking the capitalist road," was raised by Mao in connection with the Cultural Revolution, which was launched in the early months of *1966*. That Snow's date is in error is also the view of Allen Whiting, in "Probing China's Cultural Revolution," *Problems of Communism*, July–August 1973.

[28] Edgar Snow, "Aftermath of the Cultural Revolution," *New Republic*, April 10, 1971. See also Edgar Snow, *The Long Revolution* (New York: Random House, 1972).

Of course, the only "very responsible person" who could know Mao's private deliberations was the person interviewed by Snow in the article from which the quotation is taken: Mao himself.

These developments culminated in the Great Proletarian Cultural Revolution. Its relationship to the problem of succession is quite different from what some observers thought during its first months: contenders for the succession had not intensified their struggle in anticipation of Mao's passing from the scene.[29] Mao himself, partly because of concern for the fate of the revolution after his death, initiated the Cultural Revolution and, in so doing, altered his arrangements for the succession. Mao's aim in unleashing the Cultural Revolution in 1966 was, broadly speaking, three-fold. The immediate situation required him to recover power over the regime's institutions, and particularly the Party, by purging the men who no longer shared his revolutionary goals; these included Liu, who first lost his pre-eminent position as heir presumptive in August 1966, and not long after was deprived of all power. Second, Mao found it necessary to purge the regime's institutions (especially Party and government bodies in the cities) of bureaucratism and of concerns for hierarchical status and privilege. Finally, he sought once more to inspire the people with renewed revolutionary *élan*. The change in Mao's succession arrangements, therefore, did not consist simply of substituting one personality for another. The problem of succession had become inextricably entangled with the deepening problem of the future of the regime.

Mao did not expect the Cultural Revolution to be as prolonged and as destructive as it was. Initially, Mao "aimed to remove 'only a handful' from power." [30] (His target was indicated elsewhere by the formula: "the handful of persons in authority who are taking the capitalist road.") Before it had ended, however, the Cultural Revolution had overturned all the central ruling bodies in Peking, as well as much of the provincial leadership

---

29 See Barnett, *China after Mao*, pp. 102–111.

30 See Edgar Snow's interview with Mao, "Aftermath of the Cultural Revolution," *New Republic*, April 10, 1971.

throughout China. It was a veritable political revolution directed
from the top, probably matched in scope only by Stalin's "great
terror" of 1937 to 1939. But while Stalin's was a blood purge organized by the political police in which millions of persons were
imprisoned or killed, Mao's purge employed far less destructive
sanctions: it took men from their jobs and homes, dishonored
them, and on occasion subjected them to some violence as well.

Special, complementary roles were assigned to the two chief
agencies that set Mao's Cultural Revolution in motion: the Red
Guards, consisting of millions of youths loosely organized in detachments, were charged with overturning the existing structures
of authority; the People's Liberation Army was to maintain a
minimal framework of order in which the revolution could be
carried out. Their common task was to break the hold on the
Party and state of elements that had been corrupted by revisionist ideas and practices, so that the healthy elements within
them could take charge. For over three years, power ebbed and
flowed among these two agencies—the Red Guards and the army
—and a third force consisting of the healthy elements of the old
political structures. In the end, all three were combined in a new
system of "three-way revolutionary committees" that finally restored order and stability.

When he initiated the Cultural Revolution, Mao distrusted the
lieutenants who had served in the first front, particularly top
officials in the central Party apparatus. ("It was I who proposed a
struggle against the secretariat.") Consequently Mao was forced
to rely on persons with whom he had a special relationship: his
wife, Chiang Ch'ing, who till then had played no public role; his
personal secretary, Ch'en Po-ta, who till then had been an ideologist and word monger without major administrative responsibilities; and his defense minister, Lin Piao, who had given "Mao's
Thought" a special place in the army's propaganda. Ch'en Po-ta
and Chiang Ch'ing, as heads of "the Group in charge of the
Cultural Revolution under the Party's Central Committee," directed the Red Guards in their movement to purge the Party and

government. Lin controlled Mao's second major instrument, the People's Liberation Army. A fourth leader, Chou En-lai, the only experienced civilian administrator in the group, controlled the remnants of the former civilian administration. Though invariably loyal to Mao in crises, Chou was not a member of Mao's intimate circle. Of the four, Lin had by far the greatest power, and he replaced Liu as heir presumptive.

Why did Mao think a new heir was necessary? Mao's previous succession arrangements had aimed at avoiding disorder when he passed from power, but after the initiation of the Cultural Revolution disorder was held to be a virtue required to prevent corruption of the revolution. Moreover, after having just experienced at first hand the dangers of promoting the political fortunes of an heir, why did Mao select a new heir of the most dangerous type, one who had military force at his command? The reason is not clear. Mao may have thought it necessary to designate Lin as his successor in order to ensure his loyalty during the turbulence of the Cultural Revolution. He may also have feared that if his own death came during the disorder of the Cultural Revolution, it might jeopardize the regime unless the heir was someone previously designated who controlled sufficient material force to limit the severity of the crisis. Furthermore, Mao may have believed that Lin's commitment to "Mao's Thought" offered the best chance for Mao's own conception of the revolution to prevail. These possible motives suggest the weakness of Mao's position when he initiated the Cultural Revolution, and the important bargaining counters that Lin used in his dealings with Mao.

Whereas Liu Shao-ch'i, because of his long experience as an *apparachik,* had the appropriate career background for a Communist heir presumptive, Lin Piao was like no other Communist ever chosen for the role. He was a brilliantly successful general, but his experience, unlike that of other marshals, such as Chen Yi and Chu Teh, was largely restricted to military affairs, albeit in a highly politicized army. He lacked extensive experience in the

Party and government bureaucracies. Though present with Mao
on the Long March, he is said to have incurred Mao's displeasure
before coming to Yenan in 1936.[31] Whether because Mao was
displeased with Lin or, according to some versions, because Lin
had been wounded, this outstanding military commander spent
the next years of the war against the Japanese invader of China
in the USSR as a Chinese representative to the Comintern. It appears that Lin was not particularly close to Mao before the mid-
fifties, although after 1959, when he replaced P'eng Te-huai as
defense minister, he became a strong partisan of Mao's views.
Even so, there was a question of Lin's physical suitability for the
role of successor. Though his age was right (he was fifty-eight,
ten years younger than Liu and fifteen years younger than Mao),
he had been seriously ill for long periods of time and apparently
had not fully recovered.[32]

Lin Piao's designation as heir presumptive was made public at
the same time as Liu's demotion, at the August 1966 plenum of
the central committee, and by the same means. The newly published rank list of the politburo dropped Liu from the second position, immediately below Mao, to the eighth, while it raised Lin
from the sixth to the second. Since Lin previously had ranked
low in the politburo and since he still lacked the customary offices held by heir presumptives in Communist states (the second
office in the Party or, as was the case with Liu, the first in the
state), heavy symbolic reinforcement was needed to make Lin's
new status credible and authoritative. Unlike the symbols previously used in Communist states to convey a leader's status as
heir presumptive, which have usually been subtle and often ambiguous, the devices employed in the campaign to establish Lin
as Mao's heir were blatant and obtrusive. Lin's build-up took on
the proportions of a minor cult, subordinate to and closely as-

[31] Thomas W. Robinson, "Lin Piao," in William W. Whitson, ed., *The
Military and Political Power in China in the 1970s* (New York: Praeger,
1972), p. 75.
[32] He was reported to have tuberculosis.

sociated with the extravagant cult of Mao, which Lin himself had raised to new levels. "The little red book," *Quotations from Mao Tse-tung,* which had a central place in the Mao cult, was compiled on Lin's instructions and published with his foreword. In the spring of 1966, the standard designation prefixed to Mao's name became *Chairman,* instead of *Comrade,* thus setting him above all other members of the Party; soon afterward, when Lin replaced Liu as heir presumptive, he was designated "Mao's close comrade-in-arms," a unique characterization that raised him, in turn, above all the leaders except Mao. Innumerable photographs were published showing Mao alone with his "close comrade-in-arms," who frequently held aloft "the little red book"; countless captions announced their joint activities, such as receiving foreign dignitaries or mounting the rostrum together at some public rally.

New and far-reaching measures were taken by the Ninth Congress, in April 1969, to fortify Lin's position as heir, including a grotesque attempt to sanction his claim in the Party constitution. Its "General Program" asserted: "Comrade Lin Piao has consistently held high the great red banner of Mao Tsetung Thought and has most loyally and resolutely carried out and defended Comrade Mao Tsetung's proletarian revolutionary line. Comrade Lin Piao is Comrade Mao Tsetung's close comrade-in-arms and successor." [33] These words, because they were adopted by the congress and placed in the Party constitution, were given the greatest possible legalistic weight.[34] Yet there are difficulties in this attempt at constitutional designation of Mao's heir. As the highest Party authority, each congress is sovereign. No congress can bind a future congress to take any particular action. More

[33] Chapter I, "General Program," *Peking Review,* April 30, 1969, p. 36. This departure from the general practice of prefixing "Chairman" to Mao's name serves to narrow the distance between Mao and Lin, since both are designated "Comrade." Henceforth no hyphen was used in Mao's name in official Chinese publications in English.

[34] Strictly speaking, the Party does not enact *laws,* although the sanctions that are available to the state are also at the command of the Party.

important, words placed in a Communist Party's statute cannot be the ultimate authority, since they necessarily are subordinate to the revolutionary cause. Lin's designation as successor could only be legitimated by an authority higher than the congress, by the revolution itself, embodied in Chairman Mao's person and "Thought" while he lived, and in his "Thought" alone after he died.

Remarkably, neither in the Party constitution nor anywhere else is Mao directly quoted as saying that Lin is his successor. While no office is specified to which Lin is to succeed, presumably the words making him Mao's successor signified that Lin, the vice-chairman of the central committee, would succeed to Mao's post as chairman. The pre-eminence of these two offices— the only ones mentioned in the constitution—was emphasized in reporting the election of the membership of the Party's top organs: Mao and Lin, as chairman and vice-chairman, were listed first, in heavy type, while the names of the other members followed, in small type and in stroke order—that is, according to the number of strokes in their surnames.[35] This listing not only elevated Lin close to Mao's level, but it also reduced Chou En-lai to the level of an ordinary member of these bodies.

The relationship of ruler to heir presumptive, as has been observed often in this study, involves great tensions that frequently lead to a breakdown. The nature of the relationship between Mao and Lin after 1966 is not easy to grasp, especially in light of Lin's later fall from grace. What role did Mao intend Lin to play in the succession? Was Mao responsible for the extravagant propaganda on Lin's behalf, or did he at least acquiesce freely to it? If Mao distrusted Lin and secretly opposed him for the succession, he was engaged in a dangerous and even irresponsible game. If he had died or become incapacitated in the five-year interval between August 1966 and September 1971, Lin would have had a strong claim to the succession, and he conceivably might have made the claim good. It is reasonable to suppose that Mao did favor Lin to succeed him if need be, at least in the

[35] *Peking Review*, April 30, 1969.

short term, as one who could consolidate the gains of the Cultural Revolution.[36] On the other hand, a campaign on behalf of Lin of such intensity and extended duration was contrary to Mao's interest, for it left him little flexibility or room for maneuvering if he wished to reconsider his choice of an heir. Hence it seems that the blatant and unqualified campaign to establish Lin as heir presumptive went farther than Mao would have preferred, that he was in fact constrained to accept some of its more extreme features because of his dependence on Lin Piao. As previously noted, Mao did stop short of an absolute commitment on his part, inasmuch as he failed to state expressly and publicly that Lin was his personal choice as successor.

Nevertheless, the Party's extreme commitment to Lin as Mao's successor created a highly structured and potentially dangerous situation in the leadership. Lin was vulnerable to attack if he displeased Mao, who was now the single unquestioned locus of authority in China.[37] Moreover, to fall from grace almost certainly meant to fall all the way to the deepest hell, as Liu had discovered when he lost his place at Mao's right hand and was transformed into the archfiend, "renegade, traitor, and scab," guilty of "counter-revolutionary crimes." Similarly, Lin could not have been replaced as Mao's successor, in all probability, without first being destroyed politically or physically. But this circumstance, in turn, posed a danger to Mao, for it meant that Lin could contest Mao's will on important matters only if he was prepared either to sacrifice himself or to eliminate Mao. Subsequently Lin was in fact accused of secretly plotting to assassinate Mao—a charge possessed of a certain logic in circumstances where Lin could be everything or nothing but could no longer find a stable intermediate position of power.

Was it personal ambition or simple devotion to Mao that

[36] Significantly, it was only after a substantial degree of stability had been attained that Lin was purged.

[37] Lin implicitly acknowledged his vulnerability in his report to the Ninth Congress: "Whoever opposes Chairman Mao Tsetung Thought, at any time or under any circumstances, will be condemned and punished by the whole Party and the whole country" (*Peking Review*, April 30, 1969).

brought Lin to occupy such a position, at once acutely dangerous to himself and potentially all-powerful? At the beginning of the Cultural Revolution, Lin disclaimed all ambition and expressed extreme personal humility:

> We must not oppose but firmly follow the Chairman. He gives over-all consideration to problems; he is farsighted. What is more, he has his ideas, many of which we do not understand. We must resolutely carry out Chairman Mao's instructions, whether we understand them or not. I have no talent; I rely on the wisdom of the masses, and do everything according to the Chairman's directives. . . . The Central Committee has given me a task, and I know that I am not equal to it. I have thought of it many times. But since the Chairman and the Central Committee have made their decision, I can only submit myself to it and try my best to do my task. In the meantime, I am prepared to hand it over to a more suitable comrade.[38]

Lin's self-evaluation implies that he is not qualified to be Mao's successor. Since he does not understand Mao's ideas, how can he carry them out after Mao is gone? Since he has difficulty understanding Mao's instructions, how can he be relied upon to issue correct instructions himself after he has succeeded Mao? Lin claims for himself but a single virtue: loyalty to Mao's person and faithfulness to his ideas.

A decisive objection to Lin's claims of modesty and lack of ambition is the remarkable growth of the cult that grew up around his name as successor to Mao, which unquestionably was fed by his own ambitions.[39] There is actually a hint already in Lin's 1966 speech to the central committee that he was establishing a new "two-front" system like the one that had just led to the break between Mao and Liu. Lin says, "I do not interfere with him on major problems, nor do I trouble him with small matters."

[38] Speech at August 1966 plenum of central committee, JPRS, p. 17.
[39] Chou En-lai subsequently told a group of American editors that the idea of Mao's replacement by a single successor was "one of the plots" concocted by Lin Piao (*New York Times*, October 12, 1972). This is no more plausible, however, than to suppose that Lin had nothing to do with propagating his own cult.

This distinction, between what is *major* and within Mao's sphere and what is *small* and within Lin's, is seemingly reflected in a formula that Lin and his close associates used regarding the People's Liberation Army (PLA), which, they said, was "personally founded and led by our great supreme commander Chairman Mao and directly commanded by Vice-Chairman Lin Piao." [40] Subsequently, at a time when he was preparing to purge Lin, Mao criticized this formula: "It is also said that I am the founder and leader of the People's Liberation Army but Lin is the personal commander. Why can't the founder be the commander?" [41] (Mao modestly observed that he was not the founder either.) Whereas, in the fifties, Mao himself had been responsible for retreating to the second front while he assigned Liu and others to the first front, in the Cultural Revolution, if Mao is to be believed, Lin Piao, for all his humility, attempted to push Mao back to the second front, while he sought to place himself in the first front.

Whatever Lin's intentions at the outset of the Cultural Revolution, with the passage of time he maneuvered with increasing boldness to win control of the chief Party organs. After the Ninth Party Congress in April 1969, 45 percent of the central committee consisted of military personnel, and Lin's faction in the politburo included at least eight of the nineteen members. (The eight were subsequently purged in connection with Lin's alleged conspiracy.) There also seems no question that Lin attempted to tighten his control over the People's Liberation Army in order to assure his future succession to Mao, and perhaps also to acquire

[40] See, for example, the speech by Huang Yung-sheng (army chief of staff) on the forty-second anniversary of the PLA, in *Peking Review*, August 6, 1969, p. 7. Lin's allusion to a two-front system is in JPRS, p. 17.

[41] "Document No. 12 of the CCP Ceneral Committee," a summary of Mao's talks on an inspection tour from mid-August to September 12, 1971; trans. in *Issues and Studies* (Taipei), September 1971, p. 68. This is one of a series of documents which supposedly circulated inside China and which United States intelligence agencies believe to be authentic (*New York Times*, December 17, 1972). Other such documents, also published in *Issues and Studies*, are cited below.

a capacity to protect his position as heir presumptive against any change of mind on Mao's part. Lin further increased his personal power when a temporary system of administrative control, largely through military officials, was created after the Ninth Congress. During 1970, however, Mao began to reconstruct the upper levels of the provincial Party apparatus, which had been demolished in the course of the Cultural Revolution. Besides providing a more durable system of administration, the rebuilt Party structure provided a counterweight to the existing administrative structure of "revolutionary committees" dominated by the army; this no doubt was also Mao's intention.

Lin's authority and power had been built up, in the course of the Cultural Revolution, to a point approaching Mao's, creating a virtual dyarchy, which is highly unstable. Increasingly the chairman and the vice-chairman confronted each other without any mediator. Sharp conflicts arose as early as the Ninth Party Congress, in April 1969, when Lin's draft political report was replaced by one produced under Mao's "personal guidance." [42] But the real crisis in relations between the two men first came to the attention of a wide circle of the leadership in August 1970 at the Lushan plenum of the central committee.

Though Lin had been made the sole vice-chairman of the central committee and was designated Mao's "successor" in the Party constitution, within the state system Lin, as the minister of defense and deputy head of the government, was subordinate to Chou En-lai. A new draft constitution for the People's Republic of China providing for an office superior to Chou's, that of state chairman, was circulated, but in March 1970 that provision was eliminated from the revised draft.[43] Evidently at some time in the spring of 1970, Mao had decided to oppose Lin's power with that of Chou En-lai. Mao's use of this tactic did not imply that Mao

[42] Chou En-lai, report to the Tenth Party Congress; trans. in *Peking Review*, September 7, 1973, p. 17.

[43] "CCP Central Committee Circular on Distribution of the 'Revised Draft Constitution of the People's Republic of China'"; trans. in *Issues and Studies*, February 1972, p. 100.

had decided to oust Lin as successor. Mao was probably using Chou as a counterheir—a powerful leader whose function is to prevent the heir from reaching out for his inheritance prematurely.

Whatever Mao's intention, Lin did not acquiesce in the attempt to establish a more even balance in the leadership. At the Lushan plenum in August 1970, Lin again sought to make himself Chou's superior within the state apparatus by restoring to the constitution the post of state chairman. According to Mao's account of the plenum, which he presented to top leaders in the summer of 1971, Lin and his faction—including Ch'en Po-ta, Mao's former secretary, and several top military figures—engaged there "in surpise attacks and underground activities. . . . A certain person [Lin] was anxious to become state chairman, to split the Party and to seize power." [44] Actually, Lin apparently had urged Mao to assume the post of state chairman himself, no doubt expecting to be made vice-chairman, the post he already occupied in the Party. Mao, however, had already told Lin on six occasions that he would not agree to serve as state chairman. Lin nevertheless persisted, presumably in the hope that if Mao would not assume the post himself, he might still permit Lin to occupy it, just as earlier Mao had permitted Liu Shao-ch'i to become head of state. Lin evidently was able to rally some support in the central committee for his position, for Mao said that at the Lushan meeting "some of the comrades were deceived and misled." [45] Mao was adamant against Lin's proposal, however, and after several days Lin had to back down.

Mao believed Lin's activities at Lushan to have been motivated by excessive ambition. He therefore decided to disinherit Lin. But Lin, like Liu Shao-ch'i in 1965, had become strongly entrenched, and Mao had to proceed slowly and indirectly, aiming first at Lin's allies and seeking to undermine Lin's position in

[44] "Summary of Chairman Mao's Talks," *Issues and Studies*, September 1971, p. 66.
[45] *Ibid.*, p. 71.

the army. Mao first took certain military precautions, reorganizing the command of the Peking military region in January 1971 so that Lin could not use it to execute a *coup d'état*.[46] He also appointed new personnel to the Party's military affairs commission, which Lin had previously packed with his own partisans. Mao then launched a political offensive. At a work conference of the central committee in April 1971, Lin's close ally, Ch'en Po-ta, was subjected to sharp criticism, while Chou En-lai, Mao's closest lieutenant at this juncture, made a speech criticizing Lin's army subordinates. In the late summer of 1971, Mao toured crucial military regions in the country to ensure the army's loyalty before he engaged in a personal confrontation with Lin. He told his high-level audiences: "After returning to Peking I will again send for them [Lin and his partisans] for talks. They do not want to see me but I want to see them." [47] This confrontation apparently was to be followed by a central committee meeting to purge Lin's faction from the central committee. Mao characterized his comments about Lin as "personal views . . . casual remarks. Don't draw any conclusions now; let the central committee do it." [48]

Aware that Mao had become "uneasy about us," [49] Lin's faction had devised plans for a coup d'état in case Mao initiated action against it. Whether Lin, knowing that Mao was returning to Peking to confront him, tried to execute his plans for a coup is uncertain. Chou En-lai, at different times, has taken both sides of this question. In an interview with American newspaper editors on October 7, 1972, Chou said that Lin "didn't dare put his plot into practice" and that Lin had made no attempt to carry out a coup d'état or to assassinate Mao.[50] But in his report to the Tenth Party Congress, Chou said just the opposite:

---

[46] *Ibid.*, pp. 68–69.   [47] *Ibid.*, p. 71.   [48] *Ibid.*, p. 69.

[49] "The Struggle of Smashing the Counter-revolutionary Coup of the Lin-Ch'en Anti-Party Clique (Material No. 2)," *Issues and Studies*, May 1972, p. 80.

[50] *New York Times*, October 12, 1972.

[Lin] went further to start a counter-revolutionary coup d'etat, which was aborted, at the Second Plenary Session of the Ninth Central Committee in August 1970, then in March 1971 he drew up the plan for an armed counter-revolutionary coup d'etat entitled *Outline of Project* "571," and on September 8, he launched the coup in a wild attempt to assassinate our great leader Chairman Mao and set up a rival central committee. On September 13, after his conspiracy had collapsed, Lin surreptitiously boarded a plane, fled as a defector to the Soviet revisionists in betrayal of the Party and country and died in a crash at Undur Khan in the People's Republic of Mongolia.[51]

It is now generally agreed that Lin, together with his wife and son, did die in an airplane crash while trying to escape Mao's trap as it closed around him. Whether Lin actually attempted a coup d'état and Mao's assassination, or even Mao's capture, must remain open questions.

With the fall of Mao's heir, the erstwhile counterheir, Chou En-lai, exerted an increasingly powerful, if temporary, personal influence on China's policy. His influence was based less on raw power than on his great intelligence and experience as a statesman and administrator, and, more important, on the fact that Chou's understanding of the revolution's current needs was shared at this time by Mao. While the central governmental bureaucracy did not provide Chou with a durable base of personal power, its political weight in Peking in the early seventies was greater than usual because of the weakness of the central organs of the Party *apparat* and the army. The central Party apparatus had been virtually destroyed in the early months of the Cultural Revolution, when Mao launched his attack on the secretariat and purged Liu Shao-ch'i and Teng Hsiao-p'ing; the army's central organs were seriously weakened by the 1971 purge of Lin Piao and his close allies. As a result, Chou's personal position, based on the central state bureaucracy, reached a peak immediately following the purge of Lin Piao.

Sharing power with Chou in the Party politburo was the Left,

[51] *Peking Review*, September 7, 1973, p. 18.

or radical, faction, which had distinguished itself by great zeal during the Cultural Revolution. The two factions were mutually opposed, having struggled against each other since the early months of the Cultural Revolution. At that time the radical group had urged the Red Guard to attack the Establishment; the Chou group, which at times itself became a target of the Red Guards, had tried to preserve as much stability as the circumstances allowed. There were abundant signs of continuing tension between the two factions after the purge of Lin. At the center of power, balancing the two groups, as well as the regime's other contradictory elements, against each other, stood Mao, who had profited the most from Lin's defeat. Having used Lin Piao to recover control of the regime, and having then proceeded to destroy Lin, Mao, though physically weak in the ninth decade of his life, was near the peak of his power.

The army and the Party *apparat,* though each lacked a strong central headquarters and was weakly represented for a time in the Party's top central bodies, had great strength outside Peking. Regional military commanders had acquired increased responsibilities in local civil administration in the course of the Cultural Revolution. Subsequently, after the turbulence had died down, the Party apparatus in the provinces was rebuilt, to the detriment of the army. The imbalance between the *provincial* strength of the army and the Party apparatus and their weak representation in Party organs at the *center* might have given rise to political instability if it had not been remedied at the Tenth Party Congress.

The Tenth Congress, convened secretly in late August 1973, established a new balance among the main political forces. Regional Party bosses and regional military commanders acquired strong representation in the two top central Party bodies, the standing committee of the politburo and the politburo itself, moving into the places lost by Lin Piao's purged faction. Nevertheless, despite their gains in the top Party bodies, the party *apparat* and the army remained without strong central organs of their own. The new Party constitution again made no provision for a secretariat. "Under the leadership of the Chairman, Vice-Chairmen and the Standing Committee of the Political Bureau of the Central Committee, a number of necessary organs, which are compact and efficient, shall be set up to attend to the day-to-day work of the Party, the government and the Army in a centralized way." [52] This wording seemed to preclude the large, concentrated professional staff of Party officials required to operate a secretariat. Furthermore, the constitution made no provision for secretaries of the central committee, who, ever since the days of Stalin, had arrogated power by directing such a staff.[53] As a result, the *apparat* remained without the kind of centralized direction that has made similar structures powerful political forces in the countries of the Soviet bloc.

Chou En-lai, at the head of the state bureaucracy, ranked second to Mao perhaps for the first time in his five-decade career. However, no effort was made to suggest that he was Mao's heir presumptive. On the contrary, care was taken to balance Chou's eminence with that of a young new leader, Wang Hung-wen. Of the two central committee reports to the Tenth Party Congress, Chou gave the general political report; Wang, the report on changes in the Party constitution. Chou sat at Mao's left at the congress, Wang at Mao's right. In photographs of the proceedings Wang was given equal prominence with Chou. Although there is no reason to suppose that Wang's present power or authority approximated Chou's, his special place in Mao's succession plans was clearly indicated. While the standing committee of the politburo and the politburo itself are listed in stroke order, the five vice-chairmen of the central committee are listed in rank order. The implication of the rank-order listing is that this is the order of their succession to Mao's post of chairman; in this rank-order listing, Chou is placed first, Wang second.

Wang had first come to prominence in association with the

[52] Party constitution adopted August 28, 1973: Chapter IV, "Central Organizations of the Party"; trans. in *Peking Review*, September 7, 1973.

[53] "Party committees at all levels in the localities and the army units," however, elect secretaries (Chapter V, Article 10, *ibid*).

radical faction in Shanghai, where he served as Chang Ch'un-
ch'iao's deputy in mobilizing the workers for the political battles
of the Cultural Revolution. While it seems strange that Chang's
thirty-five year old protégé should have risen so quickly above
his sixty-year old patron, this may be partly explained by the
newly emphasized principle of balancing the old (Chou En-lai),
the middle-aged,[54] and the young (Wang). It seems most unlikely, however, that Wang, whom the congress gave high office
as well as public prominence, merely represented the young and
did not embody in his own person a substantial element of Mao's
plans for the succession. Wang appeared to serve two purposes
in Mao's dispositions for the period immediately ahead, as well
as for the succession. First, Wang's high rank helped maintain a
balance between the radical faction, to which he belonged, and
the faction headed by Chou En-lai; at the same time, it indicated
the limits of Chou's personal authority and made it abundantly
clear that Chou was not Mao's unique "successor," as Lin had
been according to the constitution adopted by the Ninth Party
Congress. Second, giving high rank and prestige to a young man
who had proved himself in the making of revolution rather than
in the tasks of ordinary rule served Mao's objective of providing
China with new cultural revolutions, instead of with bureaucratic stability, after his demise.

Mao's hopes for the succession did not, of course, repose solely
in Wang, whose position was by no means secure. Wang was
likely to meet opposition from Chou En-lai and members of
Chou's faction. He had yet to be tested in various capacities, a
process that might well cost him Mao's confidence. The important
question for Mao, however, was not whether he ought to make
Wang his heir, but, instead, whether he could impose "Mao's
Thought" and a commitment to new cultural revolutions upon
the post-Mao leadership. It seemed doubtful that Mao could accomplish this, even if he was able to identify the leaders whose
thought was truly congruent with his own. Political power in

---

[54] Within the politburo, Chang represents the middle-aged.

China had been dispersed, particularly after the Cultural Revolution and the purge of Lin Piao, and Mao appeared to lack the will and perhaps also the capacity to concentrate it in the degree necessary to effect a transfer of power to particular leaders of his choice. To do so would probably require the re-establishment of a strong ministry of defense or a powerful, centralized military affairs committee in the central committee; it seemed doubtful that Mao, after his experience with Lin Piao, would favor either. An alternative (or supplementary) mechanism for ordering the succession on behalf of particular leaders would be the re-establishment of a powerful secretariat of the central committee, such as formerly existed under Liu Shao-ch'i and Teng Hsiao-p'ing, but it was even less likely that Mao would willingly alter his opposition to a powerful, centralized Party *apparat*. For these reasons, Mao was limited in the extent to which he could influence the disposition of his power after his demise.

Mao, in his succession arrangements, evidently did not rely only on a capacity to choose the top leaders who would follow him. He sought, in addition, to create powerful constraints on that leadership by training "millions of successors who will carry on the cause of proletarian revolution," who when necessary would "go against the tide" and not be afraid to oppose a revisionist leadership.[55] These successors would be inspired not only by the precedent of the Great Proletarian Cultural Revolution, in the mythic version of it propagated by Mao and his close supporters, but also by the specific doctrine of mass rebellion embodied in "Mao Tse-tung Thought." This theme of the need for recurrent mass rebellion was prominent at the Tenth Congress, and was put into the newly adopted Party constitution: revolutions like the Cultural Revolution "will have to be carried out many times in the future."[56] Similarly, Wang Hung-wen, in reporting on the new constitution, quoted Mao as follows: "Great disorder across the land leads to great order. And so once again every seven or eight years. Monsters and demons will jump out

[55] *Peking Review*, September 7, 1973, p. 32.   [56] *Ibid.*, p. 26.

themselves. Determined by their own class nature, they are bound to jump out." [57] Wang applied this 1966 statement of Mao's to the situation the Party confronted at the Tenth Congress: "The living reality of class struggle has confirmed and will continue to confirm this objective law as revealed by Chairman Mao. We must heighten our vigilance and understand the protractedness and complexity of this struggle. . . . [We must] carry out many great political revolutions such as the Great Proletarian Cultural Revolution." [58] Chou's policies conformed to Mao's understanding of China's needs in the aftermath of the Cultural Revolution (just as Liu Shao-ch'i's program of recovery had conformed to Mao's view of what China needed in the aftermath of the Great Leap Forward); however, Wang's commitment to "many great political revolutions" seems in better accord with Mao's understanding of what China will need tomorrow and thereafter.

In the interval remaining before China must directly face the Mao succession, the crucial developments that may determine the outcome appear to be these: the struggle between the most powerful Party officials and the military commanders in the provinces; the struggle in Peking between the radical and the Chou En-lai factions; and finally, Mao's interventions in these struggles and, in particular, his decision whether to inaugurate a massive new personal intervention on behalf of revolution. While Mao's capacity to influence the succession remains great, the time available to him for doing so is limited. At some time in the next few years Mao will have to surrender supreme power, probably because of death or illness, though the eventuality cannot be ruled out, despite the numerous unsuccessful conspiracies of the past, that a new conspiracy may initiate the succession.

Once Mao is gone, how likely is it that his plans for the succession, in which new cultural revolutions to purify the regime are a central feature, will be realized? A new cultural revolution is

[57] *Ibid.*, p. 30.   [58] *Ibid.*, p. 31.

unlikely to take place if it is opposed jointly by the Party apparatus and the army, and it manifestly is in the interest of both institutions to prevent its occurrence. Mao devised the cultural revolution specifically as an instrument to cleanse the regime's institutions periodically of the corruption to which they are prone. Why then would the Party apparatus or the army initiate a cultural revolution, especially since a cultural revolution, once initiated, is difficult to control, as Mao himself acknowledged? [59] At the beginning of the Mao succession the Party apparatus and the army, though they will be engaged in vigorous bargaining to decide the composition and policies of the new leadership, are indeed likely to cooperate to effect an orderly transfer of power. They will probably try to ensure that the radical faction (made up of Chiang Ch'ing, Chang Ch'un-ch'iao, Wang Hung-wen, and others) is unable to mobilize elements of the "masses" by organizing the proletariat into an urban militia, the young into red guards, or the peasantry into a force of armed partisans. Though the Party apparatus and the army are likely to combine against the Left initially, however, they may fall out with the passing of time. If they fail to reach an accommodation based on an agreed definition of their respective jurisdictions, or if neither achieves a decisive victory in a struggle for supremacy, the arena of politics will tend to expand. Each side will be tempted to mobilize the masses, perhaps spurred on by fears that its rival was planning to instigate a new cultural revolution directed against itself. The outcome could be a competition between the Party apparatus and the army to mobilize elements of the masses and to deploy them in violent encounters, such as occurred in early phases of the Great Proletarian Cultural Revolution. Such internecine warfare, unregulated by Mao, could place the regime

[59] "Something disastrously wrong was done by me in the great cultural revolution, that is, I approved the big-character poster by Nieh Yuan-tzu of Peking University. . . . The time was very short, but the situation developed so rapidly as to surprise me" (speech at a Central Committee work conference, October 25, 1966, JPRS, p. 13).

itself in jeopardy. Leaders of the Party apparatus and the army doubtless will think hard before taking the first steps along a road on which such grave dangers lie open to view.

A new cultural revolution, if it is to achieve Mao's aim of purification rather than mere destruction, cannot originate as a mere by-product of struggle for the succession. To revitalize the revolution, a charismatic leadership and a revolutionary mass following seem necessary. Unless a new Mao appears to replace the present one (a most unlikely prospect), Mao's hopes for the succession are unlikely to be realized.

PART IV

CONCLUSION

12

Findings and Reflections

The thesis that the absence in Communist regimes of an orderly method of succession creates difficulties whenever supreme power is transferred is borne out by the historical account presented in Part II. But this account also indicates that the worst consequences that might be anticipated from this constitutional defect have not been realized.

Stabilizing Influence of the Party Apparatus on Succession

There has been an important source of stability in Communist succession, at least when it has occurred in the past decade, which must not be lost sight of. It stems from the crucial advantage of the senior secretary over the other candidates in the succession contest, which has favored his efforts to consolidate personal rule and thereby resolve the succession.[1] The senior secretary's advantage is due to his position at the head of the Party apparatus, which enables him to gain access to its levers of control. The extent of his advantage depends on the place of the Party apparatus in the system of ruling institutions, and this has been a variable factor. At times the Party apparatus has been a subordinate element; consequently, the senior secretary's power has been limited. When, however, the Party apparatus has controlled the other institutions of the regime and, in this sense, has

[1] The actual title of the senior secretary may be first secretary, general secretary, or simply, secretary. See note 4, below.

285

been sovereign, the senior secretary's advantage has been great, and at times decisive, in the contest for the succession.

A central feature of the politics of succession in the post-Stalin period has been the rise of the Party apparatus to a position of sovereignty in all the states of the Soviet bloc. By conferring on the senior secretary a great advantage in his struggle for the succession, this sovereignty has tended to ease the crisis of the transfer of rule.

When Stalin died in 1953, Communist regimes had existed in the various states for a total of more than eighty years, yet for only ten of those years (from approximately 1927 to 1937 in the USSR) had the Party apparatus been sovereign. Stalin had conferred sovereignty on the Party apparatus, which he headed as general secretary, in the mid-twenties; a decade later, during the "great terror," he deprived it of sovereignty. When Communist states were established in Eastern Europe after World War II, the Party apparatus in these states, though a major instrument of rule, was subject to control by the Soviet army and by the national political police, which after 1948 also was directed from Moscow.

Stalin's system of personal despotism broke down after his death. The decade that followed was crucial for the world Communist movement. These were the years when the Soviet Party apparatus, in a fateful struggle against the government and its bureaucracy, recovered sovereignty. If it had failed to do so, as it might have, events in the Communist world might have followed a radically different course: the state as representative of the people might have won sovereignty over the Party as the embodiment of the revolution. The consequences might have been a decrease in the reliance on ideology to legitimate a regime, a weakening of state control over society, and possibly an evolution of constitutional forms that might have institutionalized successions. The decade after Stalin's death was a critical juncture, since the USSR at the time still exerted a decisive influence in most of the ruling Communist parties. As it turned out, the victory of the Party apparatus in the USSR under Khrushchev led to its victory throughout the Soviet bloc. The manner in which this came about differed, however, in the various states.

1. In Czechoslovakia, Novotny's rise to power from 1953 to 1957 while heading the Party appartus, rather closely paralleled Khrushchev's rise, not only in strategy but also in the timing of tactical moves.[2]

2. In Hungary, Rakosi's strategy to recover the power he lost when Stalin died was based on his retention of the post of first secretary. Supported by Khrushchev, he succeeded, by 1955, in his efforts to make the Party apparatus supreme. The Party collapsed, along with the other agencies of Communist rule, in the uprising of the Hungarian people the following year, but Kadar subsequently rebuilt it as the sovereign institution of his rule.

3. In East Germany, Ulbricht's personal power, even while Stalin lived, was based chiefly on the Party apparatus. After the June 1953 uprising, Ulbricht consolidated his position by defeating his opponents in the political police (Zaisser) and the government (Ackermann), and by strengthening his grip on the Party apparatus, which he made the sovereign institution. Until 1960, Ulbricht's post in the government was only deputy chairman of the council of ministers; the chairman, Otto Grotewohl, on occasion cooperated with Ulbricht's opponents.

4. In Poland, after Bierut's death and the fall of Ochab (October 1956), Gomulka, as first secretary, made the Party apparatus the basis of his own rule.

5. In Bulgaria, from 1954 to 1956, Chervenkov based his authority on his post of head of the government. After he was downgraded, in 1956, Zhivkov, as first secretary, struggled for personal ascendancy. Zhivkov achieved success only in the early sixties, when he finally was able to purge his opponents in the

[2] Novotny became first secretary in September 1953, at the same time as Khrushchev. Novotny made the Party apparatus the dominant institution by 1957 and extended his authority over the state by making himself president in late 1957, just a few months before Khrushchev became head of the Soviet government.

government (Chervenkov and Yugov) and establish the supremacy of the Party apparatus.

6. In Romania, Gheorghiu-Dej continued to exercise a broadly-based personal rule after Stalin's death, even executing, in 1954, personal rivals like Patrascanu. It was only after Gheorghiu-Dej's death in 1965 that Ceausescu, as first secretary, succeeded in making the Party apparatus the sovereign institution.

Even in China, which had followed a largely independent course of development, the power of the Party apparatus, and particularly of its central secretariat and its general secretary (Teng Hsiao-p'ing), was significantly enhanced in the mid-fifties. After 1966, however, Mao Tse-tung ousted the general secretary, disbanded the secretariat, and subordinated the Party apparatus to revolutionary committees dominated by military officers.

In the Soviet bloc the Party apparatus has continued to exercise sovereignty. The Romanian succession in 1965 was the last in which the successor to the post of first secretary (Ceausescu) faced the task of establishing the sovereignty of the Party apparatus. In the three subsequent successions that have occurred in the Soviet bloc (in Czechoslovakia, Poland, and East Germany), as well as in the 1964 Khrushchev succession in the USSR, the new senior secretary has led a sovereign Party apparatus, and this has eased his problem in consolidating personal rule and resolving the succession. The senior secretary's main rivals have been members of the Party apparatus; the struggle, except in the Novotny succession, has been waged chiefly within the party apparatus.[3]

In a succession contest waged in the Party apparatus, and especially in its secretariat, the senior secretary's advantages, as this study has repeatedly had occasion to observe, are formidable. Although his powers are not defined in the Party statutes of the Communist states (hence his authority is problematic), certain functions and powers are traditionally associated with the office, or at least with the secretariat, in which he has the

---

[3] The pattern was disrupted in the Novotny succession by the intervention of the Czechoslovak people and of Moscow.

leading position. The secretariat has statutory responsibility for checking on the implementation of Party decisions, which gives it authority over the entire Party apparatus, as well as grounds for intervening in the work of other institutions. Because of the secretariat's powers of appointment at all levels but the highest, control of it confers substantial patronage. Moreover, the secretariat is responsible for preparing the agenda and necessary materials for meetings of the politburo and plenary meetings of the central committee; if the senior secretary wins a decisive voice in the secretariat, he may substantially influence these bodies' deliberations.

The senior secretary's potential *power*, his capacity to act, and to compel others to act, to promote his political ends, is indeed formidable; but his legitimate power, or authority, is less. The divergence between the two widened during the Stalin succession, owing particularly to Khrushchev's 1956 speech criticizing Stalin, which tended to cast discredit on the office he had so long occupied. Khrushchev (as well as senior secretaries in other Communist states) dealt with the problem by acquiring an additional source of legitimacy as head of the government. In the post-Khrushchev period, however, the senior secretaries' efforts have centered on building up the authority of their Party office. Thus, the more impressive title of general secretary, which had everywhere been abandoned after Stalin's death, was restored in Romania (1965), in the USSR (1966), and in Czechoslovakia (1971).[4] Moreover, the office of general secretary was made statutory in the Soviet Communist Party for the first time, so

---

[4] Except for a brief period during which the senior secretary had no special title in two parties (in the USSR and Czechoslovakia, from March to September 1953), he has been called either *general* secretary, or, more modestly, *first* secretary, of the central committee. Before 1953 the senior secretary was invariably called general secretary. Currently, in the USSR, Czechoslovakia, and Romania, he is titled general secretary of the central committee; elsewhere he is called first secretary. The difference in terminology had considerable significance in the fifties and sixties, but this may no longer be the case. Gierek, in Poland, for example, is called first secretary, and Husak, in Czechoslovakia, general secretary, although Gierek clearly is the more powerful of the two.

that henceforth the central commtitee is obliged to choose a new general secretary whenever the office is vacated.[5]

Brezhnev has carried further this process of institutionalizing the post of general secretary. Prevented till now (like Husak and Honecker), from assuming a top state or government office, he has chosen to use his Party office as the basis for engaging in summitry with foreign statesmen. In his capacity as general secretary of the central committee of the Communist Party of the Soviet Union, he has negotiated and signed state agreements with other powers. To transform the signature of a Party official into a binding obligation of the Soviet state has required a clumsy (and perhaps somewhat demeaning) device: the Soviet government submits a statement to the other party to the agreement asserting that Brezhnev has signed the document on instructions from the Soviet government. There is an element of choice in this circuitous arrangement, since Brezhnev, if he wished, could sign state agreements in his capacity as a member of the presidium of the Supreme Soviet.

The willingness of non-Communist states to acknowledge the general secretary's authority to act on behalf of the Soviet government has important implications for Soviet internal politics. It contributes to the general secretary's prestige and helps to narrow the gap between his power and his authority. As a consequence of these developments, progress has been made in the past decade toward effecting a constitutional transfer of supreme authority in the USSR, although before the task is completed much more will have to be done.

From what has been said it is apparent how closely the fortunes of the senior secretary and of the Party apparatus are intertwined. The *apparat* is naturally inclined to support the senior secretary as its candidate in a succession contest, being aware that his defeat may open the way for candidates whose strength lies in other institutions and whose fate, therefore, is linked with

[5] On the other hand, from March 1953 to September 1953, Khrushchev, the top-rank secretary, had no special title.

those institutions.[6] By giving impetus to the senior secretary's campaign to defeat his rivals for the succession, a sovereign Party apparatus has been a stablizing factor during a succession. Despite the shared aims of the Party apparatus and the senior secretary, there inevitably is tension between them. Members of the *apparat* want to be secure in their jobs, while the senior secretary wants them to be dependent so they will obey him. The tension may escalate as the senior secretary consolidates personal power. He is likely to increase his demands on the *apparat*, requiring of its functionaries work for which they may not be qualified by inclination, training, or experience. He may also at some point attempt to strengthen the role of other institutions in order to reduce his own dependence on the *apparat*. Leading *apparachiks* will resist his encroachments on their independence, but in doing so they must be wary of disrupting the regime in which the Party apparatus has the central place. Even when the senior secretary has succeeded in establishing a pre-eminent position in the politburo, the *apparat* may support the continued growth of his personal power in order to reduce the influence of competing institutions represented in the politburo (the government, the economic bureaucracy, the army, and so forth). Competition from lower-ranking Party secretaries may be an obstacle, but the centralized, hierarchical character of the Party apparatus seems to favor the concentration of its power in the hands of the senior secretary. These considerations help to account for the

[6] The senior secretary, on his part, supports the Party apparatus against the encroachments of rival institutions. Moreover, in seeking support from the Party apparatus in the early phase of a succession, the Party secretary may find it expedient to accommodate to its members' desire for security in office, as Brezhnev did, for example, in the aftermath of Khrushchev's overthrow: "The frequent reorganizations of Party, government, and economic bodies that have taken place in recent years [i.e., under Khrushchev] have had an adverse effect on the . . . selection, promotion, and training of cadres. As a rule, these changes were accompanied by an unjustified shifting and changing of officials, and this resulted in a lack of confidence among them, prevented them from making full use of their abilities, and gave grounds for irresponsibility" (*Pravda*, March 30, 1966).

otherwise puzzling fact that the senior secretary in a Communist state, initially only the most powerful member of an oligarchy, again and again has augmented his power within the oligarchy, even to a point where he has been able to subvert it and establish personal rule.

True, more than once a Party secretary has failed to consolidate power. Would-be rulers lacking firm support in the Party apparatus and faced with popular discontent, like Ochab and Gero, not surprisingly have fallen. Even ruling secretaries whose policies or mode of rule antagonized the *apparat*, like Khrushchev and Novotny, proved vulnerable to attack and were overthrown. The end result of a succession initiated by the fall of a senior secretary, however, has been the emergence of a new secretary as the predominant leader in a ruling oligarchy (this is the situation at this writing in the USSR, Czechoslovakia, and East Germany) or as the personal ruler (as in Hungary, Bulgaria, and Poland). Moreover, in Romania, after the death of the previous leader, the present senior secretary achieved personal rule; in North Vietnam, he became the dominant figure in an oligarchy. Furthermore, the original rulers in Albania and in North Korea still base their power on their position as first secretary. Only in China and Yugoslavia, where the *apparat* is not sovereign, is the senior secretary not the top-ranking leader.

It remains to be seen whether the customary price the Party apparatus must pay for its sovereignty is subjection to the limited personal rule of the senior secretary, and whether its sole means of protecting itself against his arbitrary exercise of power is to overthrow him.[7] Until now, at any rate, the *apparat*'s willing support of the senior secretary has tended to mitigate the severity of a crisis of succession and to ease the tensions of its resolution. The *apparat*'s hegemony has also provided an effective mechanism by which a ruler who seeks to arrange the succession can confer a great advantage on his heir presumptive by giving him

[7] In Tsarist Russia the aristocracy had to pay an even higher price for its power and privileges: subjection to despotism.

a strategic post in the central *apparat*. (We return to this subject below.) If the ruler chooses to avail himself of this possibility, however, he must assume a large risk that his heir may use such a powerful post to unseat him.

Granted that the *apparat* has been a stabilizing factor during periods of succession in the Soviet bloc, the question necessarily arises whether, in Communist states where the Party apparatus is not sovereign, such as China and Yugoslavia, the succession must produce crises of greater severity. The problem of arranging the transfer of power from a charismatic founder, like Mao and Tito, to an organization-minded heir, like Liu Shao-ch'i and Rankovic, is in any case extremely difficult. The initial succession arrangements of Mao and Tito providing for the transfer of power to an *apparachik* had to be abandoned. The absence of a sovereign Party apparatus that can be used as the vehicle for the transfer of power considerably complicates the succession problem that Mao and Tito are at this writing attempting to deal with. Whether the politicization of the army and the resort to constitutional enactments of various kinds in both China and Yugoslavia will provide adequate substitute mechanisms for ordering the succession remains to be seen.

Candidates and the Outcome of Succession Contests

The circle of succession comprises leaders whose high position in the political bureau and the secretariat or, in some instances, whose past careers or personal qualities make them potential candidates for the succession.

Particular ethnic and professional backgrounds may handicap ambitious leaders who otherwise might enter the circle of succession. Since entry is controlled from the top, some of the relevant criteria may change abruptly. In the early postwar period, for example, being Jewish was hardly a handicap. Jews as a persecuted minority had been recruited into the Communist parties of Eastern Europe in disproportionately large numbers. They acquired experience in upper-level posts and thus tended to rise into the top leadership in the early years of the newly established Communist regimes when no barriers were placed in their way. Subsequently, the prominence of Jewish Communists was seen as an obstacle in campaigns to win a measure of popular support for these regimes and they were forced from power. After 1952 it became virtually impossible for a Jew to enter the circle, and by the end of the decade not many Jews were left in the entire membership of the central committees of ruling Communist parties. On the other hand, members of large ethnic minorities, such as the Slovaks in Czechoslovakia, were ineligible for the most powerful posts in Prague in the late forties and early fifties; by the late sixties being Slovak was no barrier at all, and was perhaps an advantage. Accounting for this change in the eligibility of Slovaks is difficult, but no doubt the fact that Slovaks had earlier been victimized by Prague gave rise to special claims by politically active Slovaks during the period of rehabilitation.

Criteria of professional and educational experience have been more durable than ethnic criteria. Except in Yugoslavia and China, no one has entered the circle of succession in recent decades without prior top-level experience in the *apparat,* usually over an extended period of time.[8] Higher education still is not required, but future top leaders, like those who have most recently reached the top, will at least have received advanced training in a Higher Party School, whether locally or in Moscow.

No woman has yet reached the very top in a Communist state, although the wives of Mao and Lin Piao entered the Chinese Party's politburo without meeting any of the customary requirements, and Mao's wife, Chiang Ch'ing, remains in it. Ana Pauker, one of the most influential figures in the Romanian leadership in the late forties, was able, because of backing from Moscow, to hurdle the barrier faced by women. The wives

---

[8] The least experienced *apparachik* among current senior secretaries is Gustav Husak, who had only a brief tenure as first secretary in the Slovak central committee after the Soviet occupation of Czechoslovakia before receiving the top post in Prague.

of numerous high Party figures have had places just outside the succession circle in the central committees of several countries, including those of China, Albania, Romania, and East Germany. Women are considered to be particularly qualified for certain specialized posts in Communist regimes (those dealing with women's affairs and education) and, in addition, are employed by their husbands in special, confidential missions. Because, as women, they confront strong barriers to a further rise in the leadership, they may be more acceptable to their husbands' colleagues for such purposes than male relatives would be.

Closest to the center of the succession circle in Communist states is the head of the *apparat,* the senior secretary.[9] At the time of Stalin's death, in 1953, his favored position within the circle was problematic; doubt was dissolved four years later, at the time of Khrushchev's massive purge of his opponents in the Soviet government. Although the man chosen senior secretary at the onset of succession is not assured of rule, this is a decision of great moment in the succession contest. Who has the best chance of taking possession of the senior secretary's vacant post? When things go smoothly, the new head of the *apparat* is likely to be the second-rank secretary. Almost half the time, however, things have not gone smoothly.

The Second-Rank Secretary

One problem the second-rank secretary may face at the decisive moment is the fact that he lacks a special title to go with his position. This lack is an anomaly in Communist states; at all lower levels of the Party apparatus the top secretaries are ranked by title, so that the deputy to the first secretary has the title of second secretary. But in the secretariat of the central committee all the

[9] Exceptions to this and other similar generalizations are China and Yugoslavia, the two states where the central Party *apparat* does not possess hegemony.

members except the senior secretary bear the simple title of *secretary*. Nevertheless, it usually is not difficult to identify the secretary who ranks second: special devices may be used to convey his rank, as when Frol Kozlov was listed second after Khrushchev, and the other secretaries followed in alphabetical order; the second-rank secretary may deputize for the senior secretary; at Party congresses the second-rank secretary usually gives the report on organizational matters, or perhaps even the accountability report of the central committee; the second-rank secretary often, though not always, is responsible for cadre assignments.

Promotion of the second-rank secretary to a vacant top post is not automatic. On seven occasions the second secretary did receive the higher office in circumstances where this conferred primacy in the leadership. In each instance Moscow or the local leadership controlled the succession. This was true in the successions to Dimitrov, Bierut, Rakosi, Gero, Khrushchev, Gheorghiu-Dej, and Ulbricht. (In addition, the second-rank secretary was promoted to the top post of the *apparat* in Romania and Bulgaria in 1954, when the ruler vacated it to satisfy the formal requirements of "collective leadership": Stoica was thus promoted in Romania, and Zhivkov in Bulgaria.) The succession to Gottwald was equivocal. Although Novotny was not the second-rank secretary when Gottwald died in 1953, he had been until only a few weeks previously, when he was transferred to the government. At Gottwald's death Novotny returned to the secretariat, and not long afterward he was given the title of first secretary. The second-rank secretary did not succeed to the top post in the *apparat* on five other occasions: in the successions to Stalin, Ochab, Novotny, Dubcek, and Gomulka. In all but the Stalin succession the elevation of the second-rank secretary failed to occur because powerful forces outside the top leadership intervened. It can be inferred that the second secretary is expected to succeed to the office and, so long as the top leadership is free to decide, he generally is able to make good his claim.

The second-rank secretary has succeeded to the top secretariat post on the following occasions, with varying consequences:

1. Chervenkov succeeded Dimitrov as general secretary in Bulgaria in 1949, and subsequently established personal rule.

2. When Gheorghiu-Dej stepped down as first secretary in Romania in 1954, after Moscow proclaimed the doctrine of collective leadership, he temporarily promoted his second secretary, Stoica, to his former post. A year later Gheorghiu-Dej resumed the position of first secretary, subsequently making Ceausescu his deputy.

3. In Bulgaria, Chervenkov, like Gheorghiu-Dej, nominally retired in favor of his second-rank secretary, Zhivkov. When, however, Moscow ordered Chervenkov's demotion in 1956, Zhivkov became the most powerful figure in the leadership; subsequently, after a struggle of several years, he established personal rule.

4. In Poland, when Bierut died in 1956, Ochab, who had been the second-rank secretary in recent years, succeeded him, but found it necessary seven months later to relinquish the post.

5. When Rakosi was removed from his post as first secretary in Hungary, in July 1956, his second secretary and close political ally, Gero, took his place.

6. When demonstrations forced Gero from office three months later, Moscow replaced him with Kadar, who since July had been the second-rank secretary.

7. When Khrushchev was ousted from his position as first secretary in 1964, he was replaced by Brezhnev, the second-rank secretary.

8. When Gheorghiu-Dej died in April 1965, he was succeeded by the second-rank secretary, Ceausescu, who later established personal rule.

9. When Ulbricht, in East Germany, resigned as first secretary in the spring of 1971, he was replaced by Honecker, the second-rank secretary.

The fact that the second secretary ordinarily succeeds to the post of senior secretary indicates that predicting who will succeed presents few intrinsic difficulties in the short term. What is difficult to predict is not so much the identity of the successor as his capacity, once in office, to consolidate his position. Because of the crucial advantage of the post of first secretary in the succession contest, and because the second secretary is in a favored position to occupy the post of first secretary when it falls vacant, he is at the focus of attention in the initial stage of succession. In a certain respect, Communist succession resembles succession in an unstable hereditary monarchy. In such a regime, the identity of the heir apparent is known but his claim to the succession may be subject to strong challenge. On the other hand, Communist succession contests are unlike those in most modern regimes, in which several rival candidates usually compete, each with a relatively good chance to emerge victorious.

When the second secretary has been unequivocally designated by the ruler as his heir, the strength of the second secretary's claim to rule most closely approximates that of the heir apparent in a hereditary monarchy. In these circumstances, if the Party's top post falls vacant, the chances are better than even that the heir presumptive will be promoted to it. With the passage of time the ruler may, however, change his heir presumptive, thereby falsifying expectations that the incumbent second secretary would succeed. The ruler himself may lose power; in that event, expectations that the heir presumptive would succeed will be fulfilled only if he contributes to the ouster of the first secretary and consequently is able to replace him in office.

Other Secretarial Candidates

If the second-rank secretary is for some reason disqualified for the highest post in the *apparat,* the officials next in rank are in the line of succession. The number-three man in the secretariat may become the senior secretary, as happened when Khrushchev succeeded Stalin in the post. Alternatively—particularly if the central secretariat has been discredited by the opposition—the top Party post may go to the secretary of a powerful territorial

Party organization (for example, in the capital city or in a component republic). The second-rank secretary of the Czechoslovak central committee in January 1968, Jiri Hendrych, was in poor repute in 1968, together with his boss, Novotny, and in any case he had recently quarreled with him. Consequently, the succession passed to Dubcek, the first secretary in Slovakia (that is, the third- or fourth-rank post in the Czechoslovak Party apparatus), who had led the Slovak opposition to Novotny. When Dubcek was ousted after the Soviet invasion, the man chosen as the new first secretary was once more the head of the Slovak *apparat* (Gustav Husak). When Gomulka and his henchmen were ousted in the aftermath of the 1970 riots in Poland, he was succeeded as first secretary by Gierek, head of the Party organization in the key industrial province of Katowice.

In the single instance in which the successor to the post of senior secretary did not come from the Party apparatus, he came from outside the top leadership altogether.[10] Gomulka had been expelled from the community of Communists for alleged political deviations, and his first post after his political rehabilitation in the spring of 1956 was the Party's highest. In a comparable case, Kadar served in subordinate positions in the period following his 1954 political rehabilitation before becoming the second secretary of the Hungarian central committee in July 1956, and the first secretary in October. (At about the same time, Nagy became head of the Hungarian government—the dominant position for a brief moment in October 1956—only a few days after being restored to membership in the Party.)

Whatever the path that brings him to the head of the Party *apparat*, once there the incumbent is in a good position to estab-

[10] Technically Novotny and Gheorghiu-Dej (in his second tenure, beginning in 1955) also were not members of the *apparat* when they were chosen senior secretary. At the time of Gottwald's death in 1953, Novotny was deputy chairman of the council of ministers, a post he had held for less than a month; Gheorghiu-Dej, when he resumed the post of first secretary in 1955, was head of the Romanian government. (Actually he had continued to run the *apparat* while Stoica nominally headed it.)

lish his personal ascendancy. This is particularly true if he previously was responsible for cadre appointments, but even if he comes to the top office from outside the secretariat, as Gomulka did, his chances are good.[11] Because of the great possibilities of his office, the senior secretary is the natural target of those who are unwilling to subordinate themselves to a personal ruler. As a consequence, he may be prevented from winning control over the secretariat,[12] as happened to Ochab (1956) and Dubcek (1968); even if he succeeds, he may find himself blocked by a hostile majority in the politburo. Novotny and Rakosi (in the early post-Stalin years) as well as Zhivkov (in the late fifties) found themselves in this situation: each was master of the secretariat but not of the politburo. In such circumstances, the senior secretary may have to purge the politburo, as these leaders did (and as Khrushchev did in the USSR in 1957), or he may be forced to vacate the office of senior secretary, as Ochab did in 1956 and Dubcek in 1969. Even if he succeeds in winning control of the secretariat and the politburo, the senior secretary may still fail to impose his rule on a recalcitrant people.

Despite such obstacles, eight men who had succeeded to the post of senior secretary were able, in the periods indicated below, to consolidate power and establish personal rule: Chervenkov in Bulgaria, 1949–1950; Khrushchev in the USSR, 1953–1957; Novotny in Czechoslovakia, 1953–1957; Zhivkov in Bulgaria, 1956–

---

[11] Responsibility for cadres, if exercised over a long period of time or during an extensive purge, may enable the second-rank secretary to achieve considerable personal power well before the onset of the succession. Ochab, Gero, Ceausescu, and Honecker, as second-rank secretaries, were for several years in charge of cadres before succeeding to the top post. (Nevertheless, Ochab and Gero failed in their efforts to establish personal rule.) Novotny acquired important powers while assigned the task of destroying the Slansky machine in Czechoslovakia in 1951 and 1952, as did Chervenkov while conducting the purge of Kostovites in Bulgaria in 1949 and 1950.

[12] According to Gheorghiu-Dej, such a situation prevailed in Romania for several years; finally, in 1952, Moscow allowed him to purge the secretariat and make himself its master.

1962; Kadar in Hungary, 1956–1960; Gomulka in Poland, 1956–1958; Ceausescu in Romania, 1965–1968; and Gierek in Poland, 1970–1971.[13] Although these eight were able to rule for a number of years, four subsequently were forced from power: Chervenkov in 1956, Khrushchev in 1964, Novotny in 1968, and Gomulka in 1970.

Against the success of these eight rulers must be set the failure of the three men who rose to the post of senior secretary but were unable to consolidate their power. In each instance failure occurred in a matter of months after achieving the post: Ochab in Poland, between March and October 1956. Gero in Hungary, between July and October 1956; and Dubcek in Czechoslovakia, between January 1968 and April 1969. They failed in different ways. Gero had no difficulty in controlling the secretariat, but the secretariat was no longer able to dominate the Party; or the Party, the nation. On the other hand, Ochab and Dubcek did not even succeed in winning control over their respective secretariats, which had powerful opponents in them. The political incapacity of these three leaders contributed to their failure, although in less turbulent times such a lack might not have brought them down. In none of the three instances was the succession resolved within the precincts of the leadership, because the people asserted themselves. Where popular forces were not important in determining the succession, even a rather mediocre leader like Zhivkov of Bulgaria was able to consolidate power, but to do so he needed six years' time and strong Soviet support.

Candidates from Non-Party Institutions

The most powerful figures in the state and the government have been among the chief candidates for the succession. As yet,

[13] Besides these eight, the original top leaders of various Communist regimes also came to exercise personal rule: Lenin, Bierut, Dimitrov, Gottwald, Rakosi, Hoxha, Gheorghiu-Dej, Ulbricht, Tito, Kim Il-sung, Ho Chi Minh, Castro, and Mao Tse-tung.

it is true, no head of government or head of state has succeeded to a position of personal rule.[14] In the course of the Stalin succession, however, three top leaders (Georgi Malenkov, Gheorghe Gheorghiu-Dej, and Valko Chervenkov) relinquished the post of senior secretary, in the belief, apparently that they could rule from the office of head of government. Although this supposition was falsified by events, it remains true that incumbents of the offices of head of state and head of government on a number of occasions proved to be serious obstacles that an ambitious senior secretary had to overcome before he could establish personal rule.

The partial crisis of succession in Hungary after Stalin's death was centered on the struggle between Rakosi, head of the Party apparatus, and Nagy, head of the government. It reflected developments in the personal and institutional struggle between Malenkov and Khrushchev in the USSR; thus Malenkov's defeat, for example, was quickly followed by that of Nagy. When Nagy reappeared briefly eighteen months later as the most authoritative leader in Hungary, it was once more as head of the government.

When Gottwald died in 1953, his offices were split: Novotny succeeded him as senior secretary, while Zapotocky succeeded him as president of the republic. Novotny's two chief rivals were Zapotocky, the president, and Siroky, the head of the government. Both proved ineffective opponents, partly because of personal handicaps: Zapotocky was too old, and Siroky was a Slovak who had antagonized his own people. Zapotocky died in 1957, and Novotny took on his post as president. When Siroky came under political attack in 1963, Novotny simply replaced him with Lenart, another Slovak.

After Bierut's death in March 1956, the factions that emerged

---

[14] In China the head of state was for a time the heir presumptive: from 1959, when Liu Shao-ch'i became president, to 1966, when he ceased to be heir presumptive. Besides being president, however, Liu also had considerable influence in the Party apparatus during this period.

in the Polish leadership cut across institutional lines. After Gomulka's victory at the October plenum, leading figures in the opposing Natolin faction, such as Zenon Nowak, found themselves without influence in the leadership of the Party apparatus and tried briefly to enhance the role of the government, where their remaining strength was concentrated. Subsequently, Gomulka consolidated his position, and remnants of the Natolin faction accommodated to his rule.

Soviet political intervention, in 1956, against Chervenkov resulted in his replacement as head of the Bulgarian government by Anton Yugov. During the next few years Yugov built up his influence in the state bureaucracy and headed one faction opposed to the rule of Party first secretary Todor Zhivkov. (Chervenkov, relying chiefly on his continuing influence in the middle levels of the Party apparatus, headed the other faction.) Yugov's moderate draft proposal in 1958 for the next five-year economic plan was rejected in favor of a wildly ambitious plan, a Bulgarian version of China's Great Leap, that was publicly advocated by Zhivkov and Chervenkov. Although Yugov tacitly opposed this unrealistic policy, when it failed one of his subordinates, Boris Taskov, the minister of trade, became the scapegoat. Yugov maintained his influence in the state bureaucracy until the Party's Eighth Congress, in November 1962, when he suddenly was ousted from his official posts and expelled from the Party. Although Yugov had not taken reformist positions consistently, his perspective as head of the government had made him favor more rational economic planning, and this constituted one of the grounds of his opposition to Zhivkov. In the end, the Party apparatus headed by Zhivkov was a decisive victor over the government headed by Yugov. To prevent further use of the government bureaucracy as a basis of opposition to his rule, Zhivkov himself replaced Yugov as its head.

After Gheorghiu-Dej of Romania died in 1965, his offices were divided in accordance with the principal of collective leadership, just as Gottwald's had been a dozen years earlier in Czechoslovakia. Ceausescu succeeded only to Gheorghiu-Dej's post of Party first secretary, not to that of chairman of the council of state. Ceausescu's chief rivals, Chivu Stoica and Gheorghe Apostol, probably hoped to limit him to the exercise of personal authority within the Party apparatus, while they themselves were using the state council to oppose him. The maneuver failed; two years later, when he was strong enough, Ceausescu took the post of head of state.

The top state and government offices have generally been employed in a struggle against the first secretary by men who were themselves candidates for the succession, but twice they were retained by former rulers as a residual source of power. Novotny clung for a time to his post of president of the republic after he was forced out as Party first secretary, apparently hoping to use the presidential authority over the army and the government bureaucracy in his struggle against the reformers. The growth of public opinion as a political factor further weakened his position, however, and he was finally forced to resign as president. In a comparable situation, when Ulbricht was forced to resign as Party first secretary in favor of Erich Honecker, he was allowed to remain head of the state council until his death two years later. In that post he apparently did not exert much influence on his successors.

While the head of government has direct control over the administrative bureaucracy, he may be encumbered with excessive detail; on the other hand, the head of state in some Communist countries has important constitutional powers. For these and other reasons, a first secretary may choose to occupy the office of head of state, making the head of government his subordinate. First secretaries who have headed the state include Novotny, Ulbricht, Zhivkov, Gheorghiu-Dej, and Ceausescu. Lin Piao, who ranked second to Mao in the Party, tried to achieve supreme state office in order to become Cho En-lai's superior, but failed because of Mao's opposition.

Although the establishment of the sovereignty of the Party

apparatus in most Communist states in the past two decades has reduced the capacity of state and government leaders to contend for the succession, at least for the time being, the institutions they head retain their potential of serving as bases of opposition to the dominant leadership. The government bureaucracy naturally has a perspective which favors increased rationality in economic planning and administration. It tends to oppose excessive reliance on Communist doctrine in deciding policy and on Communist organizational principles in implementing it. Even if this bias does not achieve full expression, opposition leaders of diverse political tendencies no doubt will continue to utilize the government's capacity to serve as a relatively neutral instrument in the struggle against the dominant leadership entrenched in the Party apparatus.

The Fate of Defeated Candidates

After Stalin expelled Yugoslavia from the Communist bloc in 1948, he extended to Eastern Europe his long-standing practice of executing Communist leaders who opposed him. In Albania, Bulgaria, Hungary, and Czechoslovakia, political executions were preceded by public trials like those held in the USSR in the thirties. In addition, a number of Communist leaders in East Germany, Romania, and Poland were purged and imprisoned, though not executed. Where executions occurred, Stalin probably ordered or, at any rate, sanctioned them.

Did the practice of executing defeated rivals extend only to places in which Stalin's will was effective? Evidently not; executions in other Communist states compel the conclusion that Stalin's example provided Communist leaders with a weighty precedent. In Romania, Gheorghiu-Dej executed Lucretiu Patrascanu and Remus Koffler (a wartime Communist leader) after military, not public, trials. These executions of Communist leaders—apparently the only ones in Romania since the war—subsequently were condemned by Gheorghiu-Dej's successor, Ceausescu.

While the 1954 trials in Romania (and the contemporaneous trial of Slovak nationalists in Czechoslovakia, which did not lead to executions) might be regarded as a carry-over of Stalinist practices in the period before Khrushchev launched the anti-Stalin campaign in 1956, this cannot be said of the execution of Nagy in 1958 for defiance of the USSR during the 1956 Hungarian revolution. Although Khrushchev criticized Stalin's execution of innocent men, he believed it was legitimate to invoke capital punishment for what he considered real political crimes.

The execution of leaders in Communist states has occurred even when Soviet influence has not been decisive or has been completely absent. In Asia, Kim Il-sung executed his rivals in the leadership while consolidating his rule in Pyongyang after the Korean War. This was at a time when Stalin was dead and Communist China's influence had largely supplanted the Soviet Union's.[15]

Although China has announced no executions of Communist leaders, the alleged suicide in 1955 of Kao Kang, the boss of Manchuria, who had been purged the previous year, is questionable. Moreover, it is not certain that Lin Piao died in an air accident as alleged.

Why have Communist rulers, in their struggle against rivals, employed such brutal means as capital punishment? Initially, Stalin's intention in the 1930's obviously was to eliminate figures who had a certain following in the Party, and even among important groups in Soviet society, so that they could not provide a viable alternative leadership to his own. An additional motive was to *deter* opposition to Stalin. Elsewhere in Eastern Europe, in the first years after the expulsion of Yugoslavia, the intention was similar: first, to stabilize the existing leadership by eliminating viable alternative leaders, particularly such relatively

[15] In Albania, five partisans of the Soviet Union—figures of middle rank, not rivals for the succession—were sentenced to death in 1961 after a public trial. They may not have been executed, however (Nicholas Pano, *The People's Republic of Albania* [Baltimore: Johns Hopkins Press, 1968], pp. 147–148).

popular Communist figures as Rajk and Kostov, around whom nationalist sentiment might rally; second, to enforce obedience to Moscow in the existing leadership and to root out any Titoist tendencies. In the second round of purges a new motive appeared: to eliminate ethnic Communists who were objects of prejudice to part of the people and who therefore needlessly deprived the regime of possible support.[16] In Romania, in the spring of 1952, this motive led to the purge of Jews and other minority nationals from the top leadership, though they were not killed; later in the year, however, in Czechoslovakia a dozen Jews and Slovaks were executed. Although Gheorghiu-Dej may have been less compliant to Stalin's wishes than Gottwald in the matter of executing his Communist associates, he was not against execution on principle: in 1954 he executed Patrascanu, an ethnic Romanian, whom he saw as a more serious danger to his own rule than the minority nationals purged earlier. Whether the use of capital punishment by Gheorghiu-Dej was also intended to deter political opposition by his lieutenants is not clear. In the execution of Nagy in Hungary, however, the motive of deterrence clearly predominated, since Nagy himself was no longer a threat to the Hungarian leadership. The execution, in Czechoslovakia of Slansky and his fellow victims was required neither to eliminate him as a political factor nor to deter an active opposition. Instead, it aimed—like the subsequent "doctors' plot" affair in the USSR —at creating an atmosphere of terror that would reduce the political leadership in Czechoslovakia and elsewhere in the Soviet bloc to a frightened instrument for the imposition of Stalin's will.

The employment of capital punishment for political crimes has greatly affected political succession. If Rajk had not been executed, he would have provided an obvious alternative to rule in Hungary by Rakosi and his numerous Jewish associates, both in 1953 and in 1956. As it was, the search for a successor to Rakosi led in turn to Gero, to Nagy, and finally to Kadar. It may

16 This may have been a minor factor in the 1930's purges also, since many of those publicly tried were Jews.

be argued that Rajk was well suited to play the role that Gomulka played in Poland and that Kadar finally was called upon to play in Hungary itself. If Rajk had been available, the Hungarian revolution might not have occurred. Kostov might have played a similar role in Bulgaria in 1956, when Chervenkov was removed. Instead, Moscow was obliged to rely on the relatively youthful and inexperienced Zhivkov, who needed a half-dozen years, even with Soviet support, to defeat more able men. If Rajk and Kostov had survived, they probably would have forgiven any injustice done them—as Gomulka and Kadar did— and provided loyal and effective service to their parties and to Moscow. Conversely, if Gomulka had not survived, the course of Polish politics from 1956 to 1970 might have been more turbulent and less satisfactory to Moscow.

Although capital punishment for political opposition turned out to be a mistake as well as a crime, failure to impose sanctions on defeated leaders, at least by removing them from the political scene, may also be disruptive and costly. At any rate, this proved to be the case in Bulgaria after Chervenkov was demoted in 1956. The failure to remove him from the politburo hampered Zhivkov's efforts to consolidate his position as Chervenkov's successor.

Chervenkov's capacity to compete for several years with the man who succeeded him at the head of the *apparat* has been paralleled in North Vietnam, where Le Duan's predecessor as first secretary, Truong Chinh, has been his chief rival in the struggle to succeed Ho Chi Minh. On the other hand, Edward Ochab, once he was separated from the levers of power in the secretariat, posed no threat to Gomulka's position in Poland even though Ochab remained in the politburo. Likewise, Ulbricht was allowed to remain active in political life in the East German politburo. Presumably his advanced age made it unlikely, in any case, that he could cause serious difficulties for Honecker, his successor. There are as yet too few cases from which to generalize. A guess may be hazarded, however, that the political potential of an ex-head of the *apparat* typically will not be great, because the personal power of a Communist leader (at least after the first, or founding, generation) normally derives from his current control over the levers of power rather than from his possession of office, of unusual personal qualities, or of a loyal personal following.

The subsequent fate of the other ousted top leaders has been as varied as the circumstances in which they were removed from office. Rakosi was exiled to the USSR. Gero, Khrushchev, and Gomulka were pensioned off and kept isolated. Dubcek was eased from the leadership by stages and, since he was not yet eligible for an old-age pension, ended by working in relative isolation at a modest clerical job. Dubcek, Gero, and Rakosi were all expelled from the Parties they once had headed. Nagy was tried and executed.

Political Character of the Victorious Candidates

The type of succession contest that emerges in any regime is designed by its creators and in some measure shaped by the regime's history to bring to the fore candidates who embody qualities that will further the regime's chief ends. Yet Lenin's ideal of the tough-minded Bolshevik (like the non-Communist analyst's ideal type of the Communist power seeker) posits qualities that were absent from several figures who emerged from the power struggle and its culminating succession contest as leading candidates. Among them were men of uncertain or vacillating will who at crucial moments were strongly influenced by the sentiments of the society and who consequently disregarded the stark and manifest realities of power. In Hungary, for example, as unlikely a figure as Nagy could survive the bloody Rakosi period of rule and rise to hold a share of pre-eminent power. In Poland, Ochab, an *apparachik* who rose to the top in a sordid power struggle, could surrender supreme power when he found that he lacked support in the Party and the nation—an action that the Soviet leaders, who had been directly trained by Stalin, found difficult to understand. In Czechoslovakia, Dubcek—who as a child had been reared in the USSR to be a Communist, and who had been trained for several years in a Party school of the Soviet central committee—turned against his Moscow mentors and moved with the popular currents and shared the nationalist feelings of his own people, even disregarding the power balance in Eastern Europe.

Behavior of this kind is hard to reconcile with Bolshevism, and the struggle for power among Communists is supposed to eliminate men who harbor such tendencies. True, Nagy did not reach the position of duumvir that he occupied in 1953 and 1954 simply through his own efforts; he was placed there, against the resistance of the Hungarian leadership, by a Soviet faction in Moscow. Moreover, in 1956, Nagy was brought to power by the people, chiefly the youth and the workers, not by victories won in the power struggle. Ochab and Dubcek, on the other hand, did reach the top as the result of a struggle within the leadership and without decisive intervention by the USSR or by the Polish or Czechoslovak peoples. That such men could rise to the top suggests that in the Communist struggle for power the *fitness* of the survivor cannot always be defined in Bolshevik terms.

Such Communist leaders as these exist—this fact should not be lost sight of—but they are exceptions. Moreover, although they attained power, they failed to hold it. More typical of the successful survivor in a Communist succession contest are such men as Ulbricht, Chervenkov, and Rakosi, and Novotny, Zhivkov, and Honecker. The last three, incidentally, came to power after Stalin died. Tough and power-oriented, they emerged from the lower ranks of society. They were poorly educated but able, strong-willed, shrewd, and natively intelligent. If the Bolshevism of such men is not mitigated by sufficient concern for the demands of the people, they may in certain circumstances be swept from power; but it does not appear that such concern is a necessary attribute for victory in the struggle to win power.

Has the passing of the original leaders in Communist states produced successors of a different kind? The generation gap is generally greatest when the founder of a new regime is a truly charismatic figure, a hero who by his great deeds or great personal qualities has changed the life of his people. The leader who comes after such a founder is unlikely to resemble him. But the founders in Eastern Europe (except for Tito) were not charismatic figures. They were *apparachiks* who came to power with the assistance, direct or indirect, of Soviet armed force, and who ruled subject to Moscow's command.[17] Their heirs, in turn, have been *apparachiks* who rose to high office on their shoulders. The differences between a Zhivkov and a Dimitrov, between a Honecker and an Ulbricht, are not insignificant, but they are differences of degree, not of quality.

Succession to a charismatic leader is a different category of succession, and it brings a different kind of ruler. The charismatic Lenin was unlike Stalin; Stalin, who possessed his own charisma, which was the source of a new transformation of values, was qualitatively different from those who came after him. The passing of Tito and of Mao, then, unlike the passing of Gottwald and Bierut, will surely bring to power men of a different stripe from their predecessors.

Many observers have thought for some time that the second and subsequent generations of Communist leaders would be better educated than the original rulers and, more important, would be more competent to deal with technical matters and less oriented toward power and bureaucratic concerns. Such trends in those recruited to occupy leadership posts in the *central committee* may yet be shown to exist, but it is doubtful that they have seriously affected the composition of the *political*

---

[17] Fidel Castro, even more than Tito and Mao, epitomizes the charismatic leader: he created a new regime before he organized a Communist Party and gave it "a leading role."

bureaus of ruling Communist parties, and it is apparent that the *dominant* figures have by no means become technocrats.[18] Of the states that have experienced succession, Poland is the only one in which the current leader (Gierek) is obviously better qualified than his predecessors to deal with technical matters. Elsewhere, the men who have risen through the Party apparatus to the top are hardly better qualified by education or technical competence than those who preceded them up the same ladder.

Two of the current senior secretaries, Kadar and Husak, are survivors of Communist prisons and at one time were even subjected by their comrades to physical torture. Yet both men, as well as Gomulka, another former inmate of Communist prisons, responded when the call came to serve the Party once more. Although Moscow at first was reluctant to trust its erstwhile victims in the highest posts, subsequently it had good reason to be pleased with their performance. The capacity to command the loyalty of men whom the USSR has treated unjustly is an important resource that has facilitated Moscow's control of the Soviet bloc. Deep loyalty to the Communist movement has several sources. Chief among them, perhaps, is attachment to Marxist-Leninist doctrine. It is an abstract loyalty that seems well able to survive the debased practices of some of the doctrine's leading practitioners. Nevertheless, it would be wrong to see these men as merely selfless servants of the Communist ideal. They are also ambitious politicians whose only hope of returning to power was through an accommodation with Moscow, and in the end they reached such an accommodation. Those leaders who did not were cast into political limbo, like Dubcek, or even executed, like Nagy.

The Party *apparat*'s success in dominating Communist regimes in the Soviet bloc since Stalin's death has helped to lessen the severity of succession contests, hence to limit the hazards arising from crises of succession. One consequence, however, has been further to narrow the range of political types at the summit.

---

[18] For a more detailed discussion of this subject see below, p. 314.

Leaders who rise to the top of the Party apparatus and then make good their claim to rule tend to have a common political character. Typically, such a leader possesses high native intelligence; strong control over his passions, though not always over his appetites; a powerful sense of loyalty to the Party organization rather than to persons; great energy, which is channeled into the work of the Party; and great ambition, which generally reinforces his attachment to the Party apparatus. In the conditions of political life that prevail in the Soviet bloc, the Party apparatus tends to be taken as the embodiment of the Party, and the Party as the embodiment of the revolution. Thus the Party apparatus, a massive bureaucratic organization, appropriates the charisma of revolution, legitimating the personal exercise of unbridled power and the disregard of traditional canons of morality.

The fact that all the states of the Soviet bloc recruit their leaders from a pool of candidates with a similar cast of mind—one fashioned by the same ideology and by the same kind of life experience within the same kind of institution—has its advantages. For one thing, it facilitates communication among them. When Brezhnev assembles Party heads of the Soviet bloc for their periodic meetings in the Crimea, they speak a common language. Their proximate ends, of course, are by no means the same, for they exercise their minds on behalf of their own national bureaucracies and nation-states; the difference in their immediate ends leads to considerable disagreement and conflict. But they have a common mode of discourse by which to resolve their disagreements, and they share a common loyalty to the revolutionary movement that has brought them personal power and that justifies their exercise of it.

There are disadvantages in having men whose political characters were largely shaped by the Party apparatus represented in such large numbers among the leaders of Communist states. Not only are they almost always to be found in the post of first secretary, but they also tend to predominate in each Party's politburo. (On the average, 40 percent of the politburo members have built their careers chiefly in the Party apparatus.) [19] The narrow horizons and relatively stereotyped modes of thought of the *apparachik* limit the ways in which the leaders perceive and can respond to the problems their states must deal with in the years ahead. The importance of specific differences among men of this genus should not be disregarded, however, since the effects of these differences may be greatly amplified by the rulers' exercise of vast powers. Furthermore, an occasional Dubcek may rise to the top, although chances are that he will be expelled from the body politic as an alien element. Such an outcome is to be expected, at any rate, until such time as the body politic is allowed to accommodate itself better to the character of the society and the people.

Rulers' Attempts to Arrange Successions

Communist rulers, on the whole, have gone to remarkable lengths in efforts to arrange their succession. Usually they have been reluctant to call attention to these efforts, for they indicate the temporal limits of their own rule. Nevertheless, Tito, Mao,

[19] The extent to which this has been true is indicated by the following tabulation showing representation of career Party officials in the politburo:

Nations	I		II		III		IV		V	
	No.	%	No.	%	No.	%	No.	%	No.	%
Bulgaria	3	27	7	50	7	58	9	50	8	47
Czechoslovakia	2	18	4	31	6	50	11	73	6	46
Poland	7	47	6	50	4	27	7	44	10	67
Romania	8	53	6	46	2	29	5	56	—	

Roman numerals refer to the order in which Party congresses were held in each country between Stalin's death and 1973: Bulgaria and Czechoslovakia, 1954, 1958, 1962, 1966, 1971; Poland, 1954, 1959, 1964, 1968, 1971; Romania, 1955, 1960, 1965, 1969. Only four congresses were held in Romania between 1953 and 1973. A substantial proportion of the career Party officials concurrently held office outside the Party apparatus. I am indebted for the data to an important study of Communist elites: Jacob Bielasiak, "Political Change and Economic Development: A Study of Elite Composition and Decision-Making in Eastern Europe," Ph.D. dissertation, Cornell University, scheduled for completion in 1975.

and Khrushchev have spoken openly of their coming demise and of the need to prepare for their succession, although only in China has the heir presumptive, in the person of Lin Piao, been designated explicitly, in the Party constitution.[20] Even when a ruler is reticent, the character of his succession arrangements, including the designation of an heir presumptive, can usually be inferred from his political dispositions and, more particularly, from the general pattern of his relationship to a favored lieutenant.

The man designated to be heir presumptive generally ranks second in the membership of the secretariat and has delivered one of the two major reports to the preceding Party congress; his career has visibly benefited from the ruler's patronage, which may include grooming for the top office. There was considerable agreement among outside observers, even before the onset of each succession, about the designation of the eleven men treated in this study as heirs presumptive: Chervenkov, Malenkov, Liu Shao-ch'i, Ochab, Rankovic, Kozlov, Brezhnev, Ceausescu, Le Duan, Honecker, and Lin Piao.[21]

Since a Communist ruler's succession arrangements require him to delegate more power than he otherwise would, and to concentrate delegated power in fewer hands, they involve sig-

[20] In addition, Mao, during the Cultural Revolution, alluded to his early choice of Liu Shao-ch'i as his intended heir and his subsequent rejection of him, and referred to Malenkov as Stalin's heir. On first coming to power in Cuba in 1959, Fidel Castro, though still in his thirties, publicly designated his brother Raoul to succeed him.

[21] Several problematic figures have been omitted from list. Zhivkov may have been Chervenkov's heir presumptive, though it seems far more likely that Chervenkov—who was still in his fifties when he was obliged, in 1954, to vacate the office of first secretary in accordance with the doctrine of collective leadership—meant only to place in the post a very young and relatively inexperienced but (as he thought) completely loyal lieutenant. If Gottwald had in mind an heir, it may have been Novotny, during the period from Slansky's fall until February 1953, when Novotny was removed from the Party secretariat. At the time of his death in March 1953, Gottwald may have planned to take steps to establish his son-in-law, Alexis Cepicka, as his heir presumptive.

Conclusion

nificant costs and substantial risks. They have even contributed on several occasions to a Communist ruler's loss of power. Why do Communist rulers take the risk?

One basic motive for arranging the succession is the ruler's personal ambition for fame after he retires or dies. He hopes to ensure that the men who come after him are favorably disposed toward him and will commend his rule or, at least, not derogate it. Stalin, more than any other Communist ruler, seems to have been preoccupied with this concern, which helped to feed the Stalin cult but also led him to choose an heir presumptive. Patriotism is another key motive. Recognizing the weakness of Communist regimes during a transfer of supreme power, the ruler may seek to obviate disorder in the state in order to prevent a weakening of its international position during his succession. Both Tito and Mao have publicly stressed this concern, and it obviously motivated Gheorghiu-Dej of Romania. A related motive is the ruler's wish that his policies and, especially, the major programs instituted by him will not be abandoned by his heirs. They are valuable to him not merely because they are his, but also because he believes they contribute to the people's welfare and to the revolutionary cause. Arranging the succession may also have a basically negative aim: to prevent the usurpation of power by men who lack the political character of true revolutionaries. Ironically, this has been a primary motive in rulers' counteracting their own previous succession arrangements.[22]

In the Eastern European states of the Soviet bloc four of the nine erstwhile rulers groomed a youthful subordinate and later established him as heir presumptive: Dimitrov chose Chervenkov; Bierut, Ochab; Gheorghiu-Dej, Ceausescu; and Ulbricht, Honecker. On the other hand, Chervenkov, Rakosi, Novotny, and Gomulka, although each was for a number of years in a ruling

[22] Tito purged Rankovic in 1965, and Mao purged Liu in 1966 and Lin in 1971; in each instance the designated heir presumptive was alleged to have been harboring plans to usurp power.

position, did not choose heirs presumptive. If any of them intended to do so at some later time, in old age or while in ill health, he never had the opportunity; all four men were forced from power. The case of the ninth leader, Gottwald, is not so clear, although at the time of his death, in 1953, he had not designated an heir presumptive.

In the two Communist great powers, where orderly succession may be especially important, there have been five heirs presumptive: in the USSR, Stalin chose Malenkov to succeed him (1952), and Khrushchev chose first Kozlov (1960), then Brezhnev (1963); Mao had chosen Liu Shao-ch'i by the early fifties, and chose Lin Piao a decade later. Subsequently, of course, Mao came to believe that an orderly succession was far less important than one that assured future revolutionary struggle of the masses. In Yugoslavia, where Soviet intervention, if it occurs, may aim to aggravate the succession crisis rather than to mitigate it (which is its aim in the Soviet bloc), Tito favored Rankovic for the succession in the early sixties, but he has had no heir presumptive since 1966.

The four Eastern European and two Soviet rulers who designated an heir presumptive and allowed him to hold that position until the time of the succession thereby conferred on him a great advantage. All six heirs presumptive were ranked number one at the onset of succession: four when their patron died —Chervenkov (1949), Malenkov (1953), Ochab (1956), and Ceausescu (1965); two when their patron was forced from power—Brezhnev (1964) and Honecker (1971). Four erstwhile heirs presumptive never competed for the succession, having previously been deprived of their posts because they displeased their patrons: Kozlov was removed by Khrushchev (1963); Rankovic, by Tito (1965); Liu Shao-ch'i and Lin Piao, by Mao (1966 and 1971).

Although Communist rulers were able to confer an initial advantage on the six heirs presumptive who actually competed for the succession, the record of the rulers at the final outcome of the succession is not nearly as good. Two heirs presumptive consolidated personal rule (Chervenkov [23] and Ceausescu); two failed to do so and were demoted (Malenkov and Ochab); and two currently have made good, though not irreversible, progress toward achieving personal rule (Brezhnev and Honecker). The rulers' record in avoiding deep or prolonged crises by their succession arrangements in the post-Stalin period is mediocre. The single unequivocal success was the transfer of power from Gheorghiu-Dej to Ceausescu in 1965; the two moderate successes were the transfer of Khrushchev's power to Brezhnev and of Ulbricht's to Honecker. On the other hand, the Stalin and Bierut successions led to deep crises.

Of the five rulers who made little or no effort to arrange the succession—Gottwald, Chervenkov, Rakosi, Novotny, and Gomulka—the last four were ultimately deposed, somewhat complicating the transfer of power. The depositions of Rakosi and Novotny led to the two deepest succession crises that Communist states have experienced; on the other hand, Gomulka's power fell rather neatly into the hands of Gierek, and Chervenkov's finally was arrogated by Zhivkov. (The death of Gottwald, which coincided with Stalin's, led to a prolonged, moderately disruptive succession.) The effect on the succession of a ruler's deposition, then, seems to depend in some measure on whether he was ousted by a conspiracy led by a powerful heir presumptive (as were Khrushchev and Ulbricht), in which case the succession to date has been only moderately disruptive; or whether he was ousted by recognized political rivals or popular agitation (as were Rakosi, Novotny, Gomulka, and perhaps Chervenkov), in which case disruption has tended to be more serious. (We speak here only about tendencies, of course, since there are too few cases for a sweeping generalization.)

From this brief summary of the results of rulers' succession ar-

[23] Actually, Chervenkov's 1949 succession was due to Stalin's exercise of personal control in the Eastern European satellite states and has no bearing on the changed circumstances of succession in the post-Stalin period.

rangements, it is apparent that an heir presumptive poses a significant threat to a ruler's power. This threat is compounded in the Soviet bloc by the fact that Moscow may intervene to support the heir presumptive against the ruler, as it did on behalf of Honecker against Ulbricht in 1971. Why, then, in view of the potential danger, have rulers tried so often to arrange the succession? Concern for the future of the state and of the Communist movement in some measure overrides concern for their own power. In addition, the ruler (like Gheorghiu-Dej, apparently) may expect to die soon anyway, or he may hope to prevent usurpation of his power by building defenses against his own succession arrangements—for example, by altering them as necessary. This device served Mao well; on the other hand, it did not save Khrushchev, who was ousted by Brezhnev not long after Khrushchev designated him heir presumptive.

What are the risks encountered by the heir presumptive himself? He of course is vulnerable to a change of mind on the part of his patron. Four of the eleven erstwhile heirs presumptive lost their posts before the onset of the succession (Kozlov, Rankovic, Liu Shao-ch'i, and Lin Piao). The seven heirs presumptive who survived their patrons' rule, however, secured the choice position in the succession contest.[24] In mid-1974, only two of the seven, Malenkov and Ochab, have been eliminated from the contest for the succession.[25]

Interventions to change succession arrangements require of a ruler even greater power than is needed to institute them. Significantly, on three occasions the ruler who downgraded his heir presumptive was the founder of a regime. Tito did so once;

[24] The conjecture of Harrison Salisbury that "there probably is no more dangerous position which could be held by any man in a dictatorship than that of heir-presumptive" (*Ithaca Journal*, March 13, 1973) has an element of truth, but it is misleading insofar as it does not take into account the *advantages* possessed by the heir presumptive.

[25] Ochab was a victim of divisions in the leadership, reinforced by popular agitation on behalf of Gomulka; Malenkov was mainly a victim of factional struggle in the leadership.

Mao, twice. Moreover, Mao, in depriving Liu Shao-ch'i of the succession, found it necessary to incur serious political debts to Lin Piao. The fourth change of heirs presumptive was made by Khrushchev. He was aided by Kozlov's illness (April 1963). The episode may have contributed to Khrushchev's ouster from office eighteen months later, if only by forcing on the new heir presumptive, Leonid Brezhnev, an awareness of the vulnerability of his position.[26]

The problem of revising existing succession arrangements is radically different when it is a question, not of personal succession within the existing framework, but of institutional succession—of creating new institutions that are not mere agencies of personal rule and preparing them to exercise sovereignty. The ruler has a crucial service to perform by delegating major authority to the nascent institutions and conferring on them legitimacy. There is a danger, however, that the leader may not be content, like the rationalist deity of the eighteenth-century philosophes, to set the machinery in motion but may be tempted to intervene again and again to adjust or modify his original institutional arrangements. If this happens, the new institutions may not acquire the self-sufficient authority they need in order to become sovereign in the succession. This problem has developed in Yugoslavia as a result of Tito's intermittent but massive interventions since 1965, and particularly since 1971.

In the revision of arrangements for personal succession the crucial change is the removal of the heir presumptive. Almost invariably this seems to involve the discovery of some shocking act of insubordination. Khrushchev had apparently been defied by Kozlov, who in Khruschev's absence promulgated the 1963 May Day slogans. Tito learned that Rankovic had concealed a

[26] Powerful non-Communist leaders have found it even more difficult than Communist rulers to alter their succession arrangements and have usually failed. For example, though President Charles de Gaulle of France, during his last year in office, deprived Georges Pompidou of his former status of heir presumptive, he could not prevent Pompidou from succeeding to the presidency of the French republic.

microphone in Tito's bedroom. Mao was defied by Liu in the matter of the "23 Articles." The event that led Mao to disavow Lin was his campaign to make himself Chou En-lai's superior in the state apparatus, despite Mao's manifest opposition.

The personal and political relations of the ruler and heir presumptive are an intriguing subject for speculation. The relationship is a delicate one and has often proved fragile. The heir presumptive has a thin line to walk between becoming a robot at the command of the ruler and asserting his own will in ways that may awaken his patron's fears and suspicions. Since heirs are chosen because they are thought to have some capacity for rule, it is no wonder that they have tended to assert themselves. Of eleven heirs presumptive in Communist states, *two* manifestly betrayed their patrons (Brezhnev and Honecker); *three* were charged with attempted usurpation (Rankovic, Liu Shao-ch'i, and Lin Piao); and *two* evidently lost their patrons' confidence (Malenkov and Kozlov). Only *four* of the eleven retained the confidence of their patrons and (presumably) were loyal to them until the end (Chervenkov, Ochab, Ceausescu, and Le Duan).

Despite the basic fragility of the relationship between ruler and heir presumptive, on occasion it has proved remarkably durable. Honecker's close association with Ulbricht lasted a quarter of a century, including a decade during which he was heir presumptive. Ceausescu was close to Gheorghiu-Dej for over two decades, and heir presumptive for almost one. Chervenkov was associated with Dimitrov (his brother-in-law) for over a decade, and may have been his early choice for successor.

Even when the relationship between ruler and heir lasted a long time, however, it apparently was marked by considerable tension. Honecker finally seized power from Ulbricht and subjected Ulbricht to public humiliation. Honecker's conduct doubtless was politically motived, but it may also have reflected longstanding grievances against the man who, after choosing him as his political heir, required strict subordination to his will. After

Gheorghiu-Dej died, Ceausescu's open and severe criticism of important aspects of his rule suggests that he harbored serious grievances against the man who had raised him to power. Since such tensions emerged even when relationships between ruler and heir presumptive had been durable, it seems likely that they were more acute in instances where the relationship broke down. Unquestionably, one of the key obstacles to the successful arrangement of a transfer of personal rule is the complex relationship between the ruler and the heir presumptive.

Despite the problems involved in designating an heir, some Communist rulers who presently are trying to arrange the succession continue to rely on this method. Of the four present rulers in the Soviet bloc, only two (Kadar and Zhivkov) have made succession arrangements, and both have designated heirs. Kadar has groomed Bela Biszku as heir presumptive in Hungary for more than a decade. The difference in ages between the two men is nine years, which is suitable for an incumbent in his sixties (Kadar was born in 1912, Biszku in 1921). Biszku has had considerable experience in dealing with internal security affairs and was assigned the task of rebuilding the political police following the 1956 uprising. He obviously has Kadar's confidence: since 1962 he has been the second secretary in charge of cadres, internal security, and the armed forces. His great power and narrow experience make his position as heir comparable to Honecker's in the last decade of Ulbricht's rule; nevertheless, the fate Ulbricht suffered at Honecker's hands apparently did not induce Kadar to alter his basic succession arrangements. In Bulgaria, Zhivkov's second secretary, Boris Velchev, also has occupied his post for more than a decade. During this time he has been responsible for cadres but not, apparently, for security and defense matters. The difference in the ages of the two men is only three years (Zhivkov was born in 1911, Velchev in 1914). Presumably Velchev is meant to be the successor if there is an early succession, but if Zhivkov continues to rule for some time, he will probably need to groom a younger heir presumptive.

The other two Communist rulers in the Soviet bloc, Ceausescu of Romania and Gierek of Poland, have made no visible arrangements for the succession. Ceausescu, who has been in office since 1965 though he is still in his mid-fifties, appears more concerned to exercise his great powers and to make them secure against political attack than to groom an heir. His initial second secretary, Virgil Trofin, was responsible for Party organization and cadres from 1965 until 1969, when he was removed from the secretariat. He subsequently suffered further demotions. Trofin's replacement as second secretary was Gheorghe Pana. Pana was compelled to engage in self-criticism in 1971, which probably disqualified him for the role of heir presumptive. As long as Ceausescu remains jealous of his power, not only is he unlikely to choose an heir, but he probably will permit no one to serve for long as second secretary. Gierek, Poland's ruler since 1971, is too recently in office to be much concerned as yet about the succession. Husak and Honecker at this writing have not established personal rule. They are merely heads of oligarchies, and consequently are in no position to try to arrange the succession.

Of the rulers outside the Soviet bloc, Mao and Tito have been preoccupied with the problem of succession, but both decided after sad experience against choosing heirs presumptive. Hoxha, on the other hand, has shown little interest in his succession. Though still in his sixties, Hoxha has ruled Albania for a quarter of a century, and is doubtless strong enough politically to try to arrange the succession. He has not done so, however, and in the near future, at least, is not likely to. The reason is simple: Hoxha is so jealous of his own powers that he is unwilling to delegate any of them. (Hoxha actually is so fearful of attacks on his position in the leadership that for over a decade he has not absented himself from the country.) Of Communist rulers outside the Soviet bloc only Kim Il-sung in North Korea and, more definitely, Castro in Cuba appear to have designated heirs. In both cases, oddly, the heir is a younger brother: Raoul Castro in Cuba, Kim Yong-chu in North Korea.

External Factors

Soviet influence has doubtless been the most important external factor in successions in the states of the Soviet bloc. But both Moscow's will to intervene and its capacity to do so have varied markedly. The USSR seems to have played the decisive role in bringing about the ouster of top leaders chiefly during the crisis stemming from the de-Stalinization campaign in 1956 (when Chervenkov, Rakosi, Gero, and Nagy were removed), but also in the ouster of Dubcek in 1969 and Ulbricht in 1971; it was neutral in the ouster of Novotny in 1968 and of Gomulka in 1970. The Soviet leadership has been more active in the *selection* of successors: it chose Chervenkov in 1949 and Novotny in 1953; Zhivkov, Gero, and Kadar in 1956; and Husak and Honecker in the post-Khrushchev period. It was neutral in the elevation of Dubcek (1968), Le Duan (1970), and Gierek (1970). There have probably been only two instances in which Moscow was unable to prevent the elevation of a top leader whom it opposed: the brief promotion of Nagy as head of government in 1956 and the choice of Ceausescu as first secretary in 1965.

Moscow's capacity to influence succession in the Soviet bloc has depended on the unity of its leadership—particularly the leaders' capacity to take decisive action—and, even more important, the credibility of Soviet threats, which also, in some measure, has depended on the leadership's unity.[27] A simultaneous loss of unity and credibility, resulting in a reduced capacity to exert an indirect influence on succession in other Communist states, has been most evident in the periods of succession in the USSR that followed Stalin's death and Khrushchev's ouster.

The Soviet leaders' disunity and vacillation after Stalin's death

[27] Dubcek, for example, seems to have believed that divisions within the Soviet leadership reduced the risk of military intervention in Czechoslovakia.

and, in particular, the failure of the delegation sent to Warsaw in October 1956 to veto Gomulka's succession to Ochab encouraged the Hungarian opposition to Gero to believe that it was free to replace him with Nagy regardless of Soviet views on the matter. As always when the USSR has been challenged on issues that manifestly jeopardize its hegemony in Eastern Europe, Moscow belied the opposition's expectations, intervened with force, and in the process made its threats credible again. Subsequently, Khrushchev resolved the Soviet succession and brought a significant measure of unity to the leadership, but his capacity to influence successions elsewhere was not put to the test, since none occurred during his period of rule.

After Khrushchev's ouster in 1964, the USSR was unable to influence the Gheorghiu-Dej succession the following year. It played a relatively passive role, initially, in the Czechoslovak crisis of 1968, partly owing to a reduced willingness to intercede. Ultimately, the Soviet resort to force to effect a change in the Czechoslovak leadership, like its intervention in Hungary in 1956, enabled the USSR to revive fear of its threats, and hence to renew its capacity to influence succession in the Soviet bloc. Therefore, although the Soviet succession was not fully resolved in the following years, Moscow's will was not disregarded in the Gomulka and the Ulbricht successions.

For the most part, the Soviet Union has been able to exert its influence on successions by means of powerful native factions favorable to its aims or dependent on its support. Such factions enabled the USSR to oust Chervenkov, Rakosi, and Ulbricht and to replace them—as well as Dimitrov, Gottwald, and Bierut, after they died—with leaders acceptable to itself. When the Soviet leaders have been unable to act effectively by manipulating a strong native faction, they have been obliged to seek an accommodation with the incumbent (as with Ceausescu), to maintain hostile relations (as with Mao and Hoxha), or to intervene with armed force. On the three occasions when the USSR has intervened militarily—in East Germany, Hungary, and Czechoslovakia

—the application of force was massive, brutal, brief, and effective.

Moscow has generally been flexible in its support of established leaders and has judged correctly when they have lost their capacity to rule. Wisely, it did not persist in its efforts to maintain Ochab, Gero, Novotny, or Gomulka in office; even Rakosi, though he was retired belatedly, at least was not returned to power. The USSR no doubt has been influenced from moment to moment by the immediate consequences of its major political initiatives in Eastern Europe. The successful removal of Chervenkov in April 1956 may have encouraged the Soviet leaders to remove Rakosi two months later. Similarly, the ease with which Gierek supplanted Gomulka in crisis circumstances at the end of 1970 may have encouraged Moscow to replace Ulbricht by Honecker four months later. Although Moscow has made major errors in the use of its power to control succession in the Soviet bloc, on the whole it has done well in the pursuit of its overall aims.

Not only the USSR has influenced succession in the Communist states of the Soviet bloc; the states have in various ways influenced each other's successions. At times, the influence has been exerted actively and deliberately; at other times it has been a consequence of the spread of certain ideas, or of the evaluation by one state's leadership of Moscow's resoluteness in recent dealings with another Communist state. Soviet vacillation in dealing with Rakosi in the spring of 1956, for example, may have encouraged elements of the Polish leadership to polemicize openly against Moscow in the summer of 1956, and finally to defy Moscow by replacing Ochab with Gomulka. The news of this event, when it reached Hungary, in turn triggered the popular uprising against Gero and the elevation of Nagy. Throughout 1956, Yugoslavia (though it was not a member of the Soviet bloc) and China (which at that time was in the bloc but acted independently of it) influenced the successions in Poland and Hungary. Ulbricht and Novotny were adversely affected by these developments and opposed them, but they could do little, except in their own countries, until Moscow's fears finally were provoked by the Hungarian uprising and Moscow put a stop, for the time being, to the surge of reform in the bloc.

There was a new polarization of the Communist states of the Soviet bloc in 1968 on the question of reforms instituted as a consequence of the Novotny succession. Czechoslovakia, probably influenced in part by Romania's demonstration that it could act with relative independence of Moscow, even during the Gheorghiu-Dej succession, was supported by Romania and Yugoslavia. On the other side were the leaders of Poland and East Germany, who feared the spread of reformist ideas to their own countries. This time, unlike 1956, Moscow shared the fears of the conservative governments and finally joined with them in military intervention. Such joint action, however has been exceptional. Moscow seemingly has preferred to isolate political crises in other Communist states of the Soviet bloc and to deal with them by itself, as it was subsequently able to do in the Gomulka and Ulbricht successions of the early seventies.

The reciprocal effects of succession in the Communist states have extended to the rulers themselves; their succession arrangements, for example, have been influenced by developments elsewhere. Mao has said that he decided to groom Liu Shao-ch'i to rule as his successor after he observed Stalin's failure to prepare Malenkov adequately. The unseating of Khrushchev in October 1964 by his heir presumptive, Brezhnev, may have stimulated Mao's suspicions of Liu. Tito's discovery, in July 1966, that his heir presumptive, Rankovic, had bugged his quarters possibly influenced the timing, a month later, of Mao's move to purge Liu. Perhaps the purge of Lin Piao in 1971 reinforced Tito's earlier decision not to designate a new heir presumptive.

Reflections on Succession, Reform, and Stability

Succession remains a critical source of weakness in Communist regimes. True, noteworthy progress has been made in establishing an authoritative center of power at the head of a sovereign

Party apparatus, and this progress points the way toward a solution; but it has not provided one. Rule by the senior secretary in a Communist state, despite his signature on state treaties, continues to be an anomaly. Although Party members participate indirectly in the formal process by which he is elected, the rest of the nation is allowed to play no part. There is no constitutional fiction, even, to provide grounds for arguing that the people chose him as their leader. Hence, occupation of the post of senior secretary does not of itself provide a legitimate basis for the exercise of power.

The problem of the legitimacy of a Communist ruler is underscored by the growth of political forces that he has found it increasingly difficult to control. Five of the six successions that have occurred in the Soviet bloc during the past decade were initiated by the overthrow, not the death, of a ruler. Until Communist rulers can be removed from office without a death, a coup, an uprising, or a conspiracy, succession inevitably will continue to be a serious problem. Moreover, the only instance so far of a termination resulting from relatively *open* political opposition to a leader—the ouster of Novotny—had serious consequences nonetheless. Clearly, freedom to engage in political opposition to a ruler, or even a fixed limitation on his tenure of office, will not of itself solve the problem of succession. Some observers have argued that increased "development," by furthering "institutionalization," will provide the necessary basis for orderly succession; this is highly doubtful. Until now, the less highly developed Communist states of Europe (Bulgaria, Romania, and Hungary) have done no worse in ordering successions than the economically and politically more advanced states (the USSR, Poland, East Germany, and Czechoslovakia). Actually, economic progress creates unprecedented problems of management and control that the established leadership is poorly qualified to cope with; in the years ahead such difficulties may prove particularly unsettling to the leadership of the most advanced Communist states. Significantly, the overthrow of rulers during the past decade occurred in the most highly developed Communist states: the USSR (Khrushchev), Czechoslovakia (Novotny and Dubcek), Poland (Gomulka), and East Germany (Ulbricht).

The contests for the succession in all the Communist states necessarily will continue to involve illicit factional struggle, institutional rivalry, and the disruptive purging and packing of high Party bodies. But because of the protagonists' allegiance to a national state and commitment to an ideology they hold in common, and because of their common fear of so weakening the state that popular disturbances might endanger the regime, the struggle is likely to be waged in accordance with rules that limit its destructiveness. Moreover—at least in the Communist states that are in the Soviet sphere of influence—the USSR will not permit a succession contest to imperil the existence of a regime. The United States–Soviet détente may encourage liberal tendencies in the Communist states of Eastern Europe, but those tendencies will be rather narrowly restricted as long as it continues to be understood that the United States under no circumstances will intervene to protect a government in the Soviet bloc that Moscow finds unacceptable, and as long as the Soviet leaders remain adamant in their opposition to any development in Eastern Europe that they believe might jeopardize important interests.

Reform, including major economic reform, is not unlikely in the states of the Soviet bloc and may even occur without a change in leaders. However, *fundamental* reform of a kind that might, for example, significantly reduce the role of the *apparat* in the regime, if attempted at all during the next decade, is likely to be associated with a change in leadership. Radical reform is most favored, not simply by a succession (as after the death of the leader), but rather by a succession consequent upon the manifest failure of a leadership and its policies.

One possible scenario for an attempt at fundamental reform might proceed as follows: (1) The growth rate of the economy declines; attempts at piecemeal adjustment yield little improvement. (2) Popular disaffection mounts because of the reduced growth of real income, shortages of specific goods, and wage inequities; the disaffection of intellectuals rises because of cultural and ethnic restrictions on the dissemination of works of the mind. (3) Reformist groups decide that they can effect the reforms they seek only by changing the leadership. They believe they have the means to remove the dominant leader and that an acceptable candidate to replace him is available. Moreover, they are confident that Moscow will accept the outcome. (4) The dominant leader is removed as a result of one, or a combination, of the following oppositional activities: factional struggle in the leadership (as in the ouster of Novotny); popular disturbances (as in the ousters of Nagy and Gomulka); conspiracy (as in the ousters of Khrushchev and Ulbricht).[28] (5) The new leadership decides to deal with the deepening crisis, not by piecemeal reforms designed to restore the regime's equilibrium, which no longer seem adequate, but by fundamental reforms designed to modify the regime. (Such a decision probably would be made only if the successor's strategy for consolidating personal power required him to receive support from groups that favored fundamental reform.)

This scenario posits several crucial decisions that would confront the *Soviet* leadership: Should removal of the leader be permitted? Is the proposed successor acceptable? Are the proposed reforms likely to restore the regime's equilibrium, or is there a danger that they will give impetus to further reform? These are difficult questions. The USSR has a positive interest in changing a leadership if the existing one is incompetent or has been discredited. As regards any proposed successor, Moscow usually has abundant evidence on which to base a judgment, but such evidence, as the Ochab and Dubcek successions show,

---

[28] The conspiracy against Ulbricht probably required no more than a Soviet decision to replace him, which he recognized as irrevocable; the conspiracy against Khrushchev, on the other hand, almost certainly involved, in addition, extensive participation of the political police and, to a lesser degree, of the military leadership.

may be inadequate or misleading. The crucial question is whether reforms proposed by a successor administration are likely to be destabilizing. About such matters the Soviet leaders have strong and highly conservative views, and they will act on them even if the costs—as in Czechoslovakia in 1968—seem high. The Soviet leaders will probably continue to interpose their veto of radical reform in Eastern Europe so long as they perceive it as a threat to stability in the USSR.

APPENDIXES
AND INDEX

Appendix I. Successions to Former Leaders

Top-rank leader		Chief offices		Termination		Heir presumptive	Heir's chief offices		Fate of heir	
Leading oligarch	Ruler	Party	State	Mode	Date		Party	State	Leading oligarch when succession initiated?	Ruler subsequently?
	Dimitrov (Bulg.)	Gen. sec.	Govt. head	Death	1949	Chervenkov	2d sec.		Yes	Yes
	Stalin (USSR)	Gen. sec.		Death	1953	Malenkov	2d sec.	Dep. premier	Yes	No
	Gottwald (Cz.)	Chm. CC	State head	Death	1953					
	Bierut (Pol.)	1st sec.		Ouster	1956	Ochab	2d sec.		Yes	No
	Chervenkov (Bulg.)	1st sec.		Ouster	1956					
	Rakosi (Hung.)	1st sec.		Resignation	1956					
Ochab (Pol.)		1st sec.		Ouster	1956					
Gero (Hung.)		1st sec.		Ouster	1956					
Nagy (Hung.)			Govt. head	Ouster	1956					
	Khrushchev (USSR)	1st sec.	Govt. head	Ouster	1964	1. Kozlov (−1963)	2d sec.		Deposed previously? Yes	Yes
						2. Brezhnev	2d sec.		Yes	?
	Gheorghiu-Dej (Rom.)	1st sec.	State head	Death	1965	Ceausescu	2d sec.		Yes	Yes
	Novotny (Cz.)	1st sec.	State head	Ouster	1968					
Dubcek (Cz.)		1st sec.		Ouster	1969					
	Ho Chi Minh (N.Viet.)	Chm. CC		Death	1969	1. Truong Chinh (−1956)	Gen. sec.		Deposed previously Yes	?
						2. Le Duan	1st sec.		Yes	
	Gomulka (Pol.)	1st sec.		Ouster	1970					
	Ulbricht (E.Ger.)	1st sec.	State head	Ouster	1971	Honecker	2d sec.		Yes	?

Appendix II. Arrangements for Succession to Current Leaders (June 1974)

| Top-rank leader | | Approx. date of accession | Heir presumptive | Heir's chief offices | |
Ruler	Leading oligarch			Party	State
Tito (Yugo.)		1945	Rankovic (–1966)	2d sec.	Polit. police
Mao (China)		1949	1. Liu Shao-ch'i (–1966)		State head
			2. Lin Piao (–1971)	Vice-chm. CC	Vice-premier; defense
Hoxha (Alb.)		1949			
Kim Il-sung (N.Kor.)		1954	Kim Yong-chu (?; brother)	—	—
Kadar (Hung.)		1956	Bela Biszku	2d sec.	
Castro (Cuba)		1959	Raoul Castro (brother)	2d sec.	Dep. premier; defense
Zhivkov (Bulg.)		1962	Boris Velchev	2d sec.	Member, state council
Ceausescu (Rom.)		1968			
	Brezhnev (USSR)	1964			
	Husak (Cz.)	1969			
	Le Duan (N.Viet.)	1969			
Gierek (Pol.)		1971			
	Honecker (E.Ger.)	1971			

Index

How Communist States
Change Their Rulers

Designed by R. E. Rosenbaum.
Composed by Vail-Ballou Press, Inc.,
in 10 point linotype Caledonia, 3 points leaded,
with display lines in monotype Perpetua.
Printed letterpress from type by Vail-Ballou Press
on Warren's No. 66 text, 50 pound basis,
with the Cornell University Press watermark.
Bound by Vail-Ballou Press.